EBURY PRESS
INDIA'S MOST FEARLESS 3

Shiv Aroor is senior executive editor and anchor at India Today TV, and has covered the Indian military for nearly two decades. He has reported from conflict zones that include Kashmir, India's North-east, Sri Lanka and Libya. For the latter, he won two awards for war reporting. Shiv also founded the popular, award-winning military news and analysis site Livefist.

Rahul Singh is senior associate editor at *Hindustan Times* and has covered defence and military affairs for over two decades. Apart from extensive and deep reporting from the world of Indian military, including several newsbreaks that have set the national news agenda over the years, Rahul has reported from conflict zones including Kashmir, India's North-east and the Democratic Republic of Congo. The first story on the ongoing India–China border conflict appeared under his byline in 2020.

INDIA'S MOST FEARLESS 3

New Military Stories *of* Unimaginable Courage and Sacrifice

SHIV AROOR | RAHUL SINGH

EBURY PRESS

An imprint of Penguin Random House

EBURY PRESS
USA | Canada | UK | Ireland | Australia
New Zealand | India | South Africa | China

Ebury Press is part of the Penguin Random House group of companies
whose addresses can be found at global.penguinrandomhouse.com

Published by Penguin Random House India Pvt. Ltd
4th Floor, Capital Tower 1, MG Road,
Gurugram 122 002, Haryana, India

| Penguin
Random House
India

First published in Ebury Press by Penguin Random House India 2022

Copyright © Shiv Aroor and Rahul Singh 2022

Illustrations by Sandeep Unnithan

All rights reserved

10 9 8 7 6 5 4 3 2 1

ISBN 9780143451112

Typeset in Bembo Std by Manipal Technologies Limited, Manipal
Printed at Thomson Press India Ltd, New Delhi

www.penguin.co.in

MIX
Paper
FSC FSC® C010615

To the heroes who fought and died in the Galwan Valley,
their families and those who lived to tell the story

Contents

Introduction

At the time this book goes to print, it has been more than two years since the world's largest modern military standoff began in the icy hellscape of eastern Ladakh. As the two armies remain massed in war-like numbers against each other across frosted plains, frozen lakes and mountains that disappear into the clouds, the standoff between India and China is far from over. As the carnage and close-quarter suspense that defined the first few months of the conflict turn into a slower, calmer but insidiously permanent confrontation, much of what happened has lain hidden in the storm of propaganda, claims and counterclaims.

The incident that sent the unprecedented Ladakh standoff exploding into the minds of millions across India took place on 15 June 2020, on a desolate riverbend in Ladakh's Galwan River valley. Months of coverage uncovered the reality of a terrifying clash between Indian and Chinese soldiers. But the complete story of what happened that night has never been fully told.

And that's why we believe the book you are about to read is so important, not just to the legacy of the India's Most Fearless series, but in terms of giving our countrymen first-hand accounts of the biggest operations and incidents involving the Indian military. This third edition of the series begins with a first-hand account of the Galwan incident by officers and men of the 16th Battalion of the Bihar Regiment, who fought the Chinese that night and survived. Hair-raising as it was, the account proves the many shades of grey that define combat, a far cry from the black-and-white certainties they seem to us from all this distance away.

The Indian Army permitted us generous access to Colonel Ravi Kant—the officer who succeeded 16 Bihar commanding officer Colonel B. Santosh Babu, who was killed in action in the clash and awarded the hallowed Maha Vir Chakra for uncommon courage and leadership—as well as other soldiers from the battalion, allowing us to present the only first-hand account of what happened that night.

The account not only answers many questions but sets the record straight on a central bone of contention, as you will discover. The ghosts of Galwan will continue to haunt a valley that sees a tentative truce amid a larger standoff that is far from over. And the questions remain over whether an expanding hostile force at India's doorstep is a new status quo.

The lead-up to the publication of *India's Most Fearless 3* also saw the Indian military hit by one of its worst peacetime tragedies. On 8 December 2021, a helicopter crash in the Nilgiri Hills of Tamil Nadu killed the country's first chief of defence staff, General Bipin Rawat, an officer who, as chief of the army staff, was an impassioned supporter of this series, having also launched the first book. We were in constant touch with General Rawat during the course of writing this book, and he was looking forward to its release. The last conversation we had with General Rawat about *India's Most Fearless 3* was on 4 December 2021—four days before the Mi-17V5 crash—when he complained that we were taking too much time to bring out this book. He will be deeply missed.

The sole survivor of that horrific helicopter accident was a decorated young fighter pilot, Group Captain Varun Singh, whose face would become iconic across media in the days that followed. His story captivated the nation as he fought to stay alive for a week. Tragically, he didn't make it. But if a man lives on through his actions, then Group Captain Varun is as vibrant as ever in the first-ever account you will read here of his handling of a heart-stopping midair incident that won him a Shaurya Chakra.

Those are the two accounts that kick off what has been a heart-wrenching third volume of this series. You will also, for the first time, read a first-hand account of Operation Randori Behak, a fearsome Special Forces encounter in the mountains of Kashmir's Keran sector that stunned the country, which had just gone into a national COVID-19 lockdown.

You will also read, in the words of his wife, Nitika, the haunting tale of young Major Vibhuti Shankar Dhoundiyal, who was killed in action fighting terrorists in the aftermath of the February 2019 Pulwama terror attack. The tragedy persuaded Nitika to drop her corporate job and join the Indian Army. In her account is embodied the voice and grit of the many proud, grieving military families who fade completely out of view each year in the wake of gallantry awards and official recognition.

From the forests of India's North-east to the depths of the Arabian Sea, from the Line of Control to the unresponsive cockpit of a Sukhoi fighter flying at less than 50 feet, the as-yet-untold stories you're about to read here feature some of India's most fearless military personnel in their finest hours.

When *India's Most Fearless* began three books ago in 2017, we didn't think it would become a living, breathing flame that our readers would never allow to go out. If these stories inspire, thanks must go solely to the men and women we write about. When we began to write about them five years ago, it was because we believed these stories were too compelling not to share. It is, then, into the hands of the families of those we write about, their brave units and to you, the reader, once again, that we commit these ten true stories.

Delhi   Shiv Aroor
June 2022   Rahul Singh

1

'I Had Never Seen Such Fierce Fighting'

The Galwan Clash of June 2020

Even above the loud, steady roar of the Galwan River, he heard the thundering footfalls. The sound of over a thousand men reverberating through the darkness, amplified by the tunnel effect of a narrow valley flanked by steep rising mountains on both sides. Peering into the black void beyond Patrol Point 14, lit only a few metres forward by hand-held torches, the reality of those sounds dawned on Havildar Dharamvir Kumar Singh of the Indian Army's 16 Bihar infantry battalion. He clenched his eyes briefly shut to soak in every vibration. When he opened them again, he knew that the huge horde of men advancing towards his position was not marching.

They weren't even jogging.

They were sprinting.

'There were less than 400 of us,' says Havildar Dharamvir. 'We would soon discover that the number of Chinese Army soldiers running towards us was maybe three times that. We had been fighting smaller numbers of Chinese for two hours before that. But this was their main force. The all-out assault that the Chinese side was launching against us.'

An all-out assault.

Unarmed, as stipulated by decades-old protocol between the two armies, Havildar Dharamvir quickly glanced around at the soldiers with him. Even in the darkness he could tell their expressions. A curious mix of determination and fearlessness, but tinged with an edge of foreboding.

As the soldiers steeled themselves, rallied by their commanding officer and a group of younger officers, Havildar Dharamvir knew what lay ahead would need every ounce of strength the smaller force could muster. But it also made one particular man in the team even more crucial.

A non-combatant with a white suitcase.

Wading through the group of soldiers with him, Havildar Dharamvir emerged on the banks of the gushing Galwan, right where he had last seen the man he was looking for now.

With a big, unmistakable red 'plus' sign painted on to his parka, Naik Deepak Singh wasn't standing. On his knees, his suitcase open with bandages and bottles of tincture, he was crouched over what appeared to be a small group of injured men, all groaning in the darkness. Three were Indian soldiers being administered first aid.

The six other soldiers receiving emergency ministrations from the young Indian Army medic weren't Indian soldiers. They were Chinese Army personnel. Two People's Liberation Army (PLA) officers and four jawans.

'They are badly injured. They need to rest,' Naik Deepak said before Havildar Dharamvir could ask. An hour earlier, the injured Chinese soldiers had been left behind by their retreating force. Naik Deepak, the young nursing assistant, had been summoned to Patrol Point 14 by his commanding officer two hours earlier. Not he, not Havildar Dharamvir and not his commanding officer knew then how crucial his crouched figure would be in the events of that night.

'Is that your blood?' Havildar Dharamvir bent down over Naik Deepak, inspecting a gash just above the nursing assistant's right eyebrow.

'It's nothing. A piece of rock hit me. It's superficial. *Main theek hoon* [I am fine],' said Naik Deepak as he finished bandaging one of the Chinese soldiers, a young man whose face was covered with streams of blood from a head injury.

A short distance behind, at a point where the north-flowing Galwan River abruptly bent westward, Colonel Bikkumalla Santosh Babu, commanding officer of the battalion, had been alerted to the sounds of the Chinese advance. As he began to summon reinforcements and rally his much smaller force to face the arrival of the much larger Chinese advance, one thing was certain to him. No matter what transpired next in that desolate, ravine-like valley at 13,000 feet in Ladakh's Himalayan heights, history had already been made with blood and bone that day.

As word of the lethal Galwan Valley incident shocked the world at 12.21 p.m. the following day, most would see it as a spontaneous flare-up that had ended a healthy forty-five-year run of zero fatal casualties on the India–China frontier. But waiting in the darkness on the banks of the Galwan River the previous night, Naik Deepak and Havildar Dharamvir knew that nothing, including that advancing horde of Chinese soldiers, was unplanned.

* * *

On the morning of 4 May, Naik Deepak was on COVID-19 inspection rounds at the unit barracks in Leh, the capital of the new union territory of Ladakh, when he heard the booming voice of a senior soldier make the announcement.

'Orders received to proceed to KM-120,' Subedar S.R. Sahu said loudly as he poked his head into the dormitory-like hall lined with beds and lockers for the soldiers of 16 Bihar. As a subedar, he was the second senior-most junior commissioned officer (JCO) of the unit. Apart from being a combatant, his seniority also saw him charged with the upkeep and well-being of younger soldiers and men.

'*Aa gaye hain?* [So, they've come?]' Naik Deepak asked, bemused, while he conducted an examination of a soldier with a sore throat. Subedar Sahu smiled, continuing past the dormitory to the other barracks to alert the other soldiers that they would be rolling out soon. The usual bustle of the barracks settled into a quiet rhythm of movements typical of an Army unit that has just been ordered to proceed to an operational area. Boxes and equipment were loaded, bags packed, vehicles fuelled, phone calls made.

Far away in a village near Rewa, Madhya Pradesh, that afternoon, Rekha Singh, a middle school mathematics teacher, was taking a scheduled class. Her phone had been set to stay silent in class, except for calls from one person. And the tone that rang out was the distinct thrum of an incoming video call. Excusing herself, she left the classroom, accepting the call as she did so. A mess of pixelated jerks quickly took the vague shape of the man she had married less than six months earlier.

'I won't have a phone signal for a few days,' Naik Deepak said. '*Aage jaana hai* [We have to proceed to a forward area].'

Rekha tried to read her husband's expression through the glitchy, blocky video, but could only barely make out that bemused half-smile she had come to know well. She also knew not to prolong conversations, given how delicate the signal always was when he made a video call. She quickly muttered the usual hurried plea to take care, stay warm and to call her as soon as he could next. Staring into the phone after the call ended, she repeated her words as a text message and sent it. And with a quiet sigh, she returned to her waiting class.

In Leh, her husband had begun to restock his white first-aid suitcase with fresh rolls of cotton wool, combat bandages, painkillers, suturing kits and several bottles of emergency medication.

KM-120 is an Indian Army post on the western bank of the Shyok River on a highway that connects the Leh area with the more forbidding northern Ladakh. As the crow flies, KM-120 is roughly 85 km from Leh. By road, winding through craggy mountains and cold deserts, the distance is significantly more, about 220 km.

'We knew why we were being sent,' says Subedar Sahu. 'Ahead of Patrol Point 14, Chinese troops had advanced, and they had to be stopped. After getting that order, we moved with men and equipment and reached KM-120 at 1 a.m. on 5 May.'

Later that day at KM-120, the mood was calm and focused, but there was an eerie disquiet in the air. Word had spread that a violent brawl had broken out between Indian and Chinese troops on the north bank of Ladakh's Pangong Tso, the world's highest saltwater lake nestled in the mountains at more than 14,000 feet, and about 130 km south of the Galwan Valley. It was on this precise piece of land that Indian and Chinese troops had previously brawled in August 2017—a clash caught on video, clips of which quickly went viral across the media and Internet. The men at KM-120 heard that the new clash in that same area, involving the Indian Army's 17 Kumaon battalion and a Chinese patrol, was much more violent, with grievous injuries sustained on both sides.

The 5 May clash at Pangong Tso would later be regarded as the trigger point for what rapidly became a wider and far more escalatory standoff. As it happened, the most immediate fallout of the Pangong brawl was about to register in the dim valley that Naik Deepak, Subedar Sahu, Havildar Dharamvir and seventy-two other men of 16 Bihar were about to rumble into.

'It was a bleak, freezing morning on 6 May as seventy-five soldiers moved in vehicles from KM-120. We crossed the Shyok River and advanced eastward into the winding, narrow Galwan Valley to a patrol base just short of Patrol Point 14,' says Subedar Sahu.

With his white suitcase and boxes of medical supplies, Naik Deepak and his senior medic quickly set up a medical inspection (MI) room at the patrolling base—standard operating procedure for combat medics arriving in an operational area. In the brown tented structure with internal heating about 20 metres from the Galwan River, it was equipped with stretchers, gurneys and oxygen supply equipment. Bunking down for the night at the patrolling base, Naik Deepak couldn't have known that his services would be needed the very next day.

At noon on 7 May, shockwaves from the Pangong brawl reached the Galwan Valley when a small group of soldiers headed by 16 Bihar's second-in-command, Lieutenant Colonel Ravi Kant, ventured across from Patrol Point 14 to confront a Chinese patrol that had clearly strayed past its usual limits.

'*Ek chhoti jhadap thi. Baaton baaton mein hathapai ho gayi* [There was a small brawl. But it soon turned into fisticuffs],' says Subedar Sahu. 'There were injuries sustained on both sides. Lieutenant Colonel Ravi Kant was also injured.'

The men were brought to the MI room, some with serious injuries, but none in any danger. One of the injured men, barely conscious but lucid, remembers Naik Deepak administering first aid to the wounds on his arms and neck.

'He was talking to me casually, as if I was sitting up and totally okay,' the soldier recalls. 'He was talking about the weather and asked whether I would be calling my family that day. Mundane stuff to maybe divert my mind from the injuries I had sustained. As I was wheeled away in the stretcher to be taken back to KM-120 for treatment, I remember seeing Naik Deepak. He was smiling and said, "*Ek-do din mein waapis aana* [Come back well in a day or two].""

The brawl on 7 May might have been brief, but it was only a precursor to what lay in store.

'There was anger among the ranks that night,' remembers Havildar Dharamvir. 'Our second-in-command had been injured. He spoke to all the men to ensure that they remained focused and calm. But all of us, each and every man, knew that the situation was deteriorating thanks to the hostile action from the Chinese side.'

After the 7 May skirmish, Lieutenant Colonel Ravi Kant dashed to Durbuk to report details up the chain of command to the mountain brigade headquartered there. The details were serious enough for the brigade commander to arrive at the Galwan Valley the very next day.

On 9 May, the notion that the Chinese Army, already deployed in unusual numbers close to the Line of Actual Control (LAC) between both sides, had settled into a pattern of aggressive provocation was clear. As the brigade commander arrived in the Galwan Valley for a first-hand assessment of the situation, Indian and Chinese troops violently clashed in an entirely different part of their common frontier—north Sikkim. And as with the brawls at Pangong Tso and Galwan Valley thus far, the clash at Naku La in Sikkim also involved large numbers of troops and injuries on both sides.

A delicate calm descended on the Galwan Valley at Patrol Point 14. Troops and patrol parties on both sides held their positions for a month. But it was clear that the situation had transformed completely into something that could escalate very rapidly.

'Our patrols would go up to Patrol Point 14 and the Chinese troops would also come up to that point from their side. The friction between us was growing steadily,' says Subedar Sahu.

After a series of meetings between officers from both sides across the friction points in the Galwan Valley, Pangong sector—and eventually also in the Gogra Post-Hot Springs area of eastern Ladakh—it soon became abundantly clear that the situation needed a high-level intervention from the senior military brass.

So, on 6 June, the Indian Army's Leh-based Corps Commander Lieutenant General Harinder Singh and his Chinese counterpart, Major General Lin Liu, met for the first time at the desolate border personnel meeting (BPM) hut in the Chushul sector south of the Pangong Lake.

The BPM hut, used regularly by Indian and Chinese officers to hold protocol border meetings, is situated at a site drenched in history. Sitting at the western mouth of the Spanggur Gap, it is close to the famous Rezang La, a narrow mountain pass through which in the 1962 Sino–Indian war, a huge horde comprising thousands of Chinese troops attacked and, after losing huge numbers of their own, ultimately overwhelmed a much smaller 'last stand' by a company of the Indian Army's 13 Kumaon battalion. A memorial to the Indian men who stood and fought against impossible odds, while still inflicting substantial damage to the marauding force, sits on a low ridge less than 5 km away, and is regarded as hallowed ground in the annals of Indian Army war valour. It is also a reminder of the brute strength the Chinese were willing to unleash in their quest for military objectives.

Far removed from the violent clashes that had necessitated the 6 June meeting between the corps commander-ranked officers, the first round of military talks between India and China to cool border tensions turned out to be a very cordial affair— positive enough for the Indian government to issue a statement saying:

> Both sides agreed to peacefully resolve the situation in the border areas in accordance with various bilateral agreements and keeping in view the agreement between the leaders that peace and tranquillity in the India–China border regions is essential for the overall development of bilateral relations. Both sides also noted that this year marked the 70th anniversary of the establishment of diplomatic relations between the two countries and agreed that an early resolution would contribute to the further development of the relationship. Accordingly, the two sides will continue the military and diplomatic engagements to resolve the situation and to ensure peace and tranquillity in the border areas. (Source: Indian MEA Statement on 7 June 2020.)

'The corps commanders had talked, but things kept escalating 7 June onwards,' says Subedar Sahu. 'At Patrol Point 14, the Chinese soldiers came right up to a makeshift helipad on our side of the LAC and even set up tents there. One of our teams confronted them, and after some heated discussions, we were able to send them back. But they were not ready to retreat beyond Patrol Point 14, which is what we consider as the LAC.'

Subedar Sahu was summoned back to KM-120 to oversee combat logistics ahead of a situation that was clearly in freefall.

Over the next week, from 7-14 June, four separate meetings between local commanders in the Galwan Valley would take place, but the Chinese troops and officers refused to budge from Patrol Point 14. In fact, they were reinforcing their position with more tents and equipment on that triangular piece of land circumscribed by the bend in the Galwan River.

'We were deployed in our area and the Chinese side simply refused to listen to any requests not to escalate the situation,' says Havildar Dharamvir. 'Our commanding officer went up to Patrol Point 14 and spoke to his PLA counterpart, telling him that the Chinese soldiers should move back as they were on our (Indian) territory. But they were adamant that we should retreat as the area was theirs. We told them we will not go back, and the Chinese said they will not return either.'

In his bunk at the patrolling base on the night of 9 June, Naik Deepak phoned Rekha.

'He was in an unusually talkative mood, asking me about all kinds of things. He didn't usually do that,' says Rekha. 'I thought maybe he was making up for not calling for a whole week since the time he arrived in the Galwan Valley. I wasn't hard on him. I knew it was a tense situation there. But I did hope he would tell me more. I wanted to share his anxiety, but he did not seem anxious. He seemed upbeat and cheerful. I told him that I was going to my parents' place, and that the next time he called, it would need to be on my sister's phone since my signal behaved erratically there. Before he disconnected, he said yes, please go to your parents' home, I will come and fetch you in a few weeks when I come home on leave.'

Dawn on 15 June was like on any other day that week. But there was one addition to the Chinese position at Patrol Point 14 that was seen by the Indian side as a clear attempt to provoke and escalate the situation. The Chinese Army had set up an observation post (OP) at the river bend.

Colonel Santosh Babu, the commanding officer had had enough. Summoning his top men to an operations room at the patrolling base, he made it clear that the Chinese could under no circumstances be permitted to maintain an OP. It was bad enough that they had squatted with tents and equipment at

Patrol Point 14. But a position from where they could keep an eye on Indian Army movements and provide warning alerts to Chinese positions on their side was quite simply enemy action.

'On 15 June, I was at KM-120 with all the troops and equipment, and was coordinating logistics support. I got a message at around 3 p.m. from Colonel Babu to send seventy-five troops to Patrol Point 14. I had eighty-one troops with me. I arranged seven vehicles and sent seventy-five men to Patrol Point 14 at around 3.30 p.m.,' says Subedar Sahu.

When the seventy-five reinforcement troops arrived at the patrolling base about a kilometre from Patrol Point 14, Colonel Santosh Babu and a clutch of young officers from the battalion were present, including Captain Soiba Maningba. The base was bristling with an operational frisson typical of an infantry unit on the threshold of doing what it was trained for.

'At 3 p.m., we received the orders we were waiting for,' says Havildar Dharamvir. 'Colonel Babu said that a group would be proceeding towards the Chinese position, and that their tents and OP were to be dismantled and their soldiers to be pushed back from the area. We were fully pumped up and ready. We decided that we would go as a battalion . . . *josh aur jazbe ke saath* [in high spirits and morale] . . . and evict the Chinese soldiers from there. Our CO saab was leading from the front, and we said, "Sir, we are all with you on this mission."'

Naik Deepak and a team of combat medics were dispatched from the patrolling base to the MI room closer to Patrol Point 14 that had been set up the previous month.

'Before we rolled out, I saw Deepak leaving with his suitcase,' says one of the soldiers. 'He was loading additional boxes of medical supplies into a vehicle. It struck me as odd at the time that he was carrying so much. One of the men even asked him, "*Itna kyon leke ja rahe ho* [Why are you taking such a large amount of supplies]?" I guess he knew more than we did.'

Colonel Babu and his team of officers and men proceeded towards Patrol Point 14. Emerging from their vehicles, he and the others wasted no time, walking straight up to the site where the Chinese had set up their tents and OP. Spotting the approaching Indian team, a group of Chinese soldiers, led by their commanding officer, Chen Hongjun, began approaching from their side.

'Our CO had fully motivated us to evict the Chinese,' says Havildar Dharamvir, one of the soldiers in the group now face to face with the Chinese.

Colonel Babu addressed his Chinese counterpart, his voice sober, reassuring, yet firm.

'You and your men go back and we will also go back,' he told the Chinese officer.

The reaction from the group of Chinese soldiers was instantaneous and couldn't possibly have been more belligerent—they physically pushed the Indian soldiers. Worse, they dared to push Colonel Babu.

'*Unka behaviour bilkul theek nahi tha. Woh dhakka–mukki karne lage* [Their behaviour was not right, they started to push and jostle us],' says Havildar Dharamvir. He too was pushing back amid an escalating scuffle. 'Even after the pushing started, Colonel Babu was speaking in a calm manner, trying his best to defuse the situation.'

'It doesn't work like this,' Colonel Babu said, his voice momentarily raised. 'I will go back, and you will also go back.'

But every man knew in their hearts that it was too late. No soldier will tolerate his commanding officer being physically assaulted under any circumstances.

'It is like watching your parents being assaulted. Would you stand back and watch? Of course not. Nobody would,' says a soldier who was present.

When the Indian Army men pounced on the Chinese with their bare hands, things rapidly escalated. Chinese soldiers began picking up rocks and flinging them with full force at the Indian troops. Some Chinese soldiers separated from the group and ran up rocky outcrops on the mountain slopes in order to land rocks more accurately from a point of advantage. The 'no firearms' protocol prevailed, but the crossfire of brick-sized rocks was no less injurious. One large brawling group split into smaller groups of Indian and Chinese men attacking each other with their fists and stones.

After several minutes of stone pelting and fearsome hand-to-hand combat, the Indian men prevailed.

'*Bilkul* face to face *tha*,' says Havildar Dharamvir. 'But we finally managed to push them back. *Humne unko peeche dhakel diya* [We pushed them back]. They ran away.'

But in the chaos of the clash, something unthinkable had happened. Six Chinese Army personnel, including their commanding officer, Chen Hongjun, and his interpreter, Chen Xiangrong, were so badly injured that they hadn't been able to retreat with their teams. They remained with the Indian side.

'There were two or three Chinese officers and four–five Chinese jawans *jinko hum ne baitha kar ke rakha* [who were with us]. We told them, "Please do not attack like this, you must return to your area,"' says Havildar Dharamvir.

Colonel Babu knew he had an extremely delicate situation on his hands. The injuries to the Chinese men in his care meant they could only be stretchered back to their side. And the way things were at that moment, a temporary truce seemed practically impossible.

'Get the medics, get Deepak immediately from the battalion aid post,' Colonel Babu ordered, after trying to speak to the injured Chinese men. 'Ask Deepak to meet us at Patrol Point 14. These men need urgent first aid.'

'Colonel Babu was clear that the injured Chinese men needed to be treated quickly,' says Colonel (then lieutenant colonel) Ravi Kant, the unit's second-in-command.

Grim, but determined, the Indian commanding officer and his men walked back along the Galwan River to Patrol Point 14 carrying the injured Chinese men with them. Exhausted from the fighting, but energized by the action, the men proceeded to smash the Chinese observation post and tent structures. Colonel Babu rallied the team. Deep down he knew that the evening was far from over.

As if to confirm his fears, a flurry of stray rocks came hurtling down from the slopes 50 feet above. One rock struck an Indian soldier, Naik Arun, in the chest, throwing him off his feet and injuring him badly.

'I was right there when he was hit,' says Havildar Dharamvir. 'We did not have any stretcher to carry him. Somehow, I lifted him and carried him to the rear to a relatively safer place. Then I gave him some water to drink. Arun told me he was finding it hard to breathe because of the chest injury. Seeing his condition worsening, another jawan and I decided to carry him to the MI room for treatment. I was ordered to drop Arun at the MI room and return immediately, since the fighting was clearly still on. The Chinese CO and his men were all there on the ground. The situation was very volatile.'

Light was fading fast as Havildar Dharamvir and another jawan carried Naik Arun back to the MI room. Near the *nallah*, they ran into Naik Deepak, who was hauling his suitcase and hurrying towards Patrol Point 14.

'Deepak said that the CO had called him to the scuffle site as Indian and Chinese soldiers were injured. I told him I was coming from the spot and requested Deepak to attend to Naik Arun. Deepak quickly examined him and felt it was best to take Arun to the MI room, which was only 100 metres away. A medic was there along with an ambulance and oxygen support if required. Deepak said it was crucial for him to reach the scene of the fighting as ordered,' says Havildar Dharamvir. 'The CO's order was paramount for Deepak, and he wanted to reach the scene of the skirmish as quickly as possible,' adds Subedar Sahu.

'Naik Deepak moved ahead to reach where the fighting was on, and I somehow managed to carry Arun to the MI room. Then I rushed back to the scene of action where stone-pelting had intensified. The first thing I saw was Deepak treating the injured Indian and Chinese soldiers. He was giving them first aid to save their lives. Two of the Chinese men were more seriously injured than the others. He treated them first,' Havildar Dharamvir recalls.

Subedar Sahu was at KM-120 and in constant touch with the Indian soldiers at the centre of action to cater to their needs at that delicate time.

'I was told the first thing Deepak did when he arrived at Patrol Point 14 was to administer first aid to the Chinese commanding officer Chen Hongjung. He also gave first aid to two or three other Chinese PLA officials who were seriously injured. After that he treated our own Indian soldiers,' says Subedar Sahu.

'The Chinese interpreter was almost unconscious from a bad head injury and was being treated and roused by Deepak,' says Colonel Ravi Kant. 'He was barely speaking, that was the main concern. Colonel Babu's priority was to first get him sorted, since the interpreter was the one who could still translate and maybe turn the situation around quickly, or at least help ease the escalating situation.'

The Chinese soldiers pelting stones could clearly see Naik Deepak bandaging and helping the injured Chinese men at Patrol Point 14. To make it even clearer, a young Indian major got on his megaphone to communicate to the Chinese soldiers on the heights as well as in their rear positions that Indian medics were treating the Chinese commanding officer and five other personnel.

'The Chinese had seen in broad daylight that Deepak was bandaging and helping their men,' says Colonel Ravi Kant. 'Every one of their soldiers saw it and recognized that we were helping their men. The trouble was that the interpreter wasn't coming to his senses. He was the fulcrum of how we understand each other. He was crucial in such a volatile situation, and he wasn't gaining consciousness. He was the only man who could make the other side understand that we wanted to calm things down, not escalate. Deepak was trying his best. It was a race against time. Everyone saw that.'

As Naik Deepak gave the injured Chinese personnel some oxygen, a rock came like a frisbee out of the mountainside, splintered on the ground next to him, a piece of it striking him on the forehead, knocking him back. The Indian major with the megaphone once again warned, this time angrily, that the Chinese were targeting a medic administering first aid to injured Chinese personnel.

'Naik Deepak refused to stop, despite being injured,' says Colonel Ravi Kant. 'He was functioning beyond his call as a nursing assistant, treating the enemy, disregarding his own wound. That speaks of his professionalism.'

Naik Deepak understood his responsibility. It was an outside chance, but the Chinese interpreter was literally the only possible key to bringing the escalating situation to a halt. The men of 16 Bihar were well acquainted with the interpreter, having met him several times before during talks between the local battalion commanders.

'I had shared a cigarette with the interpreter on many occasions in the past. He was a pleasant, smiling guy,' says

Colonel Ravi Kant. 'He had told us he was poor, with only parents there at home. He would constantly say "let's have a solution to this dispute so I can also go back home". He always had this desire to go back home.'

And there he lay, bleeding and unresponsive, as the violence continued.

A short while later, abruptly, the stone pelting stopped, with no more projectiles landing for the next ten minutes. A sharp breeze found its way into the narrow valley, whipping itself up into a freezing, steady wind, the sound barely adding to the surging Galwan.

The sun rapidly set thereafter, putting the already extremely tense situation under a pall of total darkness. The temperature plummeted to freezing. In the distance beyond Patrol Point 14, Chinese men could be heard belting out loud threats and still hurling stones at the the Indian soldiers. Colonel Babu used a megaphone to warn the Chinese to stop, to mutually calm things down so both sides could talk peacefully the next day.

'Colonel Babu was being a professional and responsible local commander, trying to negotiate and control the situation at his end rather than involve the higher levels of the Army,' says Colonel Ravi Kant. 'If things could work out, there was nothing like it. It was also the reason why Naik Deepak was summoned—it was a gesture of goodwill by a professional soldier.'

But Colonel Babu knew that the situation had gone way past the point of no return for that night. Staring into the dark void beyond Patrol Point 14, it wasn't immediately clear what would come next. But come it would. Of this, the Indian commanding officer was certain.

It was at this point that Colonel Babu called for reinforcements from KM-120. Troops from 3 Punjab infantry battalion and two artillery units—the 81 Field Regiment and 3 Medium Regiment—would arrive in vehicles shortly thereafter, swelling the Indian force to just over 400 men.

The call for reinforcements was prescient because only minutes later, using darkness as a cover, the Chinese side launched its real assault of the night.

'*Unki main force aayi* [Their main force arrived],' says Havildar Dharamvir, who was part of the front line of troops preparing to face the Chinese. '*Adhik sankhya mein PLA ke log aaye* [PLA men arrived in large numbers].'

That 'main force' was a horde of at least 1200 men—three times the size of the Indian force waiting at Patrol Point 14.

'There was a lot of noise because of the strong water current in the Galwan River. No one could hear one another, but we could still hear the advance. There were that many men,' says Havildar Dharamvir.

'The mountains around the Galwan River are all black, adding to the total darkness that engulfed the battlefield at about 7.30 p.m.,' says Subedar Sahu. 'It was so dark that no one could recognize one another. It was in these circumstances that the huge Chinese reinforcement came from the right side of the mountain and launched an attack on us.'

But the Chinese horde that arrived was armed with more than just rocks, clubs wrapped in barbed wire and their fists. This was an entirely different PLA unit that had been waiting to attack in a sudden wave and not the regular soldiers normally deployed for patrolling the area. These were of an entirely different kind.

The Chinese horde was very well equipped, in padded riot gear and helmets, wielding batons fitted with LED incapacitators—devices that emit sudden bursts of flashing light designed to stun a person in the darkness and temporarily debilitate them. Gear and devices like these had been seen recently in the police crackdown on protesters in Hong Kong.

'They also carried carbon fibre shields which also had that bright flashing light,' says Havildar Dharamvir. 'They would flash that in the dark, and the beam would blind you. That was what they did before the final charge.'

'They charged without any regard for their own advance elements,' says Colonel Ravi Kant. 'It was like a stampede, and I would not be surprised if some of the Chinese men out front were trampled and injured. That was the intensity of the charge in the darkness. Our men were in smaller numbers, but we were ready.'

It is here that the most brutal phase of the Galwan clash began. In groups, 400 Indian Army men collided with 1200 Chinese troops in the dark winding stretch beyond Patrol Point 14 on the Chinese side. An Indian advance party had ventured even deeper into the Chinese side to confront them.

'Our advance elements, *woh aage hi reh gaye* [were left in the front],' says Subedar Sahu. 'The Chinese horde came in the middle cutting off our advance party that continued to fight where it was. *Raat mein bahut zabardast fight hui* [Intense confrontation took place at night]. There were lots of casualties. Some had their heads smashed, some had chest injuries. *Unka bhi wohi haal aur humara bhi wohi haal* [Both sides suffered the same fate].'

Metres from the swelling Galwan River, Naik Deepak continued to feverishly administer first aid. In the minute-long lulls in the savage fighting, Havildar Dharamvir remembers seeing Naik Deepak pick up his suitcase and walk into the scene of the action, following the sounds of injured personnel in order to treat them.

'There were many new injuries on the Chinese side in the fresh fighting that had broken out, and Deepak was busy flitting from one injured man to another, trying to give as much first aid as possible,' says Havildar Dharamvir.

'Imagine this happening in the middle of deafening noise and totally chaotic up-close combat. I don't know how he was managing. Some of us tried to give him cover, but there was too much fighting to do. The Chinese numbers were too large.'

By 8 p.m., when Havildar Dharamvir scanned the scene looking for Deepak, he was nowhere to be seen. The fighting had spread into several groups across a large area, including up the slopes of the mountain and the very edges of the now freezing Galwan River.

'We lost touch with him since he was in one corner busy with his first aid duties,' says Colonel Ravi Kant. 'This corner was right where the fighting was taking place. We don't quite know what happened, but I believe he continued to treat injured Indian and Chinese personnel for maybe another hour or so. There was utter chaos in the darkness. It is very likely that Deepak got encircled by the Chinese while he was doing his work. He did not stop and continued doing it.'

Naik Deepak wasn't seen again for the rest of that night.

'A battlefield nursing assistant (BFNA) buddy was supposed to be with Deepak,' says Colonel Ravi Kant. 'In the army we never leave anyone alone and there's always a buddy system in all situations. Deepak was trained at a proper nursing college. Along with him there was to be his BFNA buddy, trained at the battalion level to assist him and also for any battlefield exigencies. But the current situation was so chaotic, and Deepak was working alone.'

And the terrible cost of that night was about to unfold.

'At around 8.30 p.m. at KM-120, I got a message from the scene of action that our commanding officer was not traceable,' says Subedar Sahu. 'I tried making radio contact with Colonel Babu, but there was no response. Then I called the unit's adjutant but couldn't get through.'

Over the next half hour, a group of soldiers injured in the night fighting was ferried to KM-120 in three vehicles. Some of them had fallen into the Galwan River during the brawl and were rushed to a special 'heating room' for treatment.

'We had four or five soldiers who massaged the feet of the injured troops to stabilize them,' says Subedar Sahu, who was there when the injured men arrived. 'The temperature was well below zero. The water in the Galwan River was so cold that you couldn't be in it for even two seconds. The men were all wet and unconscious. They recovered after half an hour in the heating room. If we had not readied the heating room at KM-120, we would have lost those men.'

It is easy to forget the conditions in which this full-bodied brawl was taking place. While most casualties were caused by direct injury in the fight, weather and altitude were undoubtedly taking their toll. The Galwan Valley is the last place for such devastating energy expenditure.

'You're at over 15,000 feet in sub-zero temperatures. The air is thin, the O2 levels are as it is down by 60 per cent, so you have only 40 per cent in your body, hence with grievous injuries, it becomes ever more difficult to survive. Forget running or charging, even a brisk 200-metre walk puts you out of breath. You can imagine the toll such a brawl was taking on the human bodies on both sides,' says Colonel Ravi Kant.

Back at Patrol Point 14, there was no trace of 16 Bihar's commanding officer. His personal BSNL phone wasn't even ringing. All attempts to contact his group by radio hit a wall of silence. Meanwhile, all through the search for Colonel Babu, the fighting was getting even more fearsome.

'More Chinese reinforcements had come to the area, including their special forces,' says Havildar Dharamvir. 'The Chinese then launched a fresh attack on us. Very intense fighting went on till around 9.30 p.m. This was the fiercest fighting I have ever seen.'

One of the men involved in the 'fiercest' combat was Naib Subedar Nuduram Soren. As he fought, Havildar Dharamvir remembers seeing Soren being injured with a baton blow to his face.

'Some of the other soldiers pulled him to the side, away from the fighting and asked him to return to base,' says Havildar Dharamvir. 'But he was determined to fight. He said, "Whatever has to happen, will happen today and now. *Main peeche nahi jaunga. Mere ko maara hai PLA ne. Mein bhi unko marunga tabhi vaapas aaonga* [I will not step back. The PLA soldiers attacked me. I will return only after I have hit them too]." On the battlefield, you cannot ask for anything more inspiring than that. We advanced and fought even harder under his leadership.'

Naib Subedar Soren plunged back into the fight. Soldiers who fought near him remember his determined screams as he fought. One of them recounts, 'There was no stopping him. Naib Subedar Soren fought extremely bravely against the Chinese despite suffering serious injuries. He kept motivating us in a loud voice. He said the PLA had to be pushed back at any cost. Soren Saab motivated us so much that we thrashed the Chinese soldiers with even greater zeal.'

But the number of Chinese was so great, the soldiers soon lost sight of Naib Subedar Soren as well.

By 10.30 p.m., things fell quiet. There was a sudden shift from the savage chaos of war cries to only the sounds of the Galwan Valley. The last of the brawls broke up, with the Chinese retreating to their side. The sound of the roaring Galwan punctuated now by the sounds of the injured Indian and Chinese men. Many of them had fought to the death.

'After the Chinese were finally pushed back, we sat near the nallah. It was freezing. We were all wet. We sat there all night like that. Our officers asked us to carry out a headcount of the men, how many of us had come for the mission and how many of us were there now. Our main mission now was to find Colonel Babu. Our commanding officer was still nowhere to be seen,' recalls Havildar Dharamvir.

With flashlights, search parties fanned out from the site of the carnage, stepping between the dead and injured, hoping to find Colonel Babu, who had been missing for over two hours. Injured men on the ground were quickly carried to the MI room where a team of eight Army doctors and surgeons had arrived for emergency support.

Shortly after midnight on 16 June, the commanding officer's body was found. He had sustained a grievous head injury, most likely from a rock flung from the heights. Attempts were made to revive him.

Colonel Babu was hurriedly carried to a vehicle and dashed back to KM-120.

'At around 12.45 a.m., Colonel Babu was brought to us in a vehicle,' says Subedar Sahu. 'Doctors tried their best to revive him. *Kissi tarah unko saans aa jaaye* [If only we could make him breathe in some way]. But there was no luck. The doctors then tried to make him sit. The moment they did that, blood started oozing out of Colonel Babu's nose. It dashed our final hopes of reviving him.'

At 1.30 a.m., Colonel Babu was put back in the vehicle and sent to the Army's field hospital in Durbuk, 120 km to the south.

Back at Patrol Point 14, the search for the injured and dead continued in the freezing darkness.

'It was difficult to do a headcount as many of our soldiers were injured, and injured Chinese soldiers were also there. It was difficult to identify who was who in the darkness. We spent the entire night trying to identify our soldiers and those who belonged to the PLA. For the ones we could identify, we carried out the necessary procedure and took them to the MI room for treatment,' says Havildar Dharamvir.

At around 4 a.m., more injured Indian men were transported to KM-120. These included Subedar Anil, who had suffered serious chest injuries. An Indian Army Dhruv helicopter was called to pick up a group of the grievously injured at 6 a.m. from KM-120 and was flown to the better-equipped military hospital in Leh, which was also at a lower altitude.

Colonel Ravi Kant, then the unit's second-in-command, was in Leh on military work just before the incident. When the fighting began, he travelled all night and reached KM-120 at 4 a.m., heading straight to Patrol Point 14. There was no time to acclimatize to the steeply higher altitude. The commanding officer of the unit had been killed in action in an unthinkable sequence of events. It was upon Colonel Ravi Kant to rally his men and keep things together.

'When Lieutenant Colonel Ravi Kant reached, he assembled the battalion, briefed the men and said there was nothing to worry about, whatever had happened could not be changed, and that the battalion should be ready for any task assigned to it,' says Havildar Dharamvir. 'He told the men that their *hausla aur junoon* [courage and passion] should be higher than before. "*Main aa gaya hoon* [I am now here]," he said. He motivated us and said there was no need to be worried. He praised the way we fought against the PLA and drove them away. The battalion was fully motivated and ready to advance further, till the Chinese capital if necessary! We were grieving but that was how galvanized we were. We were prepared to do anything.'

After speaking to the men and reassuring them, Colonel Ravi Kant, now the commanding officer of the 16 Bihar battalion, ordered a team to scale one of the highest points near Patrol Point 14 and swiftly establish an OP. The events of the previous night had made it clear that border protocols and treaties between the two countries were now severely compromised, if not totally destroyed. Foreseeing more uncertainty ahead, he wanted eyes on everything the Chinese did that day. The hours gone by had extracted a terrible cost.

In vehicle after vehicle, the true extent of the human loss was brought home to KM-120, where the tragic duty of dressing wounds of the dead was conducted before the remains were boxed and dispatched down the highway to the 303 Field Hospital in Durbuk.

'At 6.15 a.m., I got a message that a havildar from our unit, Sunil Kumar, has been killed in action, and to "please come and identify him". I immediately rushed to the MI room close to Patrol Point 14,' says Subedar Sahu. 'Havildar Sunil had been in the water, face down all night. It was difficult to identify him. With some difficulty, after verifying all his details and proper identification, he was also sent to Durbuk in a vehicle.'

The next man to be identified was Havildar Palani, an artillery soldier from the 81 Medium Regiment. His body was discovered near the banks of the Galwan. Eyewitnesses had seen him valiantly fight a group of Chinese soldiers to the death, managing to subdue at least three before he fell.

As the sun rose, a search party climbed up one flank of the mountainside, hoping to find more injured men who could be saved. These had been the vantage points from where Chinese soldiers had unleashed attacks with rocks. It was behind a rocky outcrop several feet up on the flanks that the search party found Naib Subedar Nuduram Soren, the soldier whose war cries were heard loudest the previous night in the Galwan Valley. A few feet up the mountainside from his body was a rocky ledge where the search party spotted a rudimentary catapult system. The Chinese had been using a catapult to launch rocks at the Indian Army.

Over the next hour, eight more casualties, including the body of Naib Subedar Soren, arrived at KM-120.

'Soren had suffered severe injuries during the fighting, and blood was oozing out of his head. He fought valiantly and sacrificed his life for the country,' says Subedar Sahu. 'His fearlessness can never be overstated. It was superhuman. Whatever I say about him is inadequate.'

By 9 a.m., several soldiers were still unaccounted for. The brutality of the final phase of fighting had sent the brawling groups far apart, some of them deep into the Chinese side where the Indian Army's advance party had already been cut off earlier. It was almost certain at this time that Indian soldiers were either injured or forcibly held back by the Chinese on their side.

The search continued without pause, with a party led by Havildar Dharamvir venturing deeper into the Chinese side to look for casualties. Against the dark sand on the riverbank he spotted debris of used cotton wool and pieces of broken tincture bottles. He knew it before he saw it.

'Deepak was lying on the ground, his suitcase sprawled open next to him. I knew he was dead, but one never accepts it at first. He had suffered serious injuries and there was blood all over his head. We did all we could, hoping that he could be saved. We carried him to the MI room. The doctor there declared him dead on arrival,' says Havildar Dharamvir.

Just around the time that Naik Deepak's body was found, in Rewa, Madhya Pradesh, his wife had been asked to turn on her television set to catch the first newsbreak on the Galwan incident. At that point, the only confirmed information was that three men from 16 Bihar, including the commanding officer, had been killed in the deadly clash.

'I remember watching the big headlines flashing,' says Rekha. 'First it said three men were killed. A little while later, some of the names began flashing, including Colonel Santosh Babu, Havildar Palani and Sepoy Gurtej Singh (from 3 Punjab battalion). Then the headlines said a total of twenty men had lost their lives. My head was spinning. I kept telling myself that Deepak is a medic, and it's impossible that he would be at the front line in a scenario like this. *Ho hee nahi sakta* [It is not possible].'

When Rekha did not receive any phone call through the day, she called her father-in-law. He hadn't received word either, and Deepak's phone wasn't reachable. The search for the injured and dead in the Galwan Valley would take all of 16 June.

'That night, frantic and anxious, I called a cousin of mine who is also in the Army. *Andar se tension tha* [I was tense],' recalls Rekha. 'I was very emotional and nervous after receiving no news all day. My cousin received my call but was unable to help. I didn't know what to do except wait.'

Rekha didn't have to wait long. Thirty minutes after she spoke to her cousin, Naik Deepak's father finally received a phone call from Leh at 11.30 p.m.

'Deepak's father was unable to digest what he was hearing on the phone,' says Rekha. 'He handed the phone to Deepak's cousin. It was he who then called me to break the news. I thought I was hallucinating for some reason. I was very upset and angry. I disconnected the call. But he called me again. This time I listened. He told me Deepak's unit had called. I still couldn't believe it. I asked him for the number he had received the call from. I dialled, but the call wouldn't go through. You can imagine, I did not sleep that night, praying that there was some mistake. My hopes were raised by a family friend in the Army who called to say he had seen a body box of Deepak but not his body itself, and nothing was confirmed. It was only when the names were released by the Army the next day that my world came crashing down.'

'When things got so brutal, Deepak should have actually moved back but he continued to render first aid to the Indian as well as Chinese soldiers,' says Colonel Ravi Kant. 'He was encircled by the enemy. Even with all the movement of soldiers and chaotic fighting, Deepak was doing what he was trained for. Our boys had fallen, and he continued to render treatment to the maximum extent that he could. He was simply saving lives and honouring his profession. Even though he had helped their men, the Chinese either could not or refused to acknowledge the humanitarian service he was rendering. This boy was giving first aid to their soldiers just a short while ago. But he was still attacked. They could not have mistaken him for a combatant. He was clearly a medic. He did nothing but administer first aid on the battlefield.'

'I have a feeling the Chinese soldiers captured Deepak, used him to treat their injured personnel, and then killed him,' says Subedar Sahu. 'They had witnessed him treating their injured earlier. When Deepak's body was brought to KM-120 at around 1 p.m. on 16 June, the blood from his wounds was fresh. He appeared to have been attacked and killed with some sharp object. In the case of several other injured soldiers who were brought to KM-120, their blood had clotted. But in Deepak's case, the blood was fresh.

'*Deepak ko night mein capture karke rakha hoga* [He must have been held captive at night]. He was from the Army Medical Corps. The PLA must have captured him for their benefit. After getting their men treated, they must have killed him, left him there and gone back. Our boys brought him to KM-120, which is around 7 km behind Patrol Point 14. It takes about an hour and a half to reach KM-120 from Patrol Point 14. Deepak's blood was totally fresh.'

The battlefield was also littered with dead Chinese soldiers. Through the night, the injured Chinese soldiers had been pulled out of the area where the fighting took place to the PLA positions in the depth beyond Patrol Point 14.

'Since the time we had assembled in the area in the morning, we had spotted dead bodies of several Chinese soldiers lying around. Our orders were not to touch them, as the Chinese were expected to retrieve them later,' says Havildar Dharamvir.

Sure enough, late in the afternoon on 16 June, Chinese soldiers arrived with stretchers to take back their casualties. High above them, the Indian OP kept a hawk's eye on the Chinese ambulances taking the men back to a rear position. Through the day, a series of Chinese helicopters were spotted, arriving to collect the dead and wounded.

Silence pervaded KM-120. The loss of men was still sinking in.

'All the twenty fatal casualties that came were handled by me,' says Subedar Sahu. 'I got the doctors to see them and then sent the bodies to Leh and Durbuk. They were the most numbing few hours of my life. Through the night I had been pleading with my commander, saying my battalion was on the front line fighting and I had been assigned logistics support duties, organizing vehicles, rations and other tasks. When the bodies of our men were brought to me, I prayed for their peace, but wished I had been fighting alongside them. It was a painful story. For the next three days, it was almost as if I had forgotten about food, overwhelmed by the situation, the bodies, the blood.'

After all the counting and tragic paperwork, ten men were still unaccounted for. Over a series of emergency, major general-level meetings with the Chinese side, it was confirmed that the Indian Army's advance party had been cut off during the night assault and held back after the clash ended. The ten soldiers, including two majors, two captains and six men, were sent back across Patrol Point 14 at 5.30 p.m. on 18 June, formally bringing to a close the Galwan exchange.

The men of 16 Bihar remained at KM-120 and the Galwan Valley till 19 June, after which they were rotated out of the location and replaced by a new battalion. The men of 16 Bihar had just lost their commanding officer and nineteen men. While every man remained focused and galvanized, Army protocol dictated that they be given some distance, both physically and emotionally, from a location that had completely dismantled border peace and tranquillity mechanisms between the two countries. They had fought back a hostile, premeditated attack by a larger force and had paid a stinging human price.

'It was painful. But our morale was very high,' says Subedar Sahu. 'We were prepared to do anything. We would have sacrificed our lives if necessary. That is how every man in our unit felt. Our families, our wives and children are at home, but equally our families are the faujis who we are posted with. At the age of seventeen we join the Army. We spend our lives together. They are our real friends and every bit our family.'

Honouring the lasting legacy of her husband, Rekha joined the Chennai-based Officers Training Academy in May 2022 and will be commissioned into the Indian Army as a lieutenant in 2023, joining a growing list of proud army wives who have chosen to follow in the footsteps of their husbands after they were killed in the line of duty. She wants to go to the Galwan Valley at least once to see where her husband honourably gave his life treating not just his own but also the enemy.

'Deepak used to tell me he was proud that I was educated and a teacher. He did not get a chance to finish school. Because of his family circumstances, he needed to begin working early, and so he joined the Army,' says Rekha. 'He would say you have the gift of education—"*padho aur mera bhi naam ho, Deepak ki wife hai* [study and make me proud of a wife like you]". He felt he didn't have a chance, so he always encouraged me in the little time that we spent together to learn and climb higher. His English was weak, so he would always say "please only talk to me in English". He really wanted to speak fluently in the language.'

From Ladakh, 16 Bihar was sent far away to Chinthal in Hyderabad, awaiting their next deployment. Eight months later, on 11 February 2021—the raising day of the 16 Bihar Regiment, families of the men killed in action were invited to a memorial event in the city.

'Deepak's wife was also there,' says Subedar Sahu, who was tasked with coordinating logistics for the families. 'I tried to have a word with her. He was my jawan, I was his senior JCO. I was not really able to talk to her at that time. Nor was she able to speak very much. But slowly we shared our stories. Deepak's family is now the family of the unit. They are our responsibility.'

'Deepak and I met for the first time on a video call in March 2018,' Rekha told the senior soldier. 'We had an arranged marriage in December the following year, but I think it turned to love within a week. When the *rishta* came, Deepak couldn't get leave to come down, so his brother Havildar Prakash (from the Indian Army's Armoured Corps) came to see me and to introduce Deepak in some remote manner. But the very next day Deepak and I got on a video call. We met in person only in May 2019. He had strange names for me right from the start. His favourite was "Recruit". I still don't know why, and he refused to tell me.'

'I spoke with Deepak's elder brother, Havildar Prakash,' says Subedar Sahu. 'He said Rekha was like his younger sister, and if she wanted to marry again, move forward in her career or anything she chose, he would fully support her. I am in touch with Deepak's family and tell them often that 16 Bihar is always there for them.'

Havildar Prakash continues to serve in the Indian Army, proud of the stories he hears about his younger brother.

'We were very poor growing up, so both Deepak and I knew we had to take on responsibilities early to take care of the house and family,' says Havildar Prakash. 'Near our childhood home in Farenda village, there is an army range. For years we used to see army cars and cavalcades passing by. We both used to get very excited. We used to feel pride swelling in our hearts as well. Deepak, who was a biology student, enlisted with the Army Medical Corps. He plunged into it with great passion. When he came home for *chhutti*, he was basically the village doctor.'

Deepak's last visit home was in February 2020, barely four months before the Galwan Valley skirmish. The brutal fighting in the remote valley stretched the India–China bilateral relationship to a breaking point, and the trust deficit it triggered still casts a shadow over the ongoing talks to resolve the lingering LAC row that began in May 2020.

'He was to return on 14 February,' says Rekha. 'He called me from the railway station the previous day. I said, "*Jaldi aa jana, kal Valentine's Day hai* [Come soon, tomorrow is Valentine's Day]." There was a pause at the other end. He said, "*Rekha, 14 February ko Pulwama mein attack hua tha pichle saal, aur tum Valentine's Day ke baare mein baat kar rahe ho* [There was an attack in Pulwama on 14 February last year, and you are talking about Valentine's Day]." I felt a little guilty. I quickly said we wouldn't celebrate, but it would be our first Valentine's Day, and a token of our togetherness. I know he felt a little bad for reprimanding me. But I was okay with it. I know he felt strongly about it.'

When he reached home, Rekha would present him with a mobile power bank as a Valentine's Day present.

'Deepak was perplexed. I said, *Desh hai but apna relationship bhi toh hai* [We have to think about the nation, but we also have to think about our relationship]. I told him, sometimes let's talk about us and not only about the army and Pakistan and whatnot,' says Rekha. 'But I had never really felt bad. His devotion to duty was extreme—he would run to the phone every time it rang, wondering if he was being summoned back to his unit urgently. But he was very devoted to me and loved me. He never let me feel otherwise.'

'My wife tells me, if Deepak and she were watching television and if there was news of soldiers being killed in action anywhere, Deepak would simmer with anger and go silent,' says Havildar Prakash. 'And then, when the news channels flashed images of the last rites of a soldier, he would whisper to himself, "*Dekho kitna bada kaam karke gaye hai* [Look at the tremendous work he has done before sacrificing his life]."'

'Once he was talking to an Army friend, and I overheard him describe the cold and the terrain in Durbuk,' says Rekha. 'When I asked him weeks later on the phone, he was surprised. He said, "Stop googling the weather. There's a reason I don't tell you all this." He never shared details of the tough areas he was posted in so that I don't get stressed. What is that, if not love?'

On Republic Day 2021, Naik Deepak and three other men—Naib Subedar Nuduram Soren, Havildar K. Palani and Sepoy Gurtej Singh—were honoured posthumously with the Vir Chakra, India's third-highest wartime gallantry medal. Artillery soldier Havildar Tejinder Singh, who fought fiercely and survived with injuries, also received a Vir Chakra. The 16 Bihar's commanding officer, Colonel Santosh Babu, would be bestowed with a Maha Vir Chakra (MVC), the country's second-highest wartime gallantry medal.

The choice of medals—wartime decorations, as opposed to the peacetime Shaurya Chakra and Kirti Chakra medals—was also a message from the Indian Army and government that the situation in Ladakh was being formally regarded as a live conflict between the two countries.

A further sixteen officers and men from the 16 Bihar battalion would receive Sena Medal (Gallantry) decorations. These include Captain Arjun Deshpande, Subedar Amarendra Singh Parmar, Havildar Birsa Tirkey, Sepoy Nitin Khadke, Sepoy Dheerendra Yadav and Sepoy Bijay Kumar Gond. Posthumous medals were awarded to Havildar Sunil Kumar, Sepoy Ganesh Ram, Sepoy Kundan Kumar, Sepoy Kundan Ojha, Sepoy Chandrakanta Pradhan, Sepoy Rajesh Orang, Sepoy Chandan Kumar, Sepoy Ganesh Hansda and Sepoy Aman Kumar.

Last in the list of decorations to the unit for gallant action in Galwan was a lone Mention-in-Despatches for meritorious service in an operational area. The recipient was a young officer from Manipur, Captain Soiba Maningba Rangnamei. He would inadvertently be thrust into the public eye when China leaked a propaganda video of the Galwan incident on Chinese social media. The Chinese military's apparent attempt to paint the Indian side as aggressors inadvertently put a rare spotlight on the individual gallantry of Indian personnel. One particular sequence showing a defiant Captain Maningba challenging and physically stopping a group of Chinese men went viral. Viral enough that Manipur's chief minister Nongthombam Biren Singh, who hadn't noticed the honour to the young man from his state the previous month, hurriedly organized a meeting to honour the officer.

Authentic details of a military incident rarely emerge very soon after it happens. Which is why much of the detail you've just read has been written about for the first time here.

For instance, how many lives did Naik Deepak actually save that night in the Galwan Valley? His Vir Chakra citation would reveal, 'He was pivotal in rendering treatment and saving lives of more than thirty Indian soldiers, which reflects the epitome of his professional acumen.'

'What was left unsaid was his professionalism to the injured enemy. It is why, when I wrote him up for this decoration, I mentioned that his act of valour surpassed both duty and humanity,' says Colonel Ravi Kant.

But while the Indian Army would release the full list of its twenty fatal casualties on 17 June itself, the cost imposed on the other side would go on to become an object of concerted Chinese propaganda.

Eight months after the Galwan clash, in February 2021, China's official military mouthpiece formally honoured four PLA personnel posthumously—a suggestion that the Chinese Army had lost four men that night in Galwan. Two of the Chinese faces were immediately familiar to men of 16 Bihar.

The first was Chen Hongjun, commanding officer of the PLA unit involved in the first brawl.

'The second face we recognized was Chen Xiangrong, the interpreter. The man who Deepak had treated and tried to revive. Clearly, he had succumbed to his injuries. We saw him as a reasonable, friendly man who could have maybe helped communicate and calm things down. But given what came that night, I doubt it would have been possible even for him. May he find peace,' says Colonel Ravi Kant.

While the Chinese government's propaganda organs made an unseemly attempt to taunt the Indian side on the death toll it had suffered in the clash, the Indian Army maintained a studied, professional silence, unwilling to be pulled into an ugly war of claims over the bodies of the dead. Internally, however, operational reports and logs of course recorded the truth.

The Indian OP on a peak above Patrol Point 14 had been able to peep 7 km into the Chinese side and, right through 16 and 17 June, had witnessed the vehicular and air evacuation of at least thirty-six men on stretchers, though it was impossible to tell for certain how many of these were non-fatal casualties. A conservative estimate suggested about half were highly likely to be fatal, given the savagery of the clash.

While China would never comment or verify officially, a confirmation of sorts would emerge in the officers' lounge of the BPM hut at the Chushul-Moldo meeting point at one of the many rounds of talks that would be held in the weeks and months following the Galwan clash. During a chat away from the main talks, a brigadier-level officer of the PLA, who doubled as an interpreter, is said to have confirmed to an Indian colonel that the number of Chinese fatal casualties was seventeen, with over half succumbing to their injuries in the week that followed the clash.

'We have a number for how many Indian lives Deepak saved, but we don't have a number for how many Chinese men he saved that night,' says Colonel Ravi Kant. 'All I can say is that many of the injured Chinese men who survived that night definitely have Naik Deepak to thank. They were practically abandoned by their forces, while this boy was tending to their wounds. We are trained to take life to protect the country. But what can be higher than saving lives?'

At the time this book was written, the Indian Army and the PLA had held fifteen rounds of military talks to reduce border tensions in the Ladakh sector. A complete resolution is still not on the horizon, even though the ongoing negotiations have led to partial disengagement of rival soldiers from some friction areas on the LAC.

Naik Deepak's niece Palak misses the video calls with her uncle and frequently asks for him.

Her father smiles and replies, *'Woh charon taraf hai, dikhte nahi hai but aas paas hee hai hamare* [We can't see him, but he is constantly near us].'

2

'I'm Not Leaving This Cockpit'

Group Captain Varun Singh

Coonoor, Tamil Nadu
8 December 2021

The sudden roar of helicopter blades forced Joe to jerk his phone camera upward. On a walk along a verdant stretch of railway line near Kattery Park, his phone managed to capture less than two seconds of the helicopter itself, a grey silhouette against a foggy noon sky of even more grey, one half of the image filled by a burst of hillside foliage.

As the helicopter flew out of view beyond the trees, Joe jerked his phone back towards his five fellow travellers walking along the railway track, his friend Naseer, their family and friends craned their necks to follow the sound.

At precisely the eleventh second, the sudden roar of a deafening explosion from across the hill made one of the women snap her head back. Naseer, visibly shaken by the sound, turned to Joe and asked, 'What happened? Did it fall? Has it crashed?'

Still filming in the direction of the sound, Joe said, 'Yes,' unaware of what he had just managed to capture on his mobile phone. Three seconds later, the video stopped.

Hearing the sirens of emergency vehicles echo up the hillside, the six tourists hurried in the direction of the explosion. They couldn't get very near, but it was clear that fire services and the police were on their way.

Less than an hour later, news of the Indian Air Force Mi–17V5 helicopter crash broke across the news media, the story quickly overwhelmed the airwaves, social media and WhatsApp groups like no other military air accident had in living memory. On news channels, anchors and breathless reporters, fighting to digest the unbelievable flash updates, informed the country that India's first chief of defence staff (CDS), General Bipin Rawat, his wife, Madhulika Raje Singh Rawat, and twelve others were in that helicopter.

The Russian-origin helicopter had taken off from the Air Force's Sulur base at 11.48 a.m. and was to land at the helipad at the Wellington Golf Course after a twenty-seven-minute flight. However, the twin-engine helicopter—equipped with latest technology and considered to be extremely reliable—lost contact with air traffic controllers at Sulur twenty minutes after take-off and just seven minutes before it was to land.

It went into radio silence at exactly 12.08 p.m., with Joe making the video a few seconds earlier.

Overwhelmed by the breaking news updates and after word had spread in Coonoor about who was in the helicopter, Joe contacted the police and sent them the video he had filmed on his mobile phone. He wasn't aware at the time that those twenty seconds of footage would become one of the most-watched videos of the year and central to the Air Force's most crushing crash investigations in nearly sixty years.

Hours of public confusion and contradictory media reports spread, with speculation over the death toll and cause of the crash. At 6.03 p.m., nearly six hours after the accident, the Air Force finally announced on Twitter what had been most feared:

> With deep regret, it has now been ascertained that Gen. Bipin Rawat, Mrs Madhulika Rawat and 11 other persons on board have died in the unfortunate accident.

There was one final line in the Air Force's statement:

> Wing Commander Varun Singh SC, Directing Staff at
> DSSC [Defence Services Staff College, Wellington] with
> injuries is currently under treatment at Military Hospital,
> Wellington.

Given that thirteen other persons on board the helicopter
had perished in the crash, there was little doubt about the
seriousness of Wing Commander Varun's injuries. And while
no specific information emanated from the military, other than
to his wife Gitanjali and father Colonel K.P. Singh (retd), the
story of this sole survivor quickly and understandably captured
the nation's imagination. Amid the paralysing implications of
the accident, here was one military man who had managed to
evade death.

As Wing Commander Varun was transported from the
Nilgiri Hills down to Sulur in the plains near Coimbatore, a
running commentary on his condition dominated the headlines.
The enormous interest and solidarity with the officer, still in
a coma, compelled the media to satisfy audiences with more
stories about Wing Commander Varun. The 'SC' after his
name stood for Shaurya Chakra, India's third-highest gallantry
decoration for exceptional acts of valour in peacetime. It was
a medal he was awarded on Independence Day 2021, less than
four months before the crash.

It was clear that this wasn't just any soldier fighting for
his life.

The day after the helicopter tragedy, just around the
time that Wing Commander Varun was being wheeled into
an Antonov An-32 transport aircraft at Sulur to fly him to
Bengaluru for top-level intensive care treatment, a copy of a
letter he wrote to the principal of his school in Chandimandir

emerged in the media, rapidly going viral and fanning interest in the officer to a fever pitch. He had written the letter a month after he had been bestowed with the Shaurya Chakra and barely three months before the crash. He wrote:

> I write to you filled with a sense of pride and humility. On August 15 this year, I have been awarded Shaurya Chakra by the President of India in recognition of an act of gallantry on October 12, 2020. I credit this prestigious award to all those I have been associated with over the years in school, NDA and thereafter the Air Force, as I firmly believe that my actions that day were a result of the grooming and mentoring by my teachers, instructors and peers over the years.

But it was the twelfth paragraph of the letter that became a viral headline story, making Wing Commander Varun a hero on social media, even as he fought for his life in the ICU of the Air Force Command Hospital in Bengaluru:

> It is ok to be mediocre. Not everyone will excel at school and not everyone will be able to score in the 90s. If you do, it's an amazing achievement and must be applauded. However, if you don't, do not think that you are meant to be mediocre. You may be mediocre in school but it is by no means a measure of things to come in life. Find your calling, it could be art, music, graphic design, literature etc. Whatever you work towards, be dedicated, do your best. Never go to bed thinking I could have put in more effort.

When Wing Commander Varun was decorated with the Shaurya Chakra in August 2021, no one really noticed. He was one among the usual annual list of military personnel recognized for acts of valour and performance in the line of duty. As he lay suspended between life and death, the 297-word citation provided a bare glimpse of what the thirty-nine-year-old pilot had done to earn such a towering honour.

But until now, the full true story had not been told.

* * *

Hindon Air Force Station, Uttar Pradesh

12 October 2020

The vast apron of Asia's largest air force base, on Delhi's eastern suburbs, had been traditionally festooned with different types of combat aircraft just four days earlier for the annual Air Force Day event. The 'static display' which permitted attendees to do up-close walking tours of the fighter jets was a big draw, a thrill on par perhaps with watching those same jets roar overhead in the separate flypast.

But four days after the event, the apron was mostly empty. The Air Force Mirage 2000, Sukhoi Su-30, Jaguar, MiG-29 and other weapon platforms hosted at the Hindon station for spectators had gone back to their home bases. Only one 'visitor' jet remained at the base.

Tail number LA-5006, an indigenous Tejas fighter.

The fighter was among the three Tejas jets that had flown in for the Air Force Day display from their home base at the other end of the country, Sulur in Coimbatore, Tamil Nadu.

Their flight display over Hindon successful, the other two Tejas jets had since been flown back home to Sulur by two pilots, flight commander of the country's first Tejas squadron, Group Captain Syamantak Roy and commanding officer of the country's second Tejas squadron, Group Captain Manish

Tolani. They made refuelling stops in Ozar, Maharashtra, and Bengaluru before touching down in Sulur. It was the third Tejas whose homeward flight was stalled.

At 10.30 a.m., sitting in the single-seat cockpit of the Tejas with the canopy open was fighter pilot Wing Commander Varun Singh, then deputy to Group Captain Syamantak. The early winter fog had mostly lifted, revealing promising patches of blue sky wreathed in wisps of sullen cloud. Standing on the apron next to the aircraft monitoring things was Wing Commander Abhimanyu Chhetri.

Wing Commander Varun had been ferry pilot for this third Tejas, but he hadn't flown in the Air Force Day display four days earlier. At the flypast on 8 October, he was the display supervisor on the ground, tasked with the critical duty of monitoring the flights and providing real-time inputs on bird hazards.* Later that day, after the first two Tejas fighters returned to Sulur, Wing Commander Varun had encountered problems with the third aircraft while he conducted system checks for the intended return flight.

'Varun had taken off shortly after us, but he aborted the flight and landed back at Hindon and called me while still sitting in the cockpit,' says Group Captain Syamantak, who took the call at Sulur. 'While he was at 28,000 feet, there were fluctuations in the pressurization system leading to problems in the flight control performance. He told me there was an issue with the air conditioning system, which maintains temperatures of systems on board, in addition to the cockpit

---

* The Hindon Air Force station is situated close to the enormous Ghazipur garbage landfill, a mountain-sized repository of refuse from the National Capital Region. The landfill attracts large-sized scavenging birds that have posed a threat for years to flight operations at Hindon.

itself. The AC system in Tejas is important because everything is computerized.'

Over three days, the stubborn first-time glitch appeared to have been fixed. But since it was a long north-south ferry flight that had to be flown, Wing Commander Varun had conferred with his Group Captain Syamantak in Sulur and concurred that it was best to conduct a test flight near Hindon to make sure everything was okay with the Tejas before the flight home.

'We were both clear that it was critical to prove things were okay rather than encounter an emergency en route,' says Group Captain Syamantak.

With things seemingly repaired, at 10.50 a.m., Wing Commander Varun taxied the Tejas towards the tarmac, instructed by air traffic control (ATC) to hold. It was a busy morning with aircraft from Hindon—the C-130J Super Hercules and C-17 Globemaster III—departing on logistics flights.

Cleared for take-off at 11 a.m., Wing Commander Varun pushed forward on his throttle, bringing the Tejas's single General Electric F404 turbofan engine to maximum power, roaring into the air, gently banking right to take the aircraft northward into the sector designated for this test flight. Wing Commander Varun was intimately familiar with how agile the Tejas was in the air, but this was a flight to ensure all was well, so there was no need to push the aircraft to its limits.

Nearly 2000 km away in Sulur, Group Captain Syamantak monitored the test flight in real-time, receiving a live feed of what was happening with the aircraft and the pilot.

The Tejas continued to climb steadily, breaking through the cloud deck. Wing Commander Varun reported that everything seemed okay till then. It was when the fighter climbed to 23,000 feet that things began to unravel.

'At 23,000 feet, Varun got a cockpit warning of system failure,' says Group Captain Syamantak. 'He immediately descended to 18,000 feet. The warning alarm stopped. This was a test flight, so obviously he needed to check if it recurred. So, he put the jet once again into a climb.'

Almost instantaneously, another cockpit warning blared out, this time alerting Wing Commander Varun to a 'Level 1' failure in the aircraft's digital flight control computer (DFCC).

'The Tejas flight control computer is very robust, with four separate channels, so there's plenty of redundancy and fallback in case one channel fails,' says Group Captain Syamantak. 'If three channels fail, however, then you're in trouble. Serious trouble.'

While descending from 19,000 feet to 16,000 feet, that's precisely what happened.

'DFCC Level 3 fail!' Wing Commander Varun called out on his radio talkback, though ground control at Hindon and Group Captain Syamantak in Sulur already had that information, thanks to live telemetry.

The Tejas flight manual is crystal clear on courses of action to be followed by pilots for each level of failure in the DFCC:

- Level 1 Failure
  Autopilot trips out, handling becomes tricky, pilot needs to move with additional care
- Level 2 Failure
  A marked degradation in the aircraft's handling
- Level 3 Failure
  If the aircraft is out of control, the pilot must eject

'If three channels fail, the aircraft is as good as gone theoretically, and as per protocol, the pilot is fully within reason to punch out of the plane if it is out of control,' says Group Captain

Syamantak. 'But Varun reported that he wanted to try a few things to regain control of the aircraft. He pushed a switch to reset the aircraft's fly-by-wire* (FBW) system, producing an instantaneous response from the aircraft.'

After wobbling uncomfortably for a second, the Tejas abruptly pitched its nose down violently,† a jolt of a movement that sent the blood rushing to Wing Commander Varun's head and making him experience up to -4.5G, with an average of -3.5G for several seconds.

'Varun had been taken to the human endurance limit of negative G (i.e. -3G). Only display pilots train for negative G beyond that. I can only imagine how it must have felt, especially since it was unplanned and totally sudden,' says Group Captain Syamantak.

'This was a full in-flight emergency now, and Varun was practically thrown out of his seat and against his straps,' says Group Captain Syamantak. 'He was very shaken up but alert and conscious, and he knew he was even more within his rights now to bail out of the aircraft at this point.'

The dive had brought the Tejas rapidly down to 14,000 feet.

'He pulled his stick back to take the Tejas out of the bunt, allowing it a few seconds to settle,' says Group Captain Syamantak.

When Wing Commander Varun had gathered himself after the jolt, he spoke to Wing Commander Chhetri who was at the Hindon ATC.

---

* Fly-by-wire (FBW) is a system that replaces the conventional manual flight controls of an aircraft with electronic signals. The flight control computer processes these signals and carries out manual tweaks to aircraft control surfaces to produce the desired movement or response.
† The movement identified as 'bunt', where the aircraft experiences a rapid, uncontrolled, right forward pitching motion.

'The aircraft has gone out of control, I need vectors for a clear area without habitation ASAP,' came the voice from the cockpit. Ground controllers immediately sent the pilot directions, guiding the Tejas out over a desolate stretch of wilderness north-east of Delhi.

'Ejection planned?' Wing Commander Abhimanyu asked. A clear answer would allow the IAF to set in motion the recovery of the pilot once he had parachuted down.

But Wing Commander Varun replied in the negative, pointing out that he was still flying near the heavily populated Delhi suburb of Ghaziabad. He reported that he wanted to stay with the aircraft and try to nurse it back to normalcy, and only needed uninhabited ground as a precaution. After a few minutes of silence that had led to excruciating tension at both Hindon ATC and Sulur, he finally spoke.

'Aircraft is behaving,' said Wing Commander Varun. 'Will attempt return and landing. Please position me on finals for ILS [instrument landing system] approach.'

'Varun was a softspoken guy, but I could tell from his tone that his adrenaline was at its peak,' says Group Captain Syamantak. 'He had just experienced something very violent in the cockpit. It's something that can make your head spin very badly. He had recovered. He had even been asked if he wanted to punch out, because all criteria for an ejection had been met. Nobody would have blamed him for ditching the jet at that point. But he held her steady and continued to descend, determined to bring the fighter back. And that's when things spun out of control again.'

At 10,000 feet, the Tejas DFCC experienced its second Level 3 failure. This time when Wing Commander Varun reset the flight control system, the fighter aircraft violently rolled on to its back with the nose pitching down—an upside-down bunt that similarly pushed the pilot into a realm of negative G forces for four seconds. Once again, Wing Commander Varun fought to control the jet, rolling it back the right way and pulling back on the stick to get it into level flight. Once again, he initiated controlled descent.

At 8000 feet, the aircraft experienced another Level 3 failure—the third so far on the flight. Again, the plane snapped forward, throwing the pilot against his seat restraints.

'The Tejas flight reference card practically mandates an ejection below 10,000 feet if there is serious loss of control,' says Group Captain Syamantak. 'If there was a time to eject from the aircraft, it was after this third Level 3 failure. I was amazed, but I think I understood what Varun was feeling at that point.'

Wing Commander Varun and Group Captain Syamantak had been at the National Defence Academy (NDA) together at the turn of the millennium. Commissioned as fighter pilots and both going on to fly Jaguar strike jets, the two had been posted together at the Gorakhpur air force station in 2005.

'Varun was always super self-motivated,' says Group Captain Syamantak. 'As a young pilot, he quickly became a qualified flying instructor [QFI] and a test pilot. When the Tejas squadron in Sulur was hunting for a good test pilot, nobody fit the bill better than Varun. Unlike other aircraft, the Tejas is an open book. It's our own jet, designed and built by our own teams. Like all of us Tejas jocks, Varun had huge pride in this indigenous fighter, which had never been in an accident or crash. We had taken great pride in ensuring safety. Varun had therefore come up in that "zero loss" environment. This kind of ownership sentiment we feel for this aircraft is tremendous. I guess Varun was also determined not to be the one crashing a Tejas for the first time. He didn't want to create that kind of history.'

The Tejas was now at 100 feet, with its landing gear down ready for 'short finals' back to Hindon. The jet continued to descend gently, Wing Commander Varun holding it steady, the runway in sight. But 50 feet from the ground, for the fourth time, a Level 3 failure rang out.

If the Tejas pitched down now as it had during the previous failures, it would smash into the ground like a missile in seconds before any possibility of recovery. The decision now was to either eject, sending the jet careening uncontrolled towards the Hindon tarmac and hangars. Or to sign away the final chance of ejection and do everything humanly possible (apart from praying) to gently bring the aircraft down to land. The plane could have rolled or pitched violently as it had earlier in the flight. If that had happened, things would have ended very quickly.

'We were holding our breaths for that moment,' says Group Captain Syamantak. 'The aircraft could have done some other manoeuvre and endangered him. That was the moment of truth for all of us. We could lose a plane and pilot. Or we could lose a plane. For most of those monitoring those were the two main possibilities. But Varun was the pilot. Nobody knows better than the pilot in the cockpit.'

With crash tenders and emergency equipment ready near the tarmac, Hindon ATC watched as the Tejas landed safely on the main runway.

It had been fifteen minutes since the Tejas had encountered its first failure.

The first thing Wing Commander Varun did after taxiing back to the Hindon apron and powering the aircraft down was call his boss in Sulur.

'*Bach gaye* [I have escaped], sir,' said a still-shaken-up Wing Commander Varun. 'This aircraft has really taken me for a ride today.'

The pilot and his troubled jet were back safe, but those fifteen minutes in the air were serious enough for the Air

Force's Southern Air Command to suspend Tejas flights until a fleetwide investigation was conducted. The Level 3 failure had been trained for in simulators but had never happened in a real aircraft. The Air Force leadership was clear it didn't want to take any chances.

Over the following days, a court of inquiry identified the reasons for the malfunction, quickly ordering a bug fix across the two Tejas squadrons in Sulur. Test flights since have satisfactorily shown that the Tejas does not bunt or roll—or move dramatically in any manner—in the event of the DFCC Level 3 failure and reset of the flight control system.

There was a big silver lining to a mid-air incident that could easily have ended in either tragedy or the loss of a prized aircraft.

'The Tejas flight control system is among the best in the world,' says Group Captain Syamantak. 'That's why the aircraft was recoverable after a few seconds. With any other aircraft, there would have been total loss of control. The fleet underwent modifications. This was the time the early Tejas jets were ready to be upgraded with advanced software. When we stopped flying following the incident, we ensured that the upgrade involved the bug fix. That was a silver lining.'

The day after the incident, on 13 October, Wing Commander Varun was flown back to Sulur on one of the service logistics flights that criss-crossed the country. He had to leave the Tejas behind at Hindon until it could be fully fixed. The aircraft stayed for another month, with engineers from manufacturer Hindustan Aeronautics Ltd (HAL) arriving to get a closer look and ensure it was fully fit for its flight back.

'Varun returned to Sulur clearly sobered by what had happened, but he was still in good spirits,' says Group Captain Syamantak. 'That day was spent watching his cockpit and HUD (head-up display) videos of the entire incident. We already knew that his handling of the emergency was nothing short of heroic. But it was after watching the cockpit videos that the base leadership was clear that this guy deserved a gallantry decoration not less than a Shaurya Chakra.'

It was one thing monitoring data and performance of the aircraft as it went through those tribulations earlier in the month. It was entirely another watching the footage of the pilot as he bore it.

'In the second instance, when the Tejas went on its back, it was harrowing to watch,' says Group Captain Syamantak. 'He and I then left for Bengaluru to attend the court of inquiry that had been ordered. Varun had to go through all his medicals again because of the negative G he had experienced more than once. He finally returned to Sulur on 26 October, the day I took over as commanding officer of the first Tejas squadron.'

Before the end of 2020, the first Tejas jets began to be upgraded with new software that included the crucial bug fix. When it was time to test the first 'fixed' Tejas, the new commanding officer of the squadron knew who he should ask.

'Who better than him to do the test flight?' asks Group Captain Syamantak. 'Varun was a fine test pilot, and the flight was smooth and error-free. The aircraft involved in the 12 October flight had also returned to us and was ready for its own upgrade. Tail Number 5006 remains one of the best aircraft in our fleet. We love it even more because it kept our guy safe and landed back safely.'

Far from unnerving pilots and safety crews, the incident and aftermath hugely boosted confidence of Tejas pilots in Sulur. The pervasive sense was that even in such a critical emergency, it was possible to recover the jet. But the confidence was always tempered—the squadron went into deep study mode to 'wargame' what else could go wrong with systems in flight.

What happened may have been an aberration, but it triggered a deep pre-emptive safety sweep in Sulur, making the Tejas even more familiar to pilots than before.

Wing Commander Varun flew the LA-5006 again at Sulur several times with no incident.

'The incident didn't change him—he was more confident in his abilities,' says Group Captain Syamantak. 'He came out stronger. It was a contrast to how he was at that time, shaken, flustered, pumping adrenaline, but super focused.'

In April 2021, Wing Commander Varun received official word that he was being posted to the prestigious DSSC in Wellington near Coonoor in Tamil Nadu's Nilgiri Hills, alongside a promotion to the rank of group captain (equivalent to colonel in the Army).

'He knew it was an honour, but he had mixed feelings because he would not get to fly for some time,' says Group Captain Syamantak. 'But duty calls. We were expecting him to come back to the field and to the Tejas. In June 2022 he would most likely have taken over a Tejas squadron.'

On 15 August 2021, as recommended up the chain of command in the IAF, Wing Commander Varun Singh was decorated with a Shaurya Chakra. Pandemic restrictions following the second COVID-19 wave had forced the Rashtrapati Bhavan to drop plans of a traditional investiture ceremony, keeping the ritual for the following year. But the award citation itself was public:

> Faced with a potential hazard to his own life, he displayed extraordinary courage and skill to safely land the fighter aircraft. The pilot went beyond the call of duty and landed the aircraft taking calculated risks. This allowed an accurate analysis of the fault on the indigenously designed fighter and further institution of preventive measures against

recurrence. Due to his high order of professionalism, composure and quick decision making, even at the peril to his life, he not only averted the loss of an LCA [light combat aircraft], but also safeguarded civilian property and population on ground. For this act of exceptional gallantry, Wg Cdr Varun Singh is conferred with the Shaurya Chakra.

It was less than four months later that a newly promoted Group Captain Varun Singh volunteered to go down to Sulur from Wellington and escort General Rawat and his entourage in a helicopter to the Staff College for a scheduled speech by the country's top military officer.

'On that fateful day, I knew he had volunteered to be the liaison officer for the visit by the CDS because it gave him the opportunity to come down and meet us in Sulur,' says Group Captain Syamantak. 'On 8 December, Varun arrived at 8 a.m. and came straight to meet me in the squadron. He met with all the other guys from the two Tejas squadrons. His people, his buddies. Everyone knew he would be among them again as a commanding officer in six months or so.'

Group Captain Varun had always spoken of being lucky.

'Throughout his life, even with the Tejas incident, he felt he was lucky that everything worked out and he didn't eject,' says Group Captain Syamantak. 'His course mates agree he has been one lucky guy. When news initially broke that fateful afternoon that there were three survivors in the helicopter crash, everyone in the squadron immediately knew Varun had to be one of them. When he was brought to Sulur the next day, I saw a flash of him under a blanket. We prayed so hard for him.'

The Sulur base was already grieving when a comatose Group Captain Varun arrived for the emergency flight to Bengaluru. Four personnel from the base—Mi-17 helicopter pilots Wing Commander Prithvi Singh Chauhan, Squadron Leader Kuldeep Singh and airmen Junior Warrant Officer Rana Pratap Das and Junior Warrant Officer Arakkal Pradeep—had died in the crash.

The CDS's defence assistant Brigadier L.S. Lidder, Lieutenant Colonel Harjinder Singh, Havildar Satpal Rai, Naik Gursewak Singh, Naik Jitendra Kumar, Lance Naik Vivek Kumar and Lance Naik B. Sai Teja were also killed in the horrific crash, which a tri-service inquiry later established as a controlled flight into terrain (CFIT) accident. The probe found that the crash took place after the Mi-17V5 entered clouds in bad weather, leading to spatial disorientation of the pilot, which resulted in the CFIT. It refers to the accidental collision of an airworthy aircraft, under the flight crew's control, with terrain.

'After the crash, when Varun was hanging on to life, it was excruciating for us,' says a Tejas pilot from the second squadron. 'It was truly a collective prayer by us all for his recovery and for his family, including two young children. Many of us who saw him before he was flown from Sulur still have sleepless nights.'

Doctors at the Air Force Command Hospital in Bengaluru combined forces with burn and skin graft specialists from across the country to save Group Captain Varun. In media interviews, his father Colonel K.P. Singh (retd) would say that his son was a fighter and would fight this too.

On the morning of 15 December, seven days after surviving the helicopter crash that killed the other thirteen souls on board, Group Captain Varun succumbed to his injuries.

'Luck ran out for Varun, is how he would have probably described it,' says a maintenance engineer with the first Tejas squadron. 'He always wanted to shine bright, maybe be famous, be known for good.'

As Group Captain Varun had lingered between life and death for an excruciating week, his well-being went beyond just a media story. It felt personal to huge numbers of people, who perhaps felt invested in his recovery. A sliver of hope in a tragedy that could never be fully fathomed.

'A part of Varun will be smiling,' says Group Captain Syamantak. 'He would have loved to know that he is now famous and has inspired an entire nation.'

Five and a half months after Group Captain Varun's unexpected death, his mother, Uma Singh, and wife, Geetanjali, received the fighter pilot's Shaurya Chakra from President Ram Nath Kovind at a defence investiture ceremony held at the Rashtrapati Bhavan on 31 May 2022.

Mixed emotions gripped Group Capain Varun's father, Col K.P. Singh (retd), and his younger brother, Lieutenant Commander Tanuj Singh, as they sat in the imposing Durbar Hall and watched Uma and Geetanjali receive the honour from the President.

'It was a very proud moment for the family, but we missed Varun. We were told by some friends that the cameras at these ceremonies tend to focus on people who applaud the awardees with most enthusiasm. I would have climbed up my chair and clapped wildly had Varun been there to receive his medal,' says Colonel Singh.

Varun didn't really expect very much of himself when he was in school but through hard work and perseverance became one of the Air Force's finest experimental test pilots, a top-notch qualified flying instructor and was shortlisted in 2019 for the country's first crewed spaceflight, Gaganyaan.

Colonel Singh recalls that his son was among the twelve fighter pilots considered for Gaganyaan, but he could not make the cut due to a medical reason—Russian doctors ruled him out for the space mission because of issues related to jawbone density.

Varun found humour in rejection.

'Your destiny is decided by the density of your jaw.' That was Varun's WhatsApp status for the longest time.

3

'Get as Close as Possible before Dark'

Subedar Sanjiv Kumar

OP Randori Behak

The whirl of the Dhruv's rotors filled the helicopter's cabin as it climbed away from the Army helipad nestled between the hills of Trehgam in north Kashmir's Kupwara sector. Rising to only a few hundred feet, the helicopter banked southward towards terrain that rose abruptly into the forested highlands of Jumgund in Jammu and Kashmir's Keran sector.

The destination was a very short 5 km away, a distance that would be covered in a few easy minutes by the chopper. But it was the decision to use the helicopter that was the difficult part. Faced with the prospect of wasting a whole day hiking across high ridges to get to the same place, Subedar Sanjiv Kumar, grim-faced and staring out of one of the Dhruv's side windows, had finally agreed to use the chopper to transport him and his men.

In the cabin with him were five other commandos, including his buddy soldier Paratrooper Amit Kumar, another senior commando Havildar Devendra Singh and two young scouts, paratroopers Bal Krishan and Chhatrapal Singh. There was company in the air too. Flying in pursuit 400 metres behind was a second Dhruv helicopter, carrying six commandos of its own.

The two Special Forces squads of a dozen men from the 4th Battalion of the Parachute Regiment (4 Para SF) knew that this was hardly their style. Helicopters were always a noisy affair, usually unthinkable when it came to the stealthy, unannounced manner in which the men of 4 Para liked conducting their operations.

Or at least starting them.

'Anyone sitting in a valley can see, if not hear, an approaching helicopter. They can tell that helicopter *se kuchh bande aaye huwe hain* [some men have landed],' says one of the men from the second helicopter. 'Therefore, we had to account for a loss of surprise even before we were properly inducted.'

For the Special Forces unit even daunting distances were usually covered in off-road military vehicles that moved by night. But the place the commandos were headed to that morning of 4 April 2020, couldn't be reached by road. And while every man in those two helicopters had mentally factored in loss of valuable stealth, they equally agreed that the swiftness of their arrival would hopefully offset losing that element of surprise.

The two Dhruvs were flying over a country, a world really, that had come to a standstill. Ten days earlier, on 24 March 2020, Prime Minister Narendra Modi had addressed an anxious nation at the beginning of the COVID-19 pandemic. He had declared that India would be entering an unprecedented national lockdown to contain the viral spread. A quiet place like the hinterland of north Kashmir had become even quieter during the lockdown. Mirroring the tiniest detail into which Special Forces planning goes, the decision to use a helicopter also had to account for how lockdown restrictions could mean people with less to do on the ground. This could mean making them perhaps more attentive to a chopper flying nearby, a piece of information they could pass on to four men hiding somewhere on a snow-clad mountaintop. There is no eventuality, crack or weak link that Special Forces planners don't wargame in their heads before setting out for a mission.

But none of this mattered now. If Subedar Sanjiv had green-lit the helicopter ride, that was enough. Nobody needed to have any further apprehensions. Seated across from him in similar winter combat fatigues, paratroopers Amit, Bal Krishan and Chhatrapal, all three in their twenties and among the youngest in the unit, leant in close to be able to hear one another over the rotor noise. They had cut their combat teeth under the direct supervision of Subedar Sanjiv, the sullen-faced commando who wasn't just their senior. Navigating their first years into young adulthood away from their homes and families by voluntarily committing themselves to a difficult life in the Special Forces, it was in the shadow of Subedar Sanjiv that they grew into serious soldiers.

Fifteen minutes into the flight, as the two helicopters cut a lazy turn across a forested ridgeline, a pure white mountaintop came into view. Their destination had arrived. One of the pilots, speaking into the cabin address system, alerted the squad, then gently pitched the helicopter forward and descended towards the mountaintop. All six commandos used the valuable seconds of descent to cast their gaze across the terrain. It is likely that the same thought passed through each of their minds:

A pure white situation.

Miles and miles of snow.

No treeline, no cover.

Having made the difficult decision to arrive in a helicopter, it was near imperative for the commandos that they be able to exit the noisy rotorcraft in a concealed area. But the brief aerial reconnaissance of the mountaintop showed that this would have to be the second major compromise of the day—landing in an open area with plenty of visibility in every direction.

The site was about 12 km east of a stretch of the Line of Control (LoC) that Indian Air Force Mirage 2000 fighters had crossed* to bomb a Jaish-e-Mohammed terror facility near Pakistan's Balakot town just over a year earlier, in February 2019.

Around noon, the two helicopters descended to the general locations identified as Rangdoori and Teen Behak, all high-altitude sites in the Jumgund area. In coordination with Subedar Sanjiv before the flight, the pilots had brought the commando squads to the precise patch of mountaintop where an Indian Air Force Heron surveillance drone had spotted a foot trail in the snow.

The thirty-four-second video clip of the faint footprints filmed by the Heron and beamed to the Army's 68 Mountain Brigade in Trehgam on the morning of 4 April was the trigger for the urgent helicopter mission to get the dozen 4 Para commandos from the brigade helipad to the site as quickly as possible. The video clip was the first breakthrough in days.

The four terrorists had been spotted for the first time in the Rangdoori area of Jumgund three days earlier on 1 April. A patrol party from the Army's 8th Battalion of the Jat Regiment had spotted the terrorist infiltrators at a distance. The brief exchange of fire wasn't enough to eliminate the four men but forced them to abandon their heavy rucksacks and flee into a wooded area on that mountain. This was the first contact.

'The crucial thing was the terrorists had abandoned their bags, so they had no sustenance, apart from maybe some medicines or supplements in their personal pouches,' says Major Abhishek, a young 4 Para SF officer whose unit was already on standby alert by that time to join the hunt.

At dawn the next day, 2 April, troops from the Army's 41 and 57 Rashtriya Rifles counterinsurgency units arrived on site to tighten the pursuit of the terrorists. That afternoon,

---

* See *India's Most Fearless 2*.

at 4.30 p.m., the troops once again spotted the four terrorists from a distance. This time the exchange of fire was longer and more intense. But this time too, slipping off one by one from a mountain ledge, the four infiltrators managed to escape. This tense hunt would see two more exchanges of fire on the morning of 3 April. But for the rest of the day, nothing. As the troop units closed in on what was hoped to be the endgame to a frustrating forty-eight-hour hunt, the terrorists had simply evaporated. There was no sign of them in any direction.

Assisting the troops from the air, drones and helicopters had been deployed on frequent photo reconnaissance dashes to track the terrorists as they furtively moved from one hideout to another. At the 4 Para's team headquarters elsewhere in Kupwara, Subedar Sanjiv and Major Abhishek pored over the latest operational inputs as they streamed in on the morning of 3 April.

'*Jaana toh padhega,*' said Subedar Sanjiv. '*Jaldi jaana padhega, nahi toh woh wapas nikal jayenge* [We will have to get there quickly, if not, they will disappear across the LoC].'

'It had been two days since the boys from 8 Jat had recovered the terrorists' rucksacks, so Subedar Sanjiv had assessed that if we don't eliminate them quickly, they may make an attempt to fall back across the LoC,' says Major Abhishek. 'Temperatures were falling to minus, and there was a lot of snow in that general area. Surviving in those conditions is a Herculean task.'

Subedar Sanjiv knew the area well. He had served in the Jumgund area and operated with the local infantry battalions deployed there. And so, a full twenty-four hours before the 4 Para was actually summoned to help, the senior commando had already got busy with planning the mission down to its last detail.

'He was already studying the maps and recce material that was coming in, choosing the squads and selecting weapons and equipment for the mission,' says Major Abhishek. 'He did not like waiting—he knew by now it was only a matter of hours before the unit would be called in, and he didn't want to waste a minute. He had already stepped up for it.'

When Subedar Sanjiv entered 'planning mode', an unmistakable frisson would pervade the team headquarters. The sudden, hushed bustle of activity was a clear announcement to the men that some of them were about to be handpicked to roll out on their next mission.

Paratrooper Amit Kumar, Subedar Sanjiv's young buddy commando, hovered near the boss. He knew he would be part of whatever was coming next. Havildar Devendra Singh, also sullen-faced and serious, wanted in too, having operated alongside Subedar Sanjiv in dozens of operations. Paratroopers Chhatrapal Singh and Bal Krishan had already begun preparing their personal weapons and equipment. There was no way they weren't going to be on an operation with Subedar Sanjiv.

Just around the time the last firefight was erupting between the terrorist infiltrators and Rashtriya Rifles troops on 3 April, Subedar Sanjiv had finished choosing his dozen men. When the unit was finally summoned, it would take them bare minutes to roll out. This was pre-emptive planning that went to the heart of special operations preparedness.

For the rest of the day, the dozen men went through every bit of input and photographic data that had been received, using it to craft their own battle picture—another compulsion in special operations, since the very need for commandos on the ground meant that a different approach was deemed necessary.

Subedar Sanjiv ordered the squads to turn in early that night. He had made it plainly clear that the summons would arrive the following day. Flying at 12,000 feet, the Heron flying over Jumgund would prove him right.

'On the morning of 4 April, along with the drone video, orders arrived at the team headquarters to deploy as soon as possible to the brigade headquarters in Trehgam for a search-and-destroy operation,' says Major Abhishek. 'Subedar Sanjiv and his eleven men, all trained in mountain warfare, were quickly flown to Trehgam by 10.30 a.m. in two Army Dhruv helicopters.'

At Trehgam, the commando team was quickly escorted into the brigade operations room, where every bit of intelligence collected thus far was on a set of wide panel screens adorning three walls. It was here that the brigade commander first briefed Subedar Sanjiv's team, and then presented them with the choice of proceeding to the Jumgund mountaintop on foot or by helicopter.

'*Chopper se induct honge, sir. Hume jald se jald wahan pahunchne ki zaroorat hai,*' Subedar Sanjiv said. '*Agar wait karenge, toh woh bach niklenge* [The chopper is better since we need to reach at the quickest, or else they might escape].'

It was in the same two Dhruv helicopters that the two squads were now hovering over Jumgund at a drop-off site that couldn't have been more unconcealed for a Special Forces induction.

'Paratrooper Chhatrapal was the first commando to jump out of the first helicopter in low hover mode,' says a commando in the same helicopter. 'When Chhatrapal hit the ground, he sank chest-deep into the snow. He simply went inside—that's how soft and deep the snow cover was. Subedar Sanjiv immediately told the pilot to take the helicopter a little lower to the ground. The helicopter descended and shifted locations by about 10 to 15 metres. The rest of us then jumped out. The snow was very deep. The other squad in the second helicopter jumped out a short distance behind us.'

Induction complete, the two Dhruvs, vulnerable in the open, quickly climbed and peeled away from the drop-off site. On the mountaintop, it would take the dozen commandos thirty minutes to get fully out of the snow and gather their gear.

'We were waist-deep in the snow. We were not walking. We were wading,' says a member of the first squad.

About 20 metres in front were the two team scouts, Paratroopers Chhatrapal and Bal Krishan. Behind them were Subedar Sanjiv and his buddy, Paratrooper Amit. In the rear were Havildar Devendra and his buddy soldier. Just 30 metres behind the first squad were the six commandos of the second squad.

By 2 p.m. they reached the precise point where the Heron drone had spotted the foot trail in the snow. The jumbled mess of shoe impressions, in single file, had survived the light, snowless winds that morning. At regular intervals, it was clear the infiltrators had tried to cover their tracks by kicking at the snow, but the trail was clear enough to follow in a rough direction. The twelve commandos trudged on.

'It was very silent and still, with hardly any breeze,' says a commando from the second squad. 'We were following Subedar Sanjiv's lead while awaiting information from Chhatrapal and Bal Krishan, who were the eyes and ears of the pack. Around 3 p.m., the two scouts spotted something in the distance and signalled to the rest of the squad.'

About 300 metres ahead, Paratroopers Chhatrapal and Bal Krishan saw something move under a small clump of trees. Signalled by the scouts, the squads froze in their tracks.

'*Koi baitha hua hai,*' Chhatrapal signalled back to Subedar Sanjiv. 'Some kind of silhouettes with black hair. It must be them.'

There was excellent visibility in the snow. Now completely still and only signalling to each other or speaking in hushed whispers, Subedar Sanjiv initiated a 'listening drill', a field practice to squeeze every bit of intelligence out of a given situation based solely on sound. But the distance was too much to hear anything other than the dull whistle of the breeze.

'It's definitely them,' Paratrooper Bal Krishan signalled back. 'I can see movement. It looks like there is less snow under those trees and they've taken refuge there.'

Subedar Sanjiv knew the answer already, but he asked anyway, since the two scouts were in the best possible position to judge.

'Can we engage from here, or do we need to get closer?'

'Too far from here. We can't open fire from here. Low chance of hitting them and high chance of their escaping,' said Chhatrapal.

So that was settled. The commandos would need to get closer to the clump of trees to even think of firing the first shot.

'As we readied our assault weapons, Subedar Sanjiv began to plan,' says a commando from the second squad. 'Closing in directly on the location of the trees was ruled out because the sound we would make while wading and trudging through the snow would be simply too loud. If they heard it, they could have been alerted and slipped away down the slope. We needed to play it very carefully.'

With the scouts still out front, Subedar Sanjiv summoned the other nine men towards him so they could hear as he laid out his plan.

'He ordered the second squad to stay in the rear position and try to find some kind of upward slope from which we could get a height advantage to get better eyes on the infiltrators,' says the commando from the second squad. 'Immediately, six of us broke away from the larger team and slowly trudged off in search of a vantage point.'

Leading the advance squad, Subedar Sanjiv and the five other commandos knew that if they were to approach the trees without making a sound, they couldn't trudge through the snow any longer—they would need to crawl.

'We began crawling by centimetres, taking maximum care not to make any noise at all,' says a commando from the advance squad. 'We closed in a little more and stopped at a point 120 metres from the trees, where it was assessed that if we advanced any further, surprise would be lost. It was not feasible to close in any further than this also because there was simply no cover. Six of us were literally out in the open, with nothing to hide behind.'

It was 4.20 p.m. The six commandos were now separated from each other by only a few metres. Subedar Sanjiv looked to the two young scouts.

Chhatrapal and Bal Krishan, both with their TAR-21 rifles now ready, nodded an affirmative. Subedar Sanjiv had his own assault rifle ready. Paratrooper Amit and Havildar Devendra readied their multi-grenade launchers.

'I positioned my Pika machine gun,' says the sixth commando in the squad. 'We awaited word from Subedar Sanjiv to open fire. Generally, we in Special Forces engage at very close distances. In our ambushes, the engagement distance is never more than 25 to 30 metres. But this was 120 metres. But we didn't have a choice.'

Suddenly smashing the silence on that mountaintop at 4.30 p.m., the squad opened a heavy and non-stop volume of fire at the figures they had spotted under the trees ahead of them. Ammunition that included 40 mm grenades and 5.56 mm bullets tore into the target site, whipping up the snow. The firing continued for six minutes without pause.

And then Subedar Sanjiv ordered the squad to hold fire, quickly checking with the scouts for a visual report.

'Because of the distance and lack of an optimal firing position, we were not able to immediately assess the results of the fire,' says the commando with the Pika. 'Still in firing position, we couldn't tell if any of the infiltrators had been hit or had escaped down the mountain. We waited for ten minutes and conducted another listening drill. But there was no sound. Slowly, we started crawling towards the trees again.'

When the six men reached the spot near the trees, there were no bodies. Where the infiltrators had been sitting, they had left behind three syringes and a few pairs of gloves. It was clear that the infiltrators had stopped to rest and had been carrying syringes with chemical cocktails for energy or emergency sustenance. A few feet away from the syringes, the squad spotted something else.

A fresh, dark trail of blood in the snow.

It was now just past 5 p.m.

'In April, last light is about 7.30–8 p.m.,' says the sixth commando. 'Subedar Sanjiv gathered us under that tree and spoke to us in no uncertain terms.'

'*Hume jitna ho sake, unke kareeb jaane ki zaroorat hai,*' said Subedar Sanjiv. '*Andhera hone se pehle* [We need to get as close as possible to them before it gets dark].'

Since one of the terrorists was clearly injured in the firing assault, it was assessed that the infiltration party wouldn't be able to make much progress.

'Blood loss would have compounded three days without any proper food since they had lost their rucksacks. Also, they would likely have been in shock after that sudden and heavy burst of fire,' says the sixth commando. 'It looked like the endgame was in sight, but nothing could be taken for granted. Subedar Sanjiv made it clear that we had less than three hours to close in and finish the mission. We assessed that they couldn't have been more than 200–300 metres down the mountainside.'

The squad reassembled in the snow and reloaded their weapons. Over his radio, Subedar Sanjiv communicated with the rear squad, informing them to advance towards another point on the edge of the mountain and provide cover. Once in position, Subedar Sanjiv and his men began making their way down the mountainside, slowly tracking, following the intermittent spatters of blood in the snow. It was a slow, painstaking descent.

'By 7.30 p.m., light was failing fast,' says the sixth commando. 'We had now reached a steep sixty-five-degree slope.'

About 400 metres downhill from this position was a cordon that had been laid in advance by the Army's infantry and Rashtriya Rifles units that had been hunting the terrorists since 1 April. Subedar Sanjiv used a map with grid references to get a clear picture of where they were and where the 8 Jat infantry positions were down the mountainside. Subedar Sanjiv communicated over radio with the infantry positions further down the mountain, receiving confirmation that they were ready to 'receive' any terrorists attempting to make an escape down the mountain.

It was now reasonably clear that the terrorists were somewhere in the 400-metre stretch down the mountainside that passed through the thick Zurhama forest.

Though 400 metres doesn't sound like much, on a steep, icy slope filled with crags and rocks it is a daunting hunting ground. Even though the squad was taking no chances, it was evident that the terrorists had been trapped—they couldn't climb back because the squad was coming down the mountain after them. And they couldn't move further down the mountain as the infantry would be waiting for them. So, they had no choice but to hide.

The commandos in the squad were now descending the slope keeping a distance between one another. This was to ensure minimum damage in the event of an ambush. The blood trail had gone towards a *pahadi* nallah, an icy, 10-metre-wide snowmelt that streamed down the desolate mountain amid a burst of conifers.

By 8 p.m. it was totally dark. Subedar Sanjiv decided that active pursuit in the darkness was a bad idea—it was better to lay an ambush in the night. The plan was that in the morning the squad would roll down the mountain and quickly eliminate the terrorists.

'It would have been a textbook, easy kind of operation. The terrorists were properly trapped, wherever they were. There was no escape,' says the sixth commando in Subedar Sanjiv's squad.

Under a half moon and the kind of starlight that only lights up such high-altitude areas, Subedar Sanjiv and his squad began crawling out from their positions to begin laying the night ambush along the nallah.

'Try not to engage tonight. We will get them at first light,' said Subedar Sanjiv to the five men. '*Dhyan se*, Chhatrapal, Bal Krishan. *Unko pata hai ki hum yahan hain* [Be careful, they know we are here].'

Dhyan se (Carefully).

The two young scouts had always cherished that warning from their senior commando. It was of course a superfluous instruction—commandos didn't need to be told to be careful during operations. That was their nature, ingrained in their training from the start. But when Subedar Sanjiv said the words, it wasn't just as a senior soldier, but as someone who had watched the two young scouts grow.

Forty-three years old, Subedar Sanjiv had grown up in the neighbouring mountains of Himachal Pradesh. His two scouts, one from the mountains and another from the desert, were half his age. Both were now setting out to survey the nallah for the ambush plan.

But none of their training, none of the pre-emptive planning, none of the minute detailing, nor the word of warning from their senior commando could have prevented what happened next.

As the two scouts began to crawl along a shoulder of the snowmelt, they reached a cornice of snow, an icy ledge over the nallah. It felt solid, except that water from the nallah had eroded away beneath it, making it literally just a precarious overhang of brittle ice. Since the terrain was so steep, there was very little space for manoeuvre and the two scout commandos were crawling along the cornice very close together. Then, with no warning, no creaking of the ice, no heaving of the terrain, it happened.

The cornice abruptly snapped and collapsed, sending Paratroopers Chhatrapal and Bal Krishan 30 feet down into the rocky nallah in the darkness. Twenty metres behind, Subedar Sanjiv and his buddy Paratrooper Amit heard the ice break and the two scouts fall with an uncomfortable series of thuds.

'Subedar Sanjiv wanted to shout out their names to see if they were all right, but he knew that was a dangerous thing to do,' says the sixth commando in the squad who was crawling right behind Havildar Devendra. 'I could tell he was in a huge dilemma. But we needed to act fast and carefully.'

Subedar Sanjiv and Paratrooper Amit used a rope initially to attempt a rapid retrieval of the two scouts who had fallen into the nallah. There was no response or movement from below. So, they both started to crawl down towards the nallah carefully. In the darkness, it was impossible to look down and tell what the condition of the two paratroopers was. As Subedar Sanjiv collected himself as he always did, thinking of his next steps, the silence of the dark mountainside was shattered once again. This time by gunfire.

The unthinkable had happened, and it was impossible to tell in the darkness. Paratrooper Chhatrapal and Bal Krishan had fallen into the nallah and landed, badly injured, just metres from where the terrorists were hiding.

'They fell just five metres from where the infiltrators were crouched,' says the sixth commando. 'Despite the proximity of the incoming fire, they couldn't immediately make out where precisely the terrorists were hiding. Both our guys were already badly injured by the fall. But we listened carefully and could make out that the firing wasn't one-sided.'

Subedar Sanjiv and the other three commandos could clearly hear two different types of rifles being fired. The unmistakable AK-47 clatter from the infiltrators. And the pop-pop echo from the scouts' Tavor rifles. This was a veneer of good news, because it meant the two scouts weren't debilitated during the fall and were still fighting. But the mere sound of rifle fire wasn't enough to inform the rest of the squad just how fearsome the fighting in the nallah down below actually was.

'It was the closest quarter firefight that can be imagined,' says the sixth commando. 'It was all taking place with a separation of 5 to 7 metres. It was impossible to tell who killed who at precisely what point. But we knew that there was no escape from that kind of close combat.'

As the crossfire began to slow down, Subedar Sanjiv and Paratrooper Amit continued their descent. When the firing stopped, Subedar Sanjiv halted, closing his eyes, listening carefully for what the wind would bring to him up that mountainside.

'When the firing stopped, he knew it was possible, even likely, that both Chhatrapal and Bal Krishan had been killed in action,' says the sixth commando. 'But this was a live operation. There's no time to digest such things until the mission is complete. He attempted to establish radio contact with the two scouts but got no response. Even in the darkness, from the sound of his whispers, I could tell this was a very crushing moment for Subedar Sanjiv. He was like a father figure to the young paratroopers.'

In what was likely a combat stress reaction, Subedar Sanjiv refused to give up and hold position, clear in his mind that there was still a chance to get down into the nallah and pull the two scouts out. Navigating between the rocks of the nallah, he followed the lingering gun smoke to the location where the close combat had just ended. In the darkness, he spotted an injured Paratrooper Bal Krishan lying crumpled in the snow. A few metres further down, he spotted Paratrooper Chhatrapal, weapon still in hand, lying face down in the nallah.

This was a very risky exercise since it was still unclear where precisely the terrorists were hiding. If any of them had been killed in the crossfire, there were no visible bodies yet.

Crawling carefully towards the two stricken scouts, Subedar Sanjiv carefully pulled them out of the nallah and up the mountainside. Both the paratroopers were breathing, but weren't making a sound, and were clearly grievously injured. Just as Subedar Sanjiv was pulling them beyond the crossfire zone, firing suddenly burst out again. Under a hail of fire that was landing around him, Subedar Sanjiv sent out a radio message to both his buddy Paratrooper Amit as well as the second squad further up the mountain, that he was bringing the two injured paratroopers up for emergency medical help.

'Subedar Sanjiv's main priority was to pull Chhatrapal and Bal Krishan back and reassess the situation,' says the sixth commando from the squad. 'He passed on a radio message to the other squad that he was pulling the paratroopers back. Just when he had pulled the two scouts to the side, the fire assault began again.'

Positioned about 20 metres higher up the slope, Paratrooper Amit opened 'suppressing' fire in the direction of the terrorists to prevent them from firing or moving. After twenty seconds he stopped, and radioed Subedar Sanjiv for an update on his location.

There was no response.

He tried the squad's second radio, which had been with Paratrooper Chhatrapal. But there was no response from that one either.

At a slightly higher position, Havildar Devendra, the squad's second-in-command (2IC), along with his buddy, the sixth commando of the squad, held position, listening intently through the darkness and scanning the mountainside with infrared night sights on their helmets.

Creeping closer down the mountainside, they spent the night closing in and pinned down the terrorists with periodic fire. Meanwhile further down, intermittent bursts of crossfire between Paratrooper Amit and the terrorists continued at close quarters.

'Havildar Devendra couldn't make out for sure who was firing from where, so he had to be careful. Even with the night sights, it was difficult to conduct effective fire because of the close proximity of the engagement. The radios remained silent. We thought it's even possible that there's no radio response from Chhatrapal and Subedar Sanjiv because they wanted to maintain radio silence as the terrorists were close by.'

In the hail of bullets coming up the mountain, several struck Paratrooper Amit square in the chest and stomach. Bleeding heavily, the young commando trudged back up the mountain, collapsing before Havildar Devendra. He was quickly given first aid and morphine, but Paratrooper Amit had already lost too much blood. As the first rays of the sun filtered through the pines, lying in Havildar Devendra's arms, the young paratrooper took his last breath.

At 4.30 a.m. on 5 April, more firing erupted from down the nallah. The second commando squad which was positioned higher up took a decision to venture down the mountainside as a single AK-47 continued to fire intermittently from behind some rocks in the snowmelt. Morning light made the direction of fire clearer. Scouts from the second squad sent a pair of grenades careening into the hiding place, silencing the sole terrorist who was still firing.

After a night filled with gunfire, the Jumgund mountainside was totally silent once again.

Very little can conclusively be said of what happened from the time Subedar Sanjiv descended into the nallah and the end of the firefight at dawn. But when the second squad descended into the nallah for a final clearing operation, a hair-raising sight lay in wait.

Hair-raising even for commandos.

The squad first passed the body of Paratrooper Amit. The young soldier had received thirteen gunshot wounds but still managed to climb up the mountainside before succumbing to his injuries.

A short distance further down, they found the body of Havildar Devendra. He had spent the night returning fire at the terrorists. Not far from him was the sixth commando. He had sustained two gunshot wounds but was alive. His rifle lay a few metres behind him. It is most likely that it flung from his grip when he was hit. He was immediately taken up the mountainside for medical aid.

The two Dhruv helicopters had been summoned back to the mountaintop for an emergency evacuation. In communication with the second squad, one of the helicopters hovered briefly over the nallah to see if it could capture what happened. From the air, the pilots got the first glimpse of what had happened. They quickly relayed the information to the second squad which was descending to that point in the nallah.

It was when the squad reached the location of the actual crossfire that the truth of the fighting became clear. The bodies of Paratrooper Chhatrapal, Paratrooper Bal Krishan and Subedar Sanjiv were found entangled with the bodies of the terrorists. Injured in the fall and with gunshot wounds, the two young paratroopers had charged at the terrorists and killed them in fearsome hand-to-hand combat down the mountainside. Subedar Sanjiv, too grievously wounded in the crossfire, had pounced on the third terrorist and beaten him to death before life ebbed from him.

'Even for commandos like us, it was a numbing sight,' says a soldier from the second squad. 'These three guys had accepted that their life was over. They had decided that they would make it count for the mission. We still don't know how the two young scouts were able to fight after being so badly injured. We will never clearly know how they managed it.'

Only hours earlier, Subedar Sanjiv's squad had imagined the operation to be a textbook ambush that would see the four terrorists eliminated quickly the following morning.

'We just thought we would roll down and eliminate four to five guys and go back home,' says the sole surviving commando of Subedar Sanjiv's squad. 'But what happened on the ground was different. The paratroopers fell in front of the terrorists. I don't think anybody could have avoided or done better in the circumstances. It just came down to that one mishap. It was the easiest of operations. It was an unplanned contingency that changed the game against us. And the price we had to pay.'

The bodies of the five commandos, including their team leader, were carefully carried up the mountainside where the two waiting Dhruvs flew them first to the Badibai Post nearby, and then straight to the 92 Base Hospital in Srinagar—standard operating procedure even if soldiers are deemed dead at the site of an operation.

Even for a battle-hardened Special Forces unit like the 4 Para, the loss of five men in a single operation was many levels beyond a shock.

'The second squad simply could not comprehend the scale of the loss. They were devastated on that mountainside. The carnage in front of them of their own men. *Unki aatma hil gayi thi* [They were rattled to the core],' says Major Abhishek, who was tracking the operation from the 4 Para team headquarters in Kupwara and was the first to receive the news about the devastating loss.

'I got the news at 7 a.m., and was in total disbelief,' says the young officer. 'My first instinct was to reject the news, telling myself that it was impossible. This could not have happened. We were in a state of shock, it is difficult to explain how we felt. We were in denial for hours. Despite our drills and operational philosophy, this was impossible to digest. I immediately got out my quick reaction team (QRT) and started moving towards Srinagar on the morning of 5 April. It was later, after I saw the five coffins, that it finally hit me.'

'There hadn't been casualties like this since Operation Pawan in 1987,' he recalls. 'We never had such casualties despite being in Kashmir for so long. We had lost Lance Naik Sandeep Singh in 2018.* Otherwise, 4 Para had not been touched. There had been injuries, but we had eliminated so many terrorists. Not just the battalion, the entire Northern Command was in shock. Even now there's disbelief that we lost five men that day just because of a mishap.'

---

* See Chapter 7, on Lance Naik Sandeep Singh, 4 Para Special Forces.

The 4 Para, like the Army's other Special Forces units, is trained fully to prepare for combat losses—for the likelihood of death is an adjunct to operations. Training and probation in units are as raw and realistic as it is possible to be when preparing for near-death situations.

'But no amount of training could prepare us for what happened that day,' says the sixth commando, the only man from the squad who survived. 'We men in the unit live together, eat together, breathe together. Out of fifty men, you suddenly face the fact that five are no more, it's a devastating blow. We are like brothers in a unit. It was not easy to come out of that state.'

But the unit, under the watchful eye of their commanding officer, who needed to rally every ounce of strength and composure to keep his men focused, had to move on. Once the operational debriefs were complete and all information about the mission recorded, the men went back to doing the only thing they do when they're not in an operation—drawing lessons from the previous operation and training for the next one.

'The best thing was to bury ourselves back in training, remind ourselves that we are God's chosen soldiers, built for the toughest of jobs,' says the sixth commando. 'We kept ourselves busy. Telling ourselves that this might happen again, but we cannot falter in our commitment and duty. We have to be on standby for the next infiltration which can happen at any time, so we don't have the luxury to remain in shock. I cannot explain the atmosphere at that time. One could only feel it.'

The phrase 'brothers in arms' is no exaggeration in the military. And it's even more true when it comes to small, tightly knit commando units. The thirst for retribution can be overwhelming. It always comes down to the maturity and focus of the commanding officer to hold his men together and channel their anger.

'The men were full of sorrow, but also full of quiet rage,' says Major Abhishek. 'Some of them were so filled with emotion, they would go to the CO and say, *Saab aap bas aadesh do, dobara jayenge, sar kaatke layenge* [Sir, okay a mission and we will go and bring back their heads]. They wanted revenge. Nobody is a Rambo. There is a human somewhere inside each commando.'

After a numbingly silent wreath-laying ceremony at the Badamibagh cantonment in Srinagar, the remains of the five commandos were flown to their respective hometowns to their families.

On 6 April, twenty-two-year-old Paratrooper Chhatrapal Singh's casket arrived at his home in Chhavasari village in Rajasthan's Jhunjhunu district, where huge crowds from adjoining villages lined the rooftops and streets to bid the commando farewell. Images of his devastated, weeping parents being consoled by two commandos from the 4 Para would numb the nation. Images of medical staff in pandemic PPE kits delivering the body only reminded those watching that the infiltration of Pakistan-sponsored terrorists had been carried out during a global health crisis, and that the young commandos had to be sent in to battle at a time when the world had far more pressing priorities.

At around the same time, Paratrooper Bal Krishan's body arrived at his family's home in a remote part of Himachal Pradesh's Kullu district. A large *shamiana* had been erected outside the house to accommodate the mourners who had gathered there to receive the body and pay their last respects. But it was the image of a tall commando from the 4 Para breaking down while embracing Bal Krishan's grieving mother that would go viral. Special Forces men always hold their composure, trained to control their emotions. The image of the weeping commando was perhaps the most heartbreaking sign of the unit's sense of loss.

On Republic Day 2021, Subedar Sanjiv Kumar was decorated with a posthumous Kirti Chakra, the country's second-highest peacetime gallantry medal, equivalent to the wartime Maha Vir Chakra.

His citation reads, 'Subedar Late Sanjiv Kumar displayed outstanding leadership qualities, raw courage and utmost gallantry in eliminating one hardcore terrorist, injuring two terrorists, evacuating his injured scout and made the supreme sacrifice in the highest traditions of the Indian Army. His selfless action led to the subsequent elimination of five hardcore terrorists. For exhibiting conspicuous courage beyond the call of duty, Subedar Sanjiv Kumar is awarded Kirti Chakra (Posthumous).'

Subedar Sanjiv's wife Sujata Devi received her husband's medal at an investiture ceremony at Delhi's Rashtrapati Bhavan in November 2021. She lives with their teenage son, Kanishka, at their home in Bilaspur, Himachal Pradesh.

The other commandos would be decorated with Sena Medals for fearless gallantry in the operation.

The post-mortem of Subedar Sanjiv's buddy commando Paratrooper Amit Kumar Anthwal showed he had taken fifteen bullets in the operation. He was bid farewell by his parents in Pauri-Garhwal, Uttarakhand. The young commando was engaged to be married six months later in October 2020.

Thirty-nine-year-old Havildar Devendra Singh Rana's body arrived at his village Tinsoli in Uttarakhand's Rudraprayag on 6 April. His mortal remains were consigned to the flames by his parents, wife, Vineeta Devi, daughter, Aanchal, and son, Ayush. His ashes were scattered in the Mandakini River.

Thirty-eight days after the operation, the sixth commando from Subedar Sanjiv's unit was cleared to leave hospital in

Srinagar. A 7.62 mm rifle round had been removed from his shoulder, with the flesh and bone carefully reconstructed to give him back his mobility.

The first call he made was to his commanding officer at the 4 Para team headquarters in Kupwara.

'*Beta, tum kuchh hafte ke liye ghar chale jao* [Son, go home on leave for a few weeks],' said the commanding officer. '*Jab tum tayyar ho, tab wapas aa jao* [Come back when you are ready to join duty].'

The commando didn't take a moment to reply.

'Sir, *main aaj hi waapas aa raha hoon* [Sir, I am getting back to work today itself].'

* * *

Postscript

A commando from the 4 Para, Paratrooper Sonam Tshering Tamang, was decorated with a Shaurya Chakra in November 2021. The award citation noted:

> Paratrooper Sonam Tshering Tamang displayed raw courage and utmost gallantry in eliminating one hardcore terrorist, injuring one other terrorist and evacuating Subedar Sanjiv Kumar to safety. He maintained his composure and fought with nerves of steel under the most adverse circumstances wherein all other squad members of his detachment were killed in action.

4

'Where the Hell Is His Leg?'

Squadron Leader Ishan Mishra

'We're going down! Initiating ejection now!'

The Sukhoi Su-30 fighter jet was barely 23 metres from the ground, flopped on its right side and screaming downward under a moonless night sky near Tezpur, Assam, when Squadron Leader Ishan Mishra made the final call to the pilot in the second seat behind him.

The twin Saturn AL-31FP turbofans—monster engines that powered the big, heavy Su-30 and permitted the jet unusual levels of aerobatic agility for its size—couldn't have failed at a worse time. A night-training flight. A dark sky. And nearly nothing outside for the pilots to look at to orient themselves in a doomed, falling jet fighter. Not even the familiar glint of the Brahmaputra a short distance south.

And at the speed the aircraft was falling, it would smash into the ground in less than three seconds.

His left hand on the glass canopy of the fighter, Squadron Leader Ishan used his right hand to yank the ejection handle. As an explosive charge blew away the canopy and blasted the rear pilot out of the aircraft, Squadron Leader Ishan felt for a microsecond a strange mix of regret and calm.

Regret, that he wouldn't be able to speak to his wife and son one last time and prepare them for what was about to happen.

And calm, in the certainty that there was no way he was going to survive a lopsided ejection from less than 20 metres. In his final moments in the cockpit, he pushed the aircraft's left rudder pedal as hard as he could, in an effort to keep the falling jet nose-up for as long as possible.

The last thing Squadron Leader Ishan felt as the rockets under his seat flung him with bone-crushing force out of the cockpit, was a quick sharp flash of pain across his left wrist and left leg.

Then everything quickly went black.

In a separate corner of the country, 1700 kilometres away, Squadron Leader Shalika Sharma, headset on, sat hunched over a radar console at the ground control station in Punjab's front-line Halwara air base. That night of 8 August 2019, she was on the late shift guiding pilots very much like her husband in similar Su–30 MKI jets in the dark airspace that hugged the international border with Pakistan.

Only six months earlier in February 2019, the Halwara air base, situated just outside the sprawling city of Ludhiana, was on wartime alert following the Indian Air Force's air strikes in Balakot, Pakistan.* While the actual bombing was carried out by Mirage 2000 jets home-based at Gwalior, Su–30 fighters from Halwara had been part of operational support 'packages' conducting flights close to the border. As a forward base, Halwara is constantly in a state of operational alert. But after Balakot, it would be literally war-ready. The night flights being controlled by Squadron Leader Shalika that August night were part of the uninterrupted readiness training for combat pilots at the base, keeping them available to scramble at very short notice.

The night flights, a regular part of base operations, had increased in tempo and frequency, keeping the runway as active at dusk as it was in sunlight. Squadron Leader Shalika wouldn't know until hours later that while she oversaw the

---

* See *India's Most Fearless 2*.

first set of Su-30 fighters on her watch landing safely back at the Halwara base that night, her husband had hit the swampy banks of the Brahmaputra with a barely open parachute, 5 km from the Tezpur air base.

Aware that Squadron Leader Ishan was on a night mission that evening—pilots always inform their spouses or families—the young radar controller also knew that a part of her would only exhale freely once she saw that familiar WhatsApp ping after her shift had ended, and she could leave the 'no smartphones' zone that included the ground control area. A ping that would show up on her lock screen displaying the word 'landed' and that most comforting of emojis in the circumstances—a yellow 'thumbs up'. She had experienced this for nine years, but it never really got easier.

The two had fallen in love as cadets at the Air Force Academy, entering service together in 2010. As young flying officers, their paths would diverge towards the two ends of fighter operations—the cockpit and the ground control station. Not allowing the vagaries of postings in different locations to come in their way, Shalika would be married to Ishan in May 2013 in Pathankot, a short distance from her hometown, Gurdaspur. In the decade of their partnership, she couldn't remember a single instance when she hadn't received a message before and after a fighter flight.

But that never meant it interfered with work. There was more than enough on her plate, especially that night, with heavily armed fighters in the air that were depending on her to track and control.

Above all, there was Ayaan. Not far from the airfield at her family quarters on the Halwara base premises, the toddler son of the two young Air Force officers was being babysat and tucked into bed by Shalika's parents.

It was a particularly busy shift. Thirty minutes later, Squadron Leader Shalika refreshed her radar console, preparing to monitor a third formation of Su-30 jets for low-level night sorties over a stretch of airspace between the rivers Sutlej and Yamuna, unaware that in that other corner of the country, her husband had opened his eyes.

His head swimming and barely conscious, all that Squadron Leader Ishan saw was that same dark sky. He wanted to move to see if he could spot the other pilot, but not a muscle would twitch. To his right, he could feel searing heat from the flaming wreckage of his Su-30, which had impacted the ground right outside what appeared to be a village. And over the crackle of the fire and the hiss of aviation kerosene fuelling the mangled inferno, he heard human voices.

'*Tar bhori khon kat baal*? [Where the hell is his leg?],' one voice asked in Assamese.

'Yes, there's no left leg,' said another.

No left leg.

Woozy from the frightfully low ejection, Squadron Leader Ishan felt himself flinch, his mind leaping to come to terms, forced into a rictus of realization.

Then he heard a third voice from about 30 feet away.

'*Eitu ki? Eikhon niki tar bhori*!? [What's this? Is this his leg!?]'

Squadron Leader Ishan blinked away a mix of blood and sweat that had formed rivulets down his face. He knew just enough of the language to understand what had just been said. And right before things faded to black again, he wondered if, after nine years as a front-line fighter pilot, he ever wanted to wake up again.

* * *

Thirty years old and with 1600 hours of fighter flying in his logbook, Squadron Leader Ishan had arrived in Tezpur early in May 2019. As a freshly minted qualified flying instructor (QFI), he had just spent the previous twenty months training three batches of pilot cadets at the Fighter Training Wing in Hakimpet near Hyderabad. With the end of his tenure and in the tumultuous wake of the Balakot air strikes, Squadron Leader Ishan, like many other combat pilots, received postings back to front-line air bases in the northern, western and eastern sectors.

After nearly two years away from them, Squadron Leader Ishan had hoped to reunite with Shalika and Ayaan. He had barely seen his infant son who was born just months before he received orders to proceed to Hakimpet to train cadets. If video calls had bridged the distance in some small measure, the new parents also knew they couldn't really complain—the Air Force had been more than empathetic, as it usually is with serving personnel married to each other. Helped by the fact that the two were part of the same domain of operations as pilot and controller, the newly-weds had been deployed together at the Bareilly air base in 2013 and had been posted together at the Halwara base from 2016 to 2017. Four years out of six since their marriage spent in the same station was not bad. Until postings allowed them to be in the same place again, Squadron Leader Ishan would fill in the blanks with visits to Halwara to see his wife and baby son.

But once in Tezpur, there was a typically gruelling work schedule at hand. Even though Squadron Leader Ishan had flown Su-30 jets for over five years, with postings to squadron locations that included Pune, Bareilly and Halwara, he still had to 'revalidate' himself on the air superiority fighter, since he had just spent nearly two years training cadets in HJT-16 Kiran intermediate jet trainers. This wasn't a comment on the pilot's abilities by any measure—conversion and revalidation training was a standard fixture to ensure pilots are fully integrated with cockpits and systems that are either new to them or ones they may have lost touch with.

'That night of 8 August was my last revalidation flight,' says Squadron Leader Ishan. 'I had already finished twenty-four flights successfully. This was to be my final flight with a supervisor, a senior pilot from the squadron. After that, I would be back to being full ops on the Su-30 and ready for any mission.'

On an oppressively muggy north Assam evening, Wing Commander Pritam Santra, the squadron's flight commander—second-in-command in the unit—was the supervisor who climbed into the back cockpit of the Su-30. Squadron Leader Ishan wasn't exactly a 'student' here. He had just spent 700 hours in his previous posting certifying his own student pilots to cross the difficult bridge between slow propeller trainers and faster jets. But in the Air Force, training and validation is an unending exercise. Changes in software, avionics, procedures, weapons and moves made by neighbouring nations, place pilots in a constant cycle of keeping pace with technology and doctrine.

Minutes before climbing into the front cockpit, Squadron Leader Ishan called his wife on her mobile. When she didn't answer, he called his mother-in-law quickly, informing her that he was leaving for a night-flying sortie. Shalika was getting ready for her night radar controller shift. As she left home, her mother informed her that Ishan was off on a night mission.

'Yes, he sent me a text as always,' she smiled, before driving out from the quarters towards Halwara's ground control station. She made a mental note about the approximate time the mission was starting, though she knew that Su-30 missions were sometimes unexpectedly lengthy. Just around the time that she arrived at her station for a solo shift on the radar console, her husband and his supervisor were getting airborne from Tezpur.

'We took off and headed east over Chabua in upper Assam,' says Squadron Leader Ishan. 'There we carried out a couple of low-level passes over the airfield. Everything was fine. The aircraft was handling perfectly.'

The pilots then turned their aircraft around, powered up into a climb and headed back west towards Tezpur, where they proceeded to conduct more low passes over the runway.

'This was to get used to the runway at night, the pattern of the facilities and adjoining terrain—crucial elements in case of emergencies,' says Squadron Leader Ishan.

At 8.08 p.m., Wing Commander Pritam instructed the pilot in front to conduct one final overshoot, a manoeuvre in which the Su-30 was to be brought nearly all the way down to the runway as part of a normal landing approach and aborted at the last second, just before touchdown to instead climb away.

'In that last overshoot when I came four metres above the runway, just as I opened both the throttles to accelerate and get airborne again, I instantly felt the weight of the jet simply refusing to pull up properly,' says Squadron Leader Ishan. 'Right on cue, my right engine oil pressure failure indicator blinked on. This made total sense, because this is a very powerful aircraft, and it was refusing to pull up in the nice way that it usually does. We were dangerously low and turning to the right, all the while our speed dropping and altitude rising only very slowly to about 200 metres. But this climb was nothing to feel safe about, since we had no power coming from the engines. I immediately handed control back to my supervisor, Wing Commander Santra.'

Both pilots quickly guessed that if the aircraft wasn't able to climb immediately, it would take no more than eighteen seconds for their Su-30 to hit the ground. Squadron Leader Ishan heard his supervisor quickly send out a calm distress call to ground control at Tezpur, a final notification before the two men would do nothing else but try to save the jet and themselves.

'After handing control back to my supervisor in the rear cockpit, I pushed a button that engaged what is called 'combat mode', which should have given us an additional 1.5 per cent of thrust in the residual engine,' says Squadron Leader Ishan. 'The problem was we were already at very low speed. And in such a regime, opening power doesn't really pay off unless you point the nose down. And I don't need to tell you that pointing the nose down at this altitude would have simply brought things to an end much faster.'

The doomed Su-30 had entered a cruel, paradoxical situation called the 'region of reversed command', a situation where an aircraft losing power and at low speed needs to point its nose down in order to be able to accelerate enough to gain the power required to climb. At high altitudes, such a 'stall' isn't a problem since pilots have enough depth to dive their jet back into realms of control. At 23 metres, the only thing to dive into is the ground.

The fighter jet's landing gear was still down from the attempted overshoot manoeuvre, the wheels adding drag and slowing the aircraft down even further. Squadron Leader Ishan pushed a button to retract the landing gear, hoping the better aerodynamics would allow some vestiges of performance from the plane to power out of this dangerously low emergency. It was at this point that the right engine died completely, with the left engine winding down and simply unable to keep the aircraft level.

'Apart from this being a night sortie, we were also flying in overcast weather, and in the absence of the moon, the only outside feature available to us was light from a small village that happened to be in the flight path of our aircraft,' says Squadron Leader Ishan. 'Our repeated control inputs would push the aircraft to climb only slightly before dropping back down. It was a turbulent oscillation very close to the ground.'

'Ishan, engage reheat!' came the urgent call from Wing Commander Pritam in the rear cockpit, an instruction to activate the engine's afterburners, a system in many fighter aircraft engines that explosively burns additional fuel near the exhaust, adding a sudden punch of thrust to the aircraft.

'The moment I pushed my throttle up to engage reheat, the aircraft started to yaw violently from left to right—this was because we were on residual power from just one engine, while the other had given up,' says Squadron Leader Ishan Mishra. 'From the moment Wing Commander Pritam had called "engage reheat", it would be four seconds until the realization hit me.'

Amid the head rush of decision pressure, and seconds into another stomach-churning lurch downward, the younger pilot suddenly had a moment of total clarity.

'About twelve seconds into the emergency, I was totally sure that if I didn't initiate the punch out now, whatever happened to the aircraft would happen, but there was no way we both would survive,' says Squadron Leader Ishan. 'So instinctively I pulled the ejection handle with my right hand, while my left hand rested on the canopy. I felt my left wrist break in a sudden flash of pain. There was no time to attend to it. The canopy had blown off, and the wind had roared into the cockpit for a split second before Wing Commander Pritam exploded out of the rear cockpit. I used the last ounce of my power to keep the aircraft's nose pointed as far up as possible, while trying to veer it away from the village in our flight path. My eyes momentarily caught the altitude reading just as I was blasted from my cockpit at 8.10 p.m. We were at twenty-three metres and perhaps a second and a half from impact with the ground. I was certain I wouldn't survive. I just said a prayer that my supervisor makes it, and that the aircraft doesn't harm anyone in the village ahead. I felt a deep flash of regret that I could not say goodbye properly to my wife and baby boy. But the rest I had made my peace with.'

The last thing Squadron Leader Ishan saw as he bailed out was the Su-30 ploughing through a grove of bamboo trees and smashing into the ground in under two seconds, about 30 metres from the first house of the village.

'After I punched out, the Su-30 veered slightly to the left and I soared towards the right,' says Squadron Leader Ishan. 'During ejection the amount of force felt by the body is almost 20G, so for that precise moment, everything blacks out. When I hit the ground in the dark, I felt the impact. It was pitch dark and suddenly that blast happened, a big flash in front of my eyes. I landed just a few metres from the aircraft fireball. There was a lot of oil spill. It was flaming hot. Later I learnt I had sustained some burn injuries on my back too, possibly from the burning fuel from the aircraft that came close to me. It was a miracle I didn't land directly in the wreck itself.'

Squadron Leader Ishan wasn't the only one who saw the blast. Alerted to the distress call, two other Su-30 fighters flying in the area had turned towards the location just in time to see the bright orange fireball that momentarily lit up the north banks of the big river.

'When you are flying in places like Tezpur and Chabua, it's away from the big cities and completely dark,' says Squadron Leader Ishan. 'So when a blast takes place anywhere in the visual span of an aircraft, it shows very clearly. That's how the two Su-30s in the air spotted us immediately.'

Wing Commander Pritam, who was lying on his back a short distance away, was in his senses and happened to have his mobile phone with him. With difficulty, he called the Tezpur tower and informed the flight safety officer that he was alive, but that he wasn't able to immediately confirm if the younger pilot had survived the ejection.

Twenty minutes after the crash, news filtered to local TV and then social media that a fighter had crashed near Tezpur, with no information about the condition of the pilots. The reports didn't identify the aircraft type or the names of the pilots, but anyone vaguely familiar with the Indian Air Force's deployments could guess what was involved. Even before emergency response teams had reached the site of the crash, the news had broken by 8.30 p.m.

Squadron Leader Ishan's parents were watching the news at their home in Bhubaneswar when the breaking news flashed across their screens that a fighter jet had crashed in Assam. They froze, immediately picking up their phones to see if they could get more information.

In Halwara, alone in the ground control station, Squadron Leader Shalika couldn't receive calls or messages. But other colleagues had heard about the crash. Two of them rushed to the ground control station.

'Two juniors of mine showed up, and I was not expecting to see anyone on a solo shift, so I was surprised,' says Squadron Leader Shalika. 'They asked me to go home early since I had an exam to study for. I was immediately a little anxious, so I made arrangements for my relieving officer and left for home. Once outside the control station, I checked my phone as I always did, noting that there was no message from Ishan that he had landed. By now I knew something was wrong. But I wasn't panicking. Just as I reached home, the landline phone rang.'

It was Ishan's commanding officer from Tezpur, Group Captain Bopanna.

'Jai Hind, sir, *kaise ho* [how are you]?'

'Shalika, kaise ho?'

'I'm fine, sir. Anything?'

'Shalika, Ishan *ka* ejection *hua hai kuchh der pehle* [Ishan had to eject a short while ago].'

'Okay, sir,' said Squadron Leader Shalika. '*Par woh theek hai na*, sir [But he is okay, isn't he]?'

'*Haan*, we are getting him to hospital.'

She thanked her husband's CO and hung up, quickly collecting her thoughts on the next step to be taken. Most urgently, she needed to tell her parents, Ishan's parents and then travel on the first available flight to see her husband.

As she began to break the news to her mother, a group of senior personnel arrived at her quarters, including the station's chief administrative officer and the commanding officer of the local Su-30 squadron. Calm and composed thus far, Squadron Leader Shalika lost her cool.

'If you have no information about Ishan, why have you come here?' she pleaded with the visitors. 'My parents are here, and I don't want to stress them out unless I have to. Either tell me what is going on or make me speak to Ishan.'

As she waited for more information, she called her husband's uncle, who lived with her in-laws in Bhubaneswar.

'He had spoken separately with some air force people, but was keeping the information to himself,' says Squadron Leader Shalika. 'He told me Ishan is hurt but safe. "*Ghabrana mat* [Don't panic]." He switched off Ishan's parents' phones. They were made aware that Ishan had ejected from an aircraft but would not get to know any details about their only child until the following day.'

At the site of the crash, a group of locals from the village, who had just about escaped the flaming Su-30, were now gathered around the crumpled body of Squadron Leader Ishan, his flight suit caked with blood and slush. Among the villagers was a man who worked at the mess in the Tezpur air base.

Someone from the base had called him and asked him to rush to the crash site to secure the two fallen pilots.

'The last thing I heard was that voice saying they had found my leg some thirty feet away from me,' says Squadron Leader Ishan. 'After that I didn't have much consciousness. When I woke up, I was at the hospital late that night, having been brought in an Innova from the crash site. The only thing I remember was one of my squadron mates standing next to my bed with his phone in front of my face. I could vaguely make out Shalika at the other end of the video call. Luckily my face wasn't damaged.'

'Ishan, don't say anything, just give a thumbs up,' she said softly.

'Shalika, *main theek hoon*. I'm alive. Don't worry. *But tu aaja yahan par* [Please come here].'

Of course, Squadron Leader Ishan was far from fine. His spine was miraculously intact—unusual, given that compression injuries to the spine are among the commonest afflictions from an ejection—but the young pilot had suffered other terrifying injuries. He had to be given forty-two units of blood to make up for the amount he had lost at the crash site. A huge number of personnel from the Tezpur station were already there to donate blood for the injured pilot.

And the reason he couldn't give Shalika a 'thumbs up' on the video call was because all four of his limbs were shattered, broken to pieces.

And his left leg had been completely ripped off below the knee. The severed limb had been retrieved by a separate team seven hours later from the boggy swamp and placed on ice at the hospital.

'My leg got separated from my body during the ejection,' says Squadron Leader Ishan. 'It was a sleek cut like someone had cut it off with a saw. When I landed, my left leg was not connected. That is why my knee sustained injuries. I was not conscious when they brought the leg to the hospital. Had the severed leg remained inside the aircraft, it would never have been found.'

Shortly after Squadron Leader Ishan, his supervisor Wing Commander Pritam was also brought to the hospital. The senior officer had suffered injuries too, but mercifully of a less serious nature. Both men would be sedated for pain and remain unconscious through the following day as doctors dressed their wounds and stabilized the vitals of two bodies in shock. Senior medics from the Command Hospital in Kolkata and Air Force Hospital in Assam's Jorhat also arrived early on the morning of 9 August to monitor Squadron Leader Ishan and decide on the next course of action.

The doctors were unanimous—Squadron Leader Ishan needed to be flown as quickly as possible to the Command Hospital in Kolkata. So, twenty-four hours after the crash, the sedated pilot was wheeled into the cabin of an An-32, which would fly him and an icebox containing his left leg, to the eastern metropolis, better equipped to handle the injuries he had sustained.

By the time Squadron Leader Ishan was rushed into the intensive care unit (ICU) at the Eastern Army Command Hospital in Kolkata, the court of inquiry (CoI) investigating the accident had deduced that the pilot had sustained his life-altering injuries because his parachute hadn't had enough time to slow his descent fully before he hit the ground.

'When I arrived in Kolkata late at night on 9 August, two officers were there to receive me,' says Squadron Leader Shalika. 'Throughout the flight, I was preparing myself for the worst. When I saw the two officers there, I wondered if they would take me to the hospital or a wreath-laying ceremony.'

Heavily medicated, Squadron Leader Ishan vaguely remembers seeing his wife next to his bed in the ICU.

'He was barely conscious and asked me to go to the mess and take rest and come back in the morning,' she says. 'Imagine asking me to go and take rest while in that state! I was convinced that Ishan wasn't fully aware of what had happened to his leg. I was so relieved to see him alive and talking to me that the news of his lost limb didn't quite sink in. His brain was okay, his blood was flowing, he could communicate. I tried to shut out the lost limb from my mind, focus on the positive and not break down. I know how much Ishan loved his life as a pilot. I knew his heart would break, but for that moment, I was too busy thanking our stars that he wasn't dead.'

She was wrong about one thing, though. Her husband was fully aware he had lost a limb.

'When they were dressing my stump in the ICU, they would put a curtain that hid my legs from me,' says Squadron Leader Ishan. 'Everybody thought I had no idea about what had happened. But I knew from day one because *pain toh mujhe ho raha tha* [I was feeling the pain]. Initially they were giving me local morphine injections and not general anaesthesia, because the latter ran the risk of sending me into a coma.'

For five days, doctors at the Command Hospital investigated the possibility of reattaching the pilot's severed left leg in the hope that the blood vessels would work again. But the damage to the stump was too severe. And therefore, on 14 August, six days after the crash, it was decided that Squadron Leader Ishan's left leg would be amputated further, to excise the smashed portion.

That morning, the commandant of the hospital, Major General S.R. Ghosh, and a senior Army orthopaedic surgeon, Lieutenant General R.S. Parmar, came to visit the pilot. Both wanted to mentally prepare Squadron Leader Ishan for the surgery, break the news to him that he wouldn't get his leg back.

'The irony is everyone was talking to me carefully, like I didn't know what had happened,' says Squadron Leader Ishan. 'On the other hand, there I was stopping myself from discussing my injuries with my wife or squadron mates in the ICU because I thought they didn't know I'd lost a limb and didn't want to upset them. They were being strong for me. I was being strong for them. I guess that's what love and solidarity is all about.'

The advice to the injured pilot from the senior doctors was clear. Reconstructing his shattered knee would take time, and there was little or no guarantee that it would sustain. A prosthetic knee also had low chances of success given the complexity of his injury. There was only one option left.

Squadron Leader Ishan and Squadron Leader Shalika listened intently. Neither wanted to look the other in the eye in the room that day as the two doctors offered their final verdict.

'Absolutely, sir,' said Squadron Leader Ishan, careful not to allow a pause to betray any hesitation whatsoever. 'You do what you think is best. I don't have any problem.'

The amputation was scheduled for 14 August. As he waited in his hospital bed, Squadron Leader Ishan received an uninterrupted stream of visitors, mostly course mates and fellow personnel from his current and past squadrons. One course mate from Hyderabad had arrived at a time when the injured pilot had been prohibited fluids of any kind, since he was about to be operated on.

'I was simply dying of thirst but had been barred from touching any fluids,' says Squadron Leader Ishan. 'I was being given a lot of saline, so I was maddeningly thirsty. My mouth was dry, it was a horrible feeling. My course mate Sumit was there in my room. I said, "*Bhai mujhe bahut pyaas lag rahi hai*

[I am very thirsty]." He said, "*Doctor ne bola hai main nahi de sakta, teri zindagi ka sawal hai* [The doctor has said that I can't give you liquids, it's a question of your life]." I pleaded with him, saying, "*Tujhe hamare NDA days ka vasta paani pila de iss bhai ko* [For the sake of our NDA days please give your brother some water]." I was literally begging him with folded bandaged hands. He gave in and picked up a bottle and was pouring some into my mouth when the doctor walked in and saw what was going on. The doctor was furious. He said, "Don't you want your friend to remain alive during the operation? Do you want him to die?" Then he was thrown out of my room, poor guy.'

A twelve-hour surgery followed. And around the same time, the pilot's severed left leg was taken out of its icebox and sent into the hospital's incinerator. The leg that had pushed on the aircraft's rudder pedal in an effort to pull it away from the path of the village, was turned to ashes.

If the loss of his left leg wasn't traumatic enough, Squadron Leader Ishan came terrifyingly close to losing his right leg too. The latter limb had contracted a condition called acute compartment syndrome (ACS) in which elevated pressure within the leg compartment was stifling blood supply to the tissue in the limb, thereby endangering it as a whole. Amputating the right leg was discussed as a possible compulsion if things didn't improve, especially since the condition was seen to be affecting the pilot's kidneys as well. Mercifully, the doctors were able to operate on the leg, relieve the pressure and save the limb. It was still shattered in places, but the verdict was it didn't need to be amputated.

The CoI was now a week into its investigation, but nobody was clear yet as to why the accident had taken place. Whether a technical fault or engine failure, it remained unclear for a while. That a young fighter pilot's front-line combat career had ended so abruptly imbued the probe with urgency and a painful veneer.

'People were not ready to conclude why I had lost my leg,' says Squadron Leader Ishan. 'As my anaesthesia wore off, and I began to get my faculties back, the horror of realization came in waves. After my initial rehabilitation, I received my posting back to Halwara. Before proceeding, I travelled back to Tezpur in December 2019.'

Missing a leg now and in a wheelchair, the pilot was adamant that he wanted to visit the crash site.

'I asked a duty medical officer from the Tezpur base hospital to accompany me there,' says Squadron Leader Ishan. 'As we stood there, looking at where my aircraft had hit the ground and where they had found me, the medical officer got a little emotional.'

'You don't know how good it is to see you well,' said the medical officer. 'When we were cutting through your flying overalls and doing your MRI [magnetic resonance imaging] for an initial look at whether there was internal damage to your organs, you were screaming in pain. I was holding you down, trying to calm you and ask what I could give you to make you feel better.'

In convulsions of agony, Squadron Leader Ishan had screamed back, 'Sir, *mujhe* cold coffee *pila do*, I am feeling very thirsty.'

Cold coffee.

Standing at that crash site, the two men allowed themselves a laugh.

'I remember just thinking, how long will it be before I get to fly again,' says Squadron Leader Ishan. 'I was refusing to accept the reality of what had happened. I found that I was telling myself to simply be patient. And that I would get my wings again. The mind tries to protect you from the trauma you have faced. But I also knew that the most difficult part of the journey wasn't losing the leg in that ejection. It was the fight that lay ahead.'

Squadron Leader Shalika had been up for a posting to Tezpur in the weeks ahead. But after the crash, her husband would be going back to Halwara to her instead.

'Life had changed so suddenly for Ishan,' she says. 'Everyone thought he would be depressed. Who wouldn't be in such a situation? It was deeply traumatizing for us all. But I wanted to tell Ishan that I was there to be strong for us. "You can vent your emotions for a while. You don't have to put up a brave face for our sake." But he truly was extremely strong. I was worried sometimes about how matter-of-fact he was about how his life had changed. Yes, it is true that life must go on. But for a moment imagine losing a leg suddenly, doing what you love.'

When the couple returned to Halwara at the end of 2019, the first thing doctors at the base asked Squadron Leader Ishan was whether he needed more sick leave. The pilot was certain he didn't want any.

'I said no, please allow me to join back on ground duty,' I told the doctors. 'I'll do office work till the time I get medically fit. I knew in my mind that if I stayed at home, I wouldn't be able to sustain things. *Ghar mein baitha rahunga toh mein baitha hee rahunga because kaam hai jaan hai* [If I sit at home, I will always sit at home. If there is work, there is life].'

Like the morphine that had been administered to him after the accident, the self-preservatory impulse of acceptance melted in the weeks that followed. This would often manifest in loud nightmares and waking up agonized in the middle of the night.

'I would spend my days shifting between the wheelchair and bed,' says Squadron Leader Ishan. 'I was at a fighter base where I used to fly with all these guys. So, I was watching them every day, and the reality of my situation just sank in more and more.'

For months, the two young Squadron Leaders hadn't wept in each other's presence, careful to hold themselves together for the sake of the other. But back now in their private dwelling in Halwara, it was finally possible to give vent to the pain and sadness that had built up. Both knew it was important for their well-being too.

'There were times when I would cry out loud if I wasn't able to do something owing to my condition,' says Squadron Leader Ishan. '*Jab raat ko mera beta so jata hai mujhe bahut kharab lagta hai—uss samay mein apni wife ke saath phoot phoot ke rota hoon* [After my son would go to bed, strong emotions would overcome me. My wife and I would break down and cry our hearts out]. Ayaan wouldn't get up because he was small and slept deeply. But then my wife would also start sobbing. After crying I would feel a little better. *Jo hua maybe kuch aur reason tha* [There must be a reason for what happened].'

With his mother and father in Kolkata, little Ayaan had been taken by his grandparents to their native Gurdaspur. In December, before reporting to Halwara, the child's parents came to fetch him.

'As we drove to Gurdaspur, the only thought in my mind was how was I going to face my little boy,' says Squadron Leader Ishan. 'I was in a wheelchair. As expected, he seemed puzzled when he saw me, wondering, "*Arre Daddy, yeh kya gaddi gaddi* [Daddy, what is this vehicle you are on]?" I couldn't pick him up, as my hands were still heavily bandaged. Ayaan then lifted my shawl and noticed I didn't have a left leg. Children are so innocent. He simply asked me where the leg was. That was the most difficult moment for me. I had to hold back my tears until he ran off to play.'

From cockpit to wheelchair, the abruptness of his new situation was frequently overwhelming. But like his training for emergencies in the air, the pilot knew that the only thing he could do was to solve the problem in front of him. Taking on more than he could manage was an invitation to despondence, depression and frustration. He decided he needed to summon all of his pilot-like qualities to solve what lay in front him first. And only then move to the next problem.

And what was that first step?

'Going to the washroom,' he says. 'It was an enormous challenge for me. I hope nobody ever has to go through it. It is the most traumatic thing to get used to and accept. That you need help with the washroom. So, my first aim was to gain full independence in that department.'

The slow rhythm of a violently altered life was taking root when in early 2020, Squadron Leader Ishan was asked to proceed to Pune, a city he had served in and where he had flown Su-30 jets for the first time. But he wasn't being sent to the famous Lohegaon air base in the city, but an equally famous institution in the armed forces—the Artificial Limb Centre. Established in 1944, the centre provided wide-ranging rehabilitative care to injured armed forces personnel, including prosthetic limbs. And it had come a long way since the days of wooden legs strapped to amputated stumps.

'When I reached Pune, I was starting from scratch,' says Squadron Leader Ishan. 'I had foot drop, characterized by difficulty in lifting the front part of the foot, essential for any mobility. Initially I was given a rudimentary pneumatic leg.'

In April 2020, eight months after the crash, Squadron Leader Ishan stood up from his wheelchair for the first time. It was a moment of triumph, and a milestone the pilot won't forget.

'I was standing up on my old leg and new leg,' he says. 'A leg I had almost lost. I just stood there for a while, allowing my legs to take my full weight. Everything weighed a ton. I wobbled a bit, but I maintained my balance. It was a small moment, but once again, I was overwhelmed. Shalika was in Pune with me that day. She saw me, she smiled and clapped. I know she was overwhelmed too. We celebrated that day.'

A steady course of physiotherapy, counselling and exercise followed. Giving the pilot a pneumatic leg was one thing. Making him meaningfully mobile and independent was still a way off. Hopeful but impatient, Squadron Leader Ishan turned to social media for help in speeding things along on his road to recovery.

'Shalika and I came across a woman named Arpita Roy on Instagram,' he says. 'She was a double amputee yoga practitioner and fitness trainer. We put a great deal of faith in her. I signed up for a three-month course with Arpita. By December 2020, sixteen months after my accident, I was able to put my crutches aside. I started cycling. I was permitted to drive a car within the premises of the centre. But there was something else that I wanted to do, that I had been hoping against hope I would be able to.'

At the end of 2020, Shalika brought Ayaan to Pune to visit his father.

'The three of us went to the basketball court. My son played for half an hour with me. Initially Ayaan was a little concerned and didn't want me to strain myself. But then the child in him kicked in, and he enjoyed the game. The delight in his face at being able to play with me again was unforgettable. I wanted to cry, but I was too happy to do that. Shalika was also very emotional.'

That night, after Ayaan slept, husband and wife stood in the small balcony of their quarters, silently letting the glow of the day wash over them. Shalika took Ishan's hand.

'*Jo ho gaya ho gaya,*' she said. '*Tu zinda hai, sab theek ho jayega* [Whatever happened has happened. You are alive and everything will be fine].'

In early 2021, just as the COVID-19 pandemic hit, Squadron Leader Ishan returned to Halwara. The pilot's caregivers and physiotherapists wanted him to return to his place of work and get used to living in his real-world setting using his prosthetic limb. He would return every few weeks to have his prosthetic limb calibrated since the sockets would get loose with use. Each time he would return to Pune accompanied by Squadron Leader Shalika. In mid-2021, when he was summoned back to Pune for a check-up, he decided he wanted to travel alone.

'Everyone said, don't travel alone, take Shalika with you,' he says. 'But I said, "*Bhai ek baar akele jaane do* so at least I know my limitations. When there is always someone at hand, I take it for granted. If I want water, someone brings it. I need to be fully alone to know just how independent I am now. There is no other way." And so, I flew alone in that scheduled An-32 flight to Pune. It took a while to get used to getting everything myself. But I cannot tell you how exhilarating and empowering it was. The water I got up and got for myself actually tasted sweeter.'

Nearly two years since he received his prosthetic limb, Squadron Leader Ishan has begun to nurse a dream he thought would never be possible again—climbing back into an aircraft cockpit.

'I won't ever be able to fly a fighter aircraft again, I had made my peace with that,' the pilot says. 'But the Artificial Limb Centre was doing everything it could to get me fit enough to perhaps fly transport aircraft, like the An-32s that have been flying me everywhere since the accident. It would be a huge thing if that happens. I don't carry any delusions, but

I do live in hope. I cannot sit around and feel sorry for myself or angry about what happened. Ultimately, I am a national servant. It was my choice to be a fighter pilot, and I was aware of the risks. If I am paying the price for wanting to be a *fauji*, then so be it. What happened, happened in the line of duty. But I am not finished with my duties.'

Squadron Leader Ishan's hopes have remained especially high ever since a course mate sent him an article about Captain Christy Wise, a US Air Force pilot who returned to flying the C-130J Hercules transport aircraft a year after she lost her right leg in a boat accident. Captain Wise spent eight months in similar rehabilitation before she was approved to return to flying duties.

'I am doing everything I can to get back to flying,' says Squadron Leader Ishan. 'After I receive an upgraded prosthetic limb with microprocessors, I believe my case will be even stronger. I miss the cockpit. That's where I belong. I will work as hard as I can to get back into one.'

Before his more gruelling physical exercises and physiotherapy, the pilot now begins his day with multiple surya namaskars and an hour of specialized yoga. In the early days of his rehabilitation, he had taken to meditation to help organize his thoughts and channel his emotions in order to sleep better. But more recently, he finds he is much more confident and able to get rest without too much trouble.

'The Air Force has protected me like a family member,' says Squadron Leader Ishan. 'This is the real face of a war-waging organization. It isn't just about combat, but the ability to take care of your people when they are in trouble. I could not have asked for more. I'm fighting it out. I always feel the end is in sight. But I know the Air Force is looking out for me, no matter what.'

Back in Halwara in 2021, Squadron Leader Ishan met with an old friend, perhaps the current generation's most famous fighter pilot—Wing Commander Abhinandan Varthaman. The Vir Chakra-winning aviator had been shot down over Pakistan-occupied Kashmir (PoK) on 27 February 2019, after shooting down a Pakistan Air Force fighter in an air battle the morning after the Balakot air strikes.

'Once Ayaan is slightly older, people will say many things to him—"see your daddy doesn't have a leg", like my child is still told, *"Tere baap ko Pakistani maar rahe hai* [Your father was hit by the Pakistanis],"' Wing Commander Abhinandan said to Squadron Leader Ishan. '*Usko ek mazak bana* [Turn it into a joke] so that he understands that whatever happened has happened and it happened for the good.'

When Ayaan now asks his father about the missing leg, he is informed that a tiger took it away. Probed further, a full story is narrated for the child, his eyes shining in morbid fascination, tinged with the kind of open-mouthed pride only a four-year-old can show.

'He has now been told by people at the base that his father has a "Terminator" leg,' says Squadron Leader Ishan. 'I've heard him boasting about it to his friends, saying, "*Mera* dad has a Terminator leg and he can finish enemies with it." He will soon know what happened. He's a bright kid. But you know how kids live in their own world.'

As he awaits an advanced new prosthetic limb and the vistas it could reopen for him, Squadron Leader Ishan hates offering advice. But the trauma of the last two years has given him a priceless worldview he often shares with his close friends in service.

'You'll always meet people who aren't fully satisfied because *mera rank nahi aaya, mera course nahi aaya, mujhe commendation nahi mila, mujhe Shaurya Chakra nahi mila*

[I haven't been promoted or received any commendation or won a Shaurya Chakra]. I always tell them, be happy to be alive and work hard. Everything else will take care of itself.'

One of the pieces of advice Squadron Leader Ishan hears most often from civilian friends is to quit the Indian Air Force and move to the private sector.

'*Mujhe pata hai mujhe fauj nahi chhodni hai* [I don't want to quit the forces],' he says. 'I can leave, and I will probably get a disability pension as well. But I don't want people to pity me. *Main kissi ke samne haath nahi phelana chahta*. The kind of training we've undergone in NDA, we cannot plead in front of anyone or ask for anything.'

Does he miss his leg?

'I don't miss it. It went away for a reason. I don't know what that reason is. And I don't want to know. I can't see anything but what's in front of me.'

5

'I Have Never Touched Anything That Cold'

Major Vibhuti Shankar Dhoundiyal

'*Kabhi kabhi bhagwan se kuchh maang liya karo, Vibhu* [Vibhu, ask God for something once in a while].'

The WhatsApp video call had glitched out in a mess of pixels but leaning over the railing of her balcony in Dehradun, Nitika Kaul Dhoundiyal could sense her husband was smiling at the other end. She waited for the connection to strengthen, mentally reminding herself that even if it didn't, she had managed to squeeze a few seconds of a video conversation with him before he left his base. His voice came across in patches, cut by the dying mobile data signal. It didn't matter. She had learnt to piece together the snatches of speech.

'*Yaar, zindagi main bas do cheez mangi hai* [I have only asked for two things in life],' said Major Vibhuti Shankar Dhoundiyal (Vibhu), a company commander with the 55 Rashtriya Rifles in Pulwama, Jammu and Kashmir.

'*Kya* [What]?'

Nitika knew the answer, but she never tired of hearing it.

'*Ek,* I wanted to get into the Army. And two, I wanted you in my life. Both prayers have been answered. What more can I ask for?' he said.

Nitika said a quick, quiet prayer of her own.

'Be protected and be safe always,' she said with a touch of exasperation.

It was anything but an unreasonable plea. The two were talking on the evening of 15 February 2019, barely twenty-four hours after a suicide bomber had targeted a Central

Reserve Police Force (CRPF) convoy on a stretch of the Jammu–Srinagar highway that runs through south Kashmir's Pulwama district, where Major Vibhuti operated as an officer on counterinsurgency duties. Forty CRPF men had perished in the vehicle-borne attack planned and executed by the Pakistan-sponsored terrorist group Jaish-e-Mohammed. Not surprisingly, units like the 55 Rashtriya Rifles that were based in the area were on full operational alert to carry out post-attack search operations. The terrorist, a local from the district, couldn't possibly have acted alone, and it was on groups of soldiers like the one under Major Vibhuti's command to move quickly before terrorist accomplices melted back into the hinterland, or even back across the Line of Control (LoC).

Knowing she would be sick with worry after news of the suicide bombing broke on television and social media, Major Vibhu had quickly called his wife to tell her he was okay and still at his base. The scale of the loss was still sinking in.

'*Yaar,* it's a part of life,' Major Vibhu said. '*Jo hona hai woh hona hee hai* [What has to happen will happen], so no need to mess up your sleep over that.'

'Why do you always do this? Stop it.'

Nitika hated it when he spoke this way, but she also knew it was probably her husband's way of dealing with the fragility of everything around him. It had been just over a year since he had been deployed to the Kashmir Valley. Nitika had hoped her anxiety would settle but quickly learnt there was no question of that. Ever since Major Vibhuti arrived in J&K in January 2018, he had requested his commanding officer not to saddle him with desk duties. As an officer from the Army's Corps of Electronics and Mechanical Engineers (EME), his training was tuned towards the upkeep of weapons, vehicles and other hardware.

'When he came to the battalion, he made it clear from the start that he wanted operations,' says Colonel Pradeep Duggal, then commanding officer of the 55 Rashtriya Rifles. 'As a young officer from the EME, I wanted him as the unit adjutant for some time. But he said, "*Nahi sir, kuchh bhi kara do par desk pe mat bitha do mujhe* [Give me any assignment except on the desk]."'

Colonel Pradeep knew that Major Vibhuti was to be married three months later in April. He suggested to the new young officer to settle into the unit for the time being and perhaps join some operations after his wedding. But Major Vibhuti had pleaded that he didn't want to spend a moment behind a desk.

'Unknown to each other at the time, Vibhu and I took the same flight from Delhi to Srinagar on 22 January 2018, and reported to our new Rashtriya Rifles unit together,' says Major Saurabh Patni. 'We had a "dining-in" at the unit that night. Vibhu being from EME, it was unusual how keen he was on operations. It was unlike his work arm, but it was the first thing I noticed about him. "*Jo bhi ho jaye, operations mein ghusna hai* [Whatever happens, I want to be in operations]," he would insist.'

The two young majors became roommates through February as part of the mandatory pre-induction training.

Colonel Pradeep had been apprehensive about pushing Major Vibhu directly into operations, but by the middle of that year, it was clear he had a nose and heart for what was, even during a lull, a supremely difficult and dangerous job in the most restive sector of a troubled state. In October 2018, his talent in the field could no longer be ignored and he was made commander of one of the companies within the 55 Rashtriya Rifles. Nitika had known Vibhu for years and was fully aware of his eagerness to lead troops in the field, but as his newly wedded wife of six months, she received the 'good news' with mixed feelings.

'There was nothing he wanted more,' says Nitika. 'It was the beginning and end of what drove him forward. And yes, he fit me into that somewhere.'

Courtship, Wedding and Back in the Unit as Company Commander

'From the word go, with a company under his command, this boy was out to prove that we had taken the right decision to put him in operations,' recalls Colonel Pradeep. 'In November 2018, there was an operation away from his company area, but he insisted on being sent. "Sir, I can't be sitting here when my guys are out there even if it's a different location," he told me. So, I sent him. Vibhu managed to sniff out and engage a terrorist in the very first house that he searched. I immediately noticed that he had a nose for where they were hiding.'

The following month, amid an unusual flurry of confusing intelligence inputs, Major Vibhu had pieced together an operation that ended with the interception of an over-ground worker (OGW) who was transporting 200 kg of explosives in the Pulwama area.

By the end of 2018, after just three months as company commander, Major Vibhu had a reputation that stretched across the unit.

'*Jahan Vibhuti Saab honge, wahan contact ho gaya hoga* [If Vibhuti Sir was involved in an operation, it meant we have zeroed in on something],' says a soldier who served in a neighbouring company of the 55 Rashtriya Rifles. '*Agar woh operations pe nikal gaye, iska matlab tha ki kuchh hai input mein. Aur yeh baat kabhi bhi galat sabit nahi hui* [If he was out on an

operation, it meant that the intelligence input was correct. His instinct has never been proven wrong].'

The reputation was based on an uncanny consistency.

'You cannot get a more challenging environment than south Kashmir,' notes Major Saurabh. 'In the unit there would be long discussions to make sense of inputs, whether they are good or bad. Vibhu used to stay quiet. It was when he began planning and embarked on an operation that it became a reliable indication that the input was solid. I don't know how to explain it—he never went wrong.'

In January 2019, a piece of intelligence had come in suggesting that two armed terrorists were hiding in a village in Pulwama that had 120 houses.

'Six officers, including Vibhu and I, began a sweep of the houses in that village at about 1 a.m.,' says Major Saurabh. 'Four other officers and I had completed the search of around fifteen houses each. Vibhu was stuck on his first house. He simply wasn't moving from there. That turned out to be the house where the two terrorists were hiding. I can't explain how he sensed it. I can only give such examples.'

Days later, another piece of intelligence trickled in. It was the kind of input that was deemed solid—it was specific, mentioned precise coordinates, timings and more. While Major Saurabh's company was dispatched on the operation, Major Vibhu was ordered to remain at his base and provide backup if necessary.

'So, the rest of us were involved, but not him,' says Major Saurabh. 'We rolled out in an already celebratory mood since the input was that good. We were certain it would click. While we were at the location, a second intelligence input dropped, and that muddied the waters a little for the deployed men. Vibhu was dispatched to check out the second input, which was about a kilometre from our location. Moments after Vibhu

and his men arrived there, we heard firing. It turned out there was nothing in our input, but in Vibhu's they found terrorists and engaged them. I can imagine this happening once or twice. How does one explain this happening every single time?'

Major Vibhu's reputation had filtered back to his home as well, triggering a familiar mix of pride and anxiety.

'I remember once I told him, *Yaar tera phir se jaana zaroori hai andar* [Do you really need to go inside]?' remembers Nitika. 'I would keep saying *dekh ke ja* [be careful].'

Usually, he calmed his young wife's anxiety with a few loving words. But when the two were on a call a few days before the Pulwama suicide bombing, Major Vibhu found himself triggered enough to respond.

'Nikki, *ek baat bata. Main andar nahi jaunga toh kaun jayega? Jo mere peeche hain, jo mere bande hain, jo meri team hai, agar main andar nahi gaya toh unka honsla kaun badhayega? Marna-warna kya hai, marna sabko hai. Sharmindagi se marne se achha toh yeh hai, aise hee maut mil jaye, na ki team wale bole kya bhagoda banda tha, apni team ko marwane chhod ke khud chala gaya* [Tell me Nikki, if I don't go in first, who will? If I shy away who will boost the morale of my men, my team? Everyone has to die someday. I would rather die than have my men say that I left them in the lurch and ran away].'

Nitika had winced. Major Vibhu had spoken gently as he always did, but his wife could sense there was a strain in his tone. She listened in silence. Holding the phone that night she knew she would need to dig even deeper into her reserves of empathy.

'I didn't need to tread gently,' she says. 'But I knew I needed to be more aware of the constant pressure on officers and soldiers in the field. They don't get much of a break from stressful situations.'

In February 2019, the two had been married for a little over nine months but Nitika had known Major Vibhu for

over seven years. The two had met through a common friend shortly after Vibhuti was commissioned into the Army in December 2011 after graduating from the same business school in Punjab that Nitika had just enrolled herself in.

'He started off really funny—on our third meeting strictly as friends, he said he really wanted to tell me something,' says Nitika. 'I was expecting something silly. But he said, "You know we are going to be married one day." I laughed it off, feigning shock and outrage, but there was something in his manner that said he wasn't really joking.'

As a young lieutenant fresh into the Army, Vibhu had remained in touch with his friend. Through text messages over the next few months, he made it clear how he felt, even if Nitika still baulked at the thought.

'After all our chats, he would end by saying, "Baby, I love you,"' says Nitika. 'I would not reply, not knowing how to reply, and he would say, "It's fine, you don't need to say anything, I'm just portraying my love for you, yaar."'

Nitika graduated and soon began her career with a major consulting firm. As she navigated a whole new corporate world in Delhi, the one thing she found herself counting on was a daily phone call from Vibhu.

'If I missed his call, he would text me. This carried on for a few years,' she says. 'One day he didn't call, and then he didn't text. This was while he was on a weekend trip to Goa with his buddies. And then there was silence from his side for three days. When he finally called, I found myself leaping out of my chair in excitement and relief. He had dropped his phone into the sea at Anjuna Beach. He was very apologetic. It was weird. It was clear I missed him, but it was still a one-way thing.'

In the summer of 2017, Nitika found herself looking up dermatologists for a skin condition on her face. At a clinic in Delhi, while undergoing a procedure, her skin was singed, making her condition visibly worse. Nitika was gripped by panic, and her phone rang, Vibhu's name flashing across the screen. She picked up and burst out crying on the phone.

'Between sobs, I told him I had destroyed my skin and nobody would ever look at me again,' says Nitika. 'I was very distraught, and it was the first time he had heard me cry.'

The next day, while at the dermatologist to fix the damage to her skin, she received another shock. Captain Vibhu had dashed to Delhi from his military station to see his friend, arriving at the clinic that afternoon.

'I covered my face and screamed for him not to be allowed in, but he was already inside the treatment room,' she says. 'I broke down again, begging him to leave. But he sat down on the bed and prised my hands off my face. I was a mess, and he was just sitting there with a bemused look on his face.'

'What are you so worried about?' he asked, laughing and taking her hand. 'I've been asking you to marry me for years now. You're beautiful to me no matter what. And you're the person I love and want to be with.'

Nitika cried even more.

'He asked me why are you doing this? For whom are you putting yourself through all this? He could tell I was doing the treatment as a paranoid twenty-something, and he saw right through it.'

'I'm here for you. Stop all this,' Vibhu had said.

'If ever there was a moment when things changed between us, it was this,' says Nitika.

Things moved quickly thereafter. Less than a year later, in April 2018, with three months of operations with the 55 Rashtriya Rifles under his belt, Major Vibhuti returned to Delhi to marry Nitika.

On a quick honeymoon to Goa, strolling on Anjuna Beach, the newly-weds promised each other that their real honeymoon would be in the Maldives a year after on their first anniversary. The two then plunged themselves back into their work, separated by distance, but speaking many times a day. Major Vibhu immersed himself into his operations, and Nitika was back into the slipstream of her ongoing rise in the corporate world.

In December 2018, Major Vibhu came home for only the second time since the wedding. It was a last-minute plan and Nitika didn't have time to postpone the work she had scheduled for the day, a meeting with an important client.

At the meeting, as Nitika briefed the people present, a member from the client's team asked her how her husband was, aware that he was in the Army and deployed in J&K. A little embarrassed, Nitika mentioned that he was fine and had actually just arrived in town for a break. The client was shocked.

'What are you doing here?' he had said. 'Work doesn't stop. Stop losing precious time with your husband. He knows he can't always be here because he's on duty protecting the country. So please don't put anything above family time. And please thank him for his service.'

Nitika had rushed home in the metro, leaping into Major Vibhu's arms on the platform where he said he would wait. After a few blissful days in Delhi's glorious winter, the officer once again returned to duties in south Kashmir.

February began ominously and with a tragedy. On the first day of the month, as Major Vibhuti and his company conducted a morning search operation in a Pulwama village, a Mirage 2000 fighter aircraft crashed in a ball of flame during take-off at Bengaluru's HAL airport. Two young test pilots, Squadron Leader Samir Abrol and Squadron Leader Siddhartha Negi, had died in the accident. Negi had been Major Vibhuti's classmate in school in Dehradun and a close friend.

On 16 February, two days after the Pulwama suicide attack, while Major Vibhuti and his company were preparing for a gruelling week of cordon-and-search operations, news arrived that another childhood friend and classmate from Dehradun, Major Chitresh Bisht, had been killed while attempting to defuse an improvised explosive device (IED) in the Rajouri sector along the LoC.

'I was very worried about his mental state,' says Nitika, who had travelled to Dehradun for the weekend to see her mother-in-law. 'This was a lot of personal and professional tragedy to deal with in a month. We spoke many times that day. What could I say apart from the usual comforting words? He was very stoic about it.'

On the night of 16 February, Major Vibhuti called again. Speaking first to Nitika and then his mother. But before disconnecting, he asked for Nitika to be put back on the line.

'Nikki, promise me no matter what happens to me, you will not stop living your life,' he said, his voice still gentle and unstrained. 'You are not going to spoil your life. Promise me that you will move forward, find love again, marry and have children.'

'Are you stupid? Don't talk such rubbish,' Nitika shouted back. She could feel her hairs standing on end. 'You please go to sleep. I hope there's no going out right now?'

'No, winding down for the day, will call you tomorrow,' he said.

'I love you, baby.'

Late next night, on 17 February, the familiar thrum of an incoming video call woke up Nitika. She had slept early to catch the morning train back to Delhi the following day.

'I'm missing you a lot,' Major Vibhu said.

Nitika could make out even in the grainy visual that her husband was in his field fatigues.

'We are going out for an operation soon. I love you so much.'

Nitika rubbed her eyes sleepily, telling her husband to be safe and take all precautions like she had said so many times before. Major Vibhuti paused, staring into the phone, his face soft but serious.

'Nikki, you take care, and make sure you take care of the family also.'

Nitika felt that familiar feeling of her skin crawling, holding her breath for a second, staring into the phone with no words to say. Major Vibhuti smiled, waved and hung up.

'For the first time, he forgot to say I'll call you back,' says Nitika. 'He never forgot to say that.'

Returning to bed, Nitika could barely sleep. Fifteen minutes later, she turned to her bedside table, picked up her phone and dialled her husband.

'Nikki, *kya hua* [what happened]?' he asked softly. He realized what he had forgotten to say.

'I love you, Vibhu.'

Major Vibhuti paused, smiling.

'Nikki, you know what I do before going for an operation? I take my phone out, and I look at a picture of you and then of my mother.'

Nitika felt tears well up in her eyes.

'Don't talk like this, my love.'

'If someday something happens to me and if I haven't seen your face, then I won't be at peace.'

Nitika was crying now but said nothing.

'Go to sleep, baby. I'll call you in the morning.'

Earlier that day, the 55 Rashtriya Rifles had received fresh intelligence on the whereabouts of three terrorists who were believed to be hiding in Pinglana, a neighbourhood near Kakapora, the home village of Adil Ahmed Dar, the

Jaish-e-Mohammed suicide bomber who had carried out the devastating attack three days earlier.

'Our commanding officer personally briefed us that day,' says Major Saurabh. 'There was palpable excitement in the ranks. After three days of night searches and interrogations we finally had a chance to get the guys who had facilitated such terrible damage to the country.'

Before departing from the battalion headquarters with his team, Major Vibhuti went to seek his commanding officer's permission to move.

'Just go all out, take care of yourself, don't be in a hurry,' Colonel Pradeep told his company commander.

These brief meetings were common, but they always weighed heavily on the unit boss.

'Whenever someone moves out on an operation, you know it could be their last. I remember Vibhu's last words before he left that night: "Sir, *bas main nikal raha hoon, aur kuchh hai toh batao* [Sir, I am leaving now, is there anything else you want to tell me]." There was no drama. We do this every day.'

Major Vibhu and Major Saurabh rolled out with their respective teams at 10.30 p.m. and headed straight towards Pinglana.

Totally dark in the hinterland, the landscape was a luminescent white that night with many inches of freshly fallen snow as the vehicles rumbled towards the village. Pinglana consisted of two rectangular clusters of about sixty houses divided by a road running through the middle.

Arriving on site, Major Vibhu and his team threw a cordon on one side of the road, preparing to begin their side of the search, as Major Saurabh and his team did the same on the other side of the road.

'Vibhu and I had a quick word before setting up the cordon—he simply said, search carefully,' recalls Major Saurabh.

'We were pumped up and ready to get this done. And as always, Vibhu's nose for terrorists didn't fail him that night.'

Of the thirty-odd houses that comprised his cordon-and-search area, Major Vibhuti carefully approached the second house in the row.

'Our teams were in touch via radio, so we were updating each other in real time,' says Major Saurabh. 'I received an update that Vibhu and his team had moved the family out of the second house and taken them a safe distance away. And just as we received word that Vibhu and his men were starting their search in that house, I heard the firing begin.'

After forty seconds of heavy assault-rifle fire from inside the house, Vibhu's team sent a radio confirmation to Major Saurabh and other units on standby in the area that contact had been established with the terrorists.

'Now everyone was in the picture as to where the action was,' says Major Saurabh. 'Once again, Vibhu had homed in perfectly. It was around 11.30 p.m., and the temperature was minus 8 degrees Celsius. It had begun to snow heavily. Minutes later, another radio update came that one terrorist had been killed while two terrorists had been injured. But both were still firing.'

Four minutes later, a search party led by 55 Rashtriya Rifles second-in-command, Lieutenant Colonel Rahul Gupta, closed in on the firefight, acquiring first visual contact of the encounter. They noticed that both Major Vibhuti as well as three soldiers from his team were flat on their stomachs, clearly injured, but still firing back. Major Vibhuti had crawled forward, gesturing to the other men to find cover.

'He was leading from the front,' says a soldier who was part of the six-member team inside the compound of the house. 'He was telling us to move to the left and out of the line of fire. He refused to turn back.'

The sound of rifle fire punctuated a steady howling wind, bringing with it even more snow.

Colonel Pradeep was also in radio contact nearby, tracking each move.

'As Vibhu was clearing the house, the terrorists shifted to a cowshed in the same compound,' says Colonel Pradeep. 'After Vibhu cleared the house with his buddy, they approached the cowshed. Suddenly there was a volley of fire from inside the cowshed and Vibhu took a few bullets. Badly injured, he still held his ground, pushed his buddy away to safety, and he returned fire. He did not let the terrorist break contact and escape. He maintained his composure, continuously passing on information to the other team members. Once hit, people usually give up. But badly injured, Vibhu still remained strong and eliminated the terrorist. Then he changed position with his buddy. There was another terrorist behind the first one, who he also managed to injure with a few shots. But by then he had lost too much blood.'

During a brief lull in the firing, as both sides paused to reload, Lieutenant Colonel Rahul dashed into the house and pulled out the six men who had gone in to engage the terrorists. Major Saurabh's team had now also arrived on site and was providing cover fire to facilitate the evacuation. Four, including Major Vibhuti, had multiple gunshot wounds.

'A helicopter evacuation was impossible in that weather,' says Major Saurabh. 'So, I was coordinating vehicles to dash them immediately to the 92 Base Hospital in Srinagar. Three of the men were motionless. But Vibhu was still breathing.'

In Dehradun, at half past midnight, Nitika stirred awake.

'When I opened my eyes, I could not see anything. You know how you can still see things when it's dark. But I couldn't. It was pitch black. I felt for my phone and switched on its light. I couldn't see that either. I thought I may be dreaming, but then I heard and smelt something that made my blood run cold. I could hear Vibhu's voice whispering, "Nikki, I love you." And I smelt cigarette smoke. Vibhu and I used to smoke sometimes. Nobody else in the house did. My head was spinning, and I was very scared. I was sure I was dreaming. I just whispered *I love you* twice and then pulled the sheet over my head. I mumbled the Gayatri Mantra to myself. When I opened my eyes again, I could see pale light streaming in from the window. I got up and had a glass of water. There was no smell in the room. I tried my best to sleep the rest of the night.'

In Pinglana, Major Saurabh and another soldier carried Major Vibhuti to a waiting stretcher.

His eyes were almost closed, and he was breathing very slowly. There was no movement. All we could do was hold his hand. The team's nursing assistant came and started administering first aid. Vibhu and injured soldiers Havildar Sheoram and Sepoy Ajay Kumar were in one vehicle. The fourth man, Sepoy Hari Kumar, had already succumbed to his gunshot wounds. In a furious snow blizzard, the vehicles rumbled north in the darkness towards Srinagar's 92 Base Hospital.

'There was no time to rest, the operation was still on,' says Major Saurabh, who was now in front of the house and directly engaging fire with the terrorists. 'At 1.15 a.m., I received a radio input that Vibhu and his three men had been pronounced dead. Standing there in the snow, crouched behind a parapet wall, I felt the wind being knocked out of me. My friend. My men. I had commanded the same company just a few months earlier before Vibhu had taken it over.'

The house now surrounded by troops, Major Saurabh allowed himself a few minutes to digest what had just happened.

'It was in the middle of an operation. We could not stop. It was the first time I had faced such a situation. While the firing paused, I gave a call to one of our unit officers who was on leave at the time—Lieutenant Colonel Vipul Narain. He was a mentor to Vibhu and me. I just needed some strength.'

Firing resumed an hour later and continued through the night and much of the next morning. Major Saurabh, who attempted to advance towards the house at dawn, received gunshot wounds in both legs. Lying in the snow, in great pain, he crawled to safety before passing out. By morning, the two remaining terrorists were finally cornered and killed, one near the cowshed and the other two houses away.

In Dehradun, Nitika was up early after a night of fitful sleep. Bleary-eyed, she began packing her suitcase for the journey back to Delhi. She tapped on her phone to see if she had missed any calls or messages. It was unlikely, her phone was always kept on loud volume. There were no messages or calls from her husband.

While she sipped from a cup of tea before leaving for the railway station, Vibhu's mother said, 'I had a funny dream last night, of Vibhu massaging my feet.'

Vibhu's sister, who was also in the room, said she had dreamt of Vibhu as well.

Nitika smiled, finished her tea and then got into the car so the family could drop her to the station.

'That morning I didn't feel right,' says Nitika. 'Vibhu always texted me the morning after an operation saying, "Baby I'm back, I love you." A friend of mine was on the same train. He could see how agitated I was getting and suggested I call someone from the unit to reassure myself. There could be many reasons why Vibhu had not called. I wasn't panicking, but my nerves were shot.'

At 7.30 a.m., while she was on the train, Nitika's phone rang. It was from an officer at the 55 Rashtriya Rifles.

'He has received injuries, we are trying to revive him, ma'am,' said the voice at the other end.

Nitika felt a flood of anger rise from within.

'Please just tell me the truth,' she said. 'I can already sense what has happened. Just give it to me straight.'

The officer at the other end paused before breaking down.

'Please don't worry about me, just give me the information I am asking for,' said Nitika. 'When will I see his body? Give me a proper time.'

'Vibhu Sir's body is in Srinagar. It will be flown to Dehradun via Palam (Delhi) by this evening.'

'Okay, thank you,' Nitika said before hanging up.

The train had left Dehradun and was picking up speed.

'I didn't know what to do,' remembers Nitika. 'I asked a ticket collector where the next station was. Thirty minutes later, as the train slowed down, I got off. The first thing I did was call Vibhu's sister. She was closest to him. She broke down and wept uncontrollably. I remember staying very calm on that empty railway platform.'

Next, Nitika called her mother in Delhi.

'My mother's painful screams tore my heart apart,' she says. 'I was petrified of one thing. How was I going to break the news to Vibhu's mother?'

On her way back to Dehradun in a taxi, she remained in a daze.

'I was wearing my *chura* and *mangalsutra* [wedding bangles and necklace] at that time. Suddenly, I just couldn't bear the weight of those bangles and other adornments of marriage. I found myself removing my mangalsutra, *payal* [anklets] and my *dejihor* [earrings]. I just couldn't bear anything on me. *Mera dil beth jata hai yeh yaad karke* [My heart sinks when I remember that time].'

Arriving back at Vibhu's family home, Nitika stood in front of the house just as a few close relatives and media personnel began to arrive.

'I didn't have the heart to break the news to Vibhu's mother,' she says. 'It was only after she was told the news that I went into the house. We ran to each other, hugged and fell down to the ground wailing.'

Major Vibhuti Shankar Dhoundiyal's flag-draped casket arrived at the family home at 8 p.m. that day.

The next morning, the casket was opened for the family to have one final look at Vibhu.

'I have never touched anything as cold as my husband's face,' says Nitika. 'When they put the lid back on the casket, my family tells me I was knocking on it. I guess I was hoping for some miracle. Maybe he would wake up. I recall how my grandmother had once lost her pulse but had been revived. I kept knocking on the wood of that casket. I wanted to see him again, but I didn't have the heart to open it again. I wanted him to rest.'

The 55 Rashtriya Rifles were grieving too.

'I lost four brave men that night,' says Colonel Pradeep. 'Vibhuti's spirit stays with us. He always took care of his men. Even in Pinglana, two of the men in his team survived because he led from the front and ensured they remained out of the line of fire. I remember how Vibhuti would sometimes be harsh on troops during training. Back at the base, while eating together, he would tell the men, "My anger can save our lives, that's why I lose my cool, don't take it any other way." This was always appreciated by the men. They would say, "*Vibhuti Saab hain toh dhyan rakhenge hamara* [If Vibhuti sir is there, he will take care of us]."'

Major Saurabh Patni, who received bullet injuries in both legs, remained unconscious for two days. It would be seven months before he walked again. Metal rods were inserted into both his legs, with one of the rods only removed in late 2021. The officer's WhatsApp DP hasn't changed since he regained consciousness after the encounter—a happy picture of him with Vibhu in their barracks during pre-induction training.

'I don't think I will ever change that picture,' says Major Saurabh. 'One of the things I keep going back to is something that happened during that training period before we were thrown into ops. There was a 5 km run we had to do weekly with a bulletproof jacket, *patka* and full load of ammunition. Most of us preferred to run as a group, because it's easier to blend in and keep up. But the area also had a night duty checkpost. The person manning that post had to run a day later alone, which nobody wanted to do. We decided to draw lots. But before we could do that, Vibhu volunteered and ran alone. It was never visible on his face that he was sacrificing anything.'

Back in Delhi, Nitika returned to work two weeks later.

'For a time, I had the profoundest hallucinations in which Vibhu would manifest in front of me almost every day,' she says. 'One of the most common visions I saw was Vibhu and me shackled in different rooms, struggling to break free and run to each other. We were scratching the walls, desperate to be together.'

Her grief would also lead Nitika to immerse herself in her phone, obsessively texting her husband on WhatsApp.

'I would send him texts like, "Where have you reached, baby, please call back." Nothing would be delivered. I tried to call him, but the phone was switched off. Then when the trance ended, it would hit me that he is no longer with me, and I would break down. My parents were very worried about me. I didn't feel like talking to anyone. Like so many people, I drowned myself in my work. I would demand even more work from my clients. I buried myself in my career.'

Nitika continued to be haunted by visions of Vibhu in shackles. The vision wore her down mentally. On a particularly low day, as she stood on her balcony, thinking about whether life was worth living any longer, she saw her phone screen blink.

'When I tapped open the phone, it went straight to a voice note that Vibhu had sent me many months earlier,' she says. 'It was him singing a song. I can't tell if I'm imagining all of this, but I know it happened.'

When April 2019 arrived, the month of their first anniversary, Nitika took seriously ill.

'I stopped eating. I was like a skeleton. I was admitted to a hospital for a few days. I was administered shots to help me sleep. In that state, I remember having a vision of Vibhu and me sitting on what looked like a white cloud. He is holding my hand and saying, "Yaar, what are you doing to yourself." And I say, "*Yaar mazaa nahi aa raha hai, mujhe bhi saath le chalo* [Nothing feels good. Take me with you]." And then he refuses.'

Such conversations would continue, says Nitika.

'In one particular dream or vision, Vibhu appeared to read my mind. He said you must be wondering how much pain I felt *jab goli lagi* [when I was shot]. He said he felt no pain and it was very quick. The first bullet itself ended everything. I know this wasn't true, but he needed to reassure me, and I have since accepted that he's telling me the truth.'

The visions would sometimes have very specific conversations, says Nitika.

'In one of these dreams, Vibhu told me I would soon be speaking with a woman who had lost her husband. And that I needed to tell her that he was safe and sound with Vibhu. Some days later, towards the end of April, I got a call from a naval officer who asked if I could speak with Karuna Chauhan, a newly-wed lady who had lost her husband, Lieutenant Commander Dharmendra Singh Chauhan, in a fire accident on board the aircraft carrier INS *Vikramaditya*. I realized she was the one Vibhu was telling me about.'

During another bout of ill health and hospitalization, Nitika dreamt of Vibhu sitting in the chair next to her bed.

'He said, "Nikki, when you wake up there will be a nurse who will be holding your hands. She will be reviving you. Just tell her I said thank you and kiss her hands. Say your husband is eternally grateful to her for saving your life." When I woke up, I did exactly that. And when I was alone in the room again, I whispered to Vibhu that he is free. I told him that he doesn't need to worry about me any more. I was sure I wanted to live.'

In August 2019, the Indian Army announced that Major Vibhuti Shankar Dhoundiyal would be decorated with a posthumous Shaurya Chakra. The medal citation noted his 'unparalleled courage, conspicuous bravery and exceptional leadership qualities'.

'When I was discharged from hospital, I saw Vibhu again only once in my visions,' says Nitika. 'But I also had total clarity on what I wanted to do next.'

Taking the fourteenth Services Selection Board (SSB) examination, Nitika joined the Officers Training Academy (OTA) in Chennai.

'During physical endurance training one day, I was exhausted and about to give up on a long run. I didn't even look up, and I knew he was standing there with a big grin on his face. I heard him whisper, "*Arre bhaag, moti, bhaag, fail ho jaogi* [Run, or else you will fail]!"'

In May 2021, Lieutenant Nitika Kaul Dhoundiyal was commissioned into the Indian Army, her officer stars pipped on her shoulders by the then northern commander of the Indian Army, Lieutenant General Yogesh Kumar Joshi. In November, in full uniform and accompanied by Vibhu's mother, Nitika received her husband's Shaurya Chakra from the President at a Rashtrapati Bhavan investiture ceremony.

'I don't get visions any more,' says Nitika. 'Vibhu never wanted death. He loved our life together. We had so many plans. He wanted a certain house. We talked about children. We were thinking about life.'

With her unit now, Lieutenant Nitika hopes Vibhu is aware of the tribute she's trying to pay him.

'And I hope he isn't laughing,' she says.

6

'They Were Coming to Behead'

Sepoy Karmdeo Oraon

Line of Control, Naugam Sector
4.25 p.m.
29 December 2018

The only sound that could be heard from inside the light machine gun nest was a slow, cold breeze through the pines that lined the track leading down the mountainside to a bend 100 metres away. The only smell was the familiar tingle of frozen conifer-scented air mixed with gun grease.

Sepoy Karmdeo Oraon strained at the peephole, holding his breath so he could look as steadily and clearly through the little square of vision as possible. His hands rested instinctively on the weapon that gave the mini bunker its identity. A battered black machine gun with a distinct orangish brown buttstock. One hand curled around the pistol grip of the weapon. The other on the handguard.

He shifted his gaze up over the trees, scanning a brief horizon that held territory just across the Line of Control (LoC). And he knew even before they landed that weapons had been fired on the other side, the frozen calm broken by a series of whistling and hissing sounds that ended in earth-shaking thuds around the bunker. A fearsome, uninterrupted mortar and rocket-propelled grenade attack had begun on India's Karalkot Post, a cluster of five bunkers—including Sepoy Karmdeo's light machine gun (LMG) nest—spread across a 50-metre frontage at LoC, Naugam.

Even though it pushed him instantly into ready-to-retaliate mode, the incoming attack didn't startle Sepoy Karmdeo. The battalion was already on high alert following an exchange that had taken place in the same area thirteen days earlier. Ceasefire violations by the Pakistan Army at the LoC were more than routine at the time. The year 2018 had seen a staggering 1600 ceasefire violations by the Pakistan Army. That December alone had already witnessed 175, an average of nearly six each day. The soldier from the Charlie Company of the 8 Bihar infantry battalion adjusted his protective headgear and bulletproof vest and turned his head for a moment to count the number of hand grenades he had stacked in a wooden ammo box.

The firing was coming from hundreds of metres away across the LoC, too far to humanly fling a hand grenade. But there was a good reason why the grenades—a French word meaning pomegranate—were available in Sepoy Karmdeo's bunker. The post was perched atop a hill that straddled a route notorious for infiltration by Pakistan Army-aided terrorists. And only ninety seconds into the high-tempo bombardment from the other side, Sepoy Karmdeo saw them.

Five shadowy figures, 100 metres away.

In single file and in a crouched manner, they emerged from around the mountain bend. Their Kalashnikov rifles in firing posture, the five men edged forward under protection from a fresh blaze of cover fire that was now raining down on the Indian machine gun nest from two hill ridges emanating outward.

Apart from the mortars and rockets still smashing into the ground around the bunker, rifle fire tore into the bunker's walls, filling the air with a deafening clatter. Squinting through his peephole but holding fire, Sepoy Karmdeo noticed flashes of light from the combat fatigues of two of the men creeping forward.

It was only after they had crept closer that the Indian soldier realized what that was. Tucked into the belts of two of the approaching figures, glinting in the early evening sun, were 12-inch-long hunting daggers.

They were coming not just to kill and overrun the Karalkot Post.

They were coming to behead.

* * *

Thirteen days earlier
Line of Control, Naugam Sector
16 December 2018

The wireless intercepts couldn't have been clearer. Two Pakistan Army personnel had been seriously wounded on the other side of the LoC. The chaotic static and crackle of the intercepts also indicated that the injured men were officers—a brigadier who commanded Pakistan's 75 Infantry Brigade and was visiting forward positions to meet troops, and a colonel who commanded Pakistan's 37 Punjab infantry battalion. In a blood-drenched year that had seen multiple soldier casualties on both sides, the wounding of two senior Pakistan Army officers in an Indian retaliation was deemed an escalation—an invitation for the cycle of violence to climb to the next level.

Not that the location wasn't a raw nerve anyway.

The Karalkot Post was located 2 km ahead of the 8 Bihar battalion headquarters in the Kaiyan bowl, an area that had been grabbed back from the Pakistan Army during the 1971 war. For a half century since, the Pakistan Army had been attempting to either take back the Kaiyan bowl, or at least dominate it in such a manner as to make it simply too dangerous for Indian posts to remain. The men of 8 Bihar therefore not only had to defend the frontage in that area, but constantly retaliate to ceasefire violations. The Army unit that had been deployed in the area before 8 Bihar arrived eleven months earlier, had suffered several casualties and bore the scars of a particularly ill-tempered sector on an aggressively lit-up LoC.

Corroborating the wireless intercepts, informers in Pakistan-occupied Kashmir confirmed to the 8 Bihar battalion headquarters that a Pakistani brigadier and colonel, who had been hit on 16 December, were battling for their lives in a military hospital not far from the location. The confirmation triggered an instantaneous level of higher alert, courtesy 8 Bihar's commanding officer.

'They will try to even the score,' said Colonel Debashis Nath in a signal to his front-line posts, including Karalkot. 'Don't let your guard down against counter-retaliatory action by the Pakistan Army and terrorist infiltrators. Not even for a second. Be alert at all times for a strike on your posts.'

'Leave of all soldiers was cancelled to beef up the strength at each post. Multiple inputs were received from higher headquarters too that Pakistan was planning to retaliate and strike Indian Army posts on the LoC. Our unit was deployed ahead of the LoC fence, and it had been on red alert. Drills to counter any contingency were rehearsed and troops were fully prepared,' says an officer from the battalion.

This LoC fence, built in early 2000, is a meandering 550 km fence mounted with modern electronic surveillance gadgets along stretches of the 740 km LoC on the Indian side. The reason the fence isn't continuous is because of the forbidding high-altitude terrain in several sectors. Built with two rows of fencing and concertina wire, it is designed to obstruct infiltrators. The Indian Army mans posts on either side of the fence. The Karalkot Post, for instance, is located 900 metres ahead of the fence, making it the first line of

India's defence against the Pakistan Army in this pocket of the Naugam sector.

The alert was more detailed than just a general call to a higher state of readiness. It predicted the possibility of Pakistani retaliation in the form of a Border Action Team (BAT) operation, referring to an attack launched from across the LoC by mixed squads of Pakistan Army Special Service Group (SSG) commandos and terrorist infiltrators. In BAT actions, the commandos and specially trained terrorists would work together, performing a military-style covert assault that was notorious for the intended endgame—the decapitation of any Indian soldiers they managed to kill—and going back across the LoC with their heads. These attacks were designed not just to exact revenge, but to instil a deep sense of fear and unease in the minds of the units deployed at the LoC. The most infamous beheading, one that made national headlines, took place six years earlier in January 2013, when an Indian Army patrol party was ambushed, and one of the soldiers decapitated and mutilated.

Line of Control, Naugam Sector
4.30 p.m.
29 December 2018

The five men were slowly creeping closer, their movement covered by a hail of fire directed at Sepoy Karmdeo's bunker and the four other bunkers a few metres behind his, up the mountainside.

But it was Sepoy Karmdeo's bunker that was nearest to the advancing terrorists. They would make the first close-range 'contact' with the Indian soldier and attempt to overrun the post, trying to kill as many soldiers as possible. The other Pakistani attack squads—it was now clear there were at least three more in addition to the terrorist squad—would focus on providing an incessant volley of cover fire from the mountain flanks and from across the LoC.

About 2 km away at his battalion headquarters, Colonel Debashis heard the explosions and the sound of machine gun fire. None of these were unusual sounds in the sector under his watch, but as he prepared to take the daily 'all OK' report from his second-in-command (2IC) over the phone, the forty-year-old commanding officer could tell this wasn't just another ceasefire violation.

'The moment my 2IC wished me "good evening" and started giving me the all-OK report, I could hear unusually intense firing in the area. But it wasn't immediately clear which of my posts was bearing the brunt of the multiple explosions and the raging, high-intensity firing producing powerful echoes in the mountain side. However, I could make out that this was happening nearby, in my backyard,' Colonel Debashis says.

Backyard, indeed.

Twelve minutes into the firing, Colonel Debashis received an urgent signal from one of his company commanders manning a post not far from Karalkot. The message also contained a crucial input, mentioning that this appeared to be a BAT action, likely vengeance for the 16 December injuries inflicted on the two senior Pakistan Army officers.

The Pakistani brigadier was back to work a week after his injuries, but the Pakistani colonel, initially presumed dead, was still fighting for his life in a military hospital. But the Pakistani revenge mission was now in full flow.

'We tried to speak to the Karalkot Post but the telephone lines were cut off by the raiding teams. It took us a while to connect with the post commander over the radio set to find out what was happening,' the CO recalls.

Naik Deepak Singh at an Army base

Naik Deepak Singh with his wife, Rekha Singh

Rekha receiving Naik Deepak Singh's Vir Chakra from President Ram Nath Kovind at an investiture ceremony at Rashtrapati Bhavan in New Delhi

Colonel B. Santosh Babu's wife, Santoshi, and mother, Manjula, receiving his Maha Vir Chakra from the President of India

Naib Subedar Nuduram Soren's wife, Laxmi Soren, receiving his Vir Chakra from President Ram Nath Kovind

Havildar K. Palani's wife, Vanathi Devi, receiving his Vir Chakra from the President of India

Sepoy Gurtej Singh's parents, Prakash Kaur and Virsa Singh, receiving his Vir Chakra from the President of India

President Ram Nath Kovind presenting the Vir Chakra to Havildar Tejinder Singh

Still from a video released by the Chinese; Captain Soiba Maningba Rangnamei of 16 Bihar challenges a Chinese officer during the Galwan confrontation

Group Captain Varun Singh's mother, Uma Singh, and wife, Geetanjali, receiving his Shaurya Chakra from the President of India

Group Captain Varun Singh

Subedar Sanjiv Kumar (*centre*); (*clockwise from top left*): Paratrooper Bal Krishan, Paratrooper Amit Kumar, Havildar Devendra Singh and Paratrooper Chhatrapal Singh

Paratrooper Sonam Tshering Tamang was decorated with a Shaurya Chakra for his role in Operation Randori Behak

Subedar Sanjiv Kumar

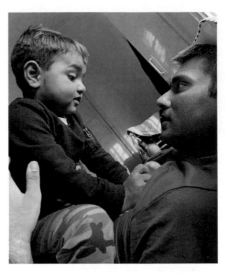

Squadron Leader Ishan Mishra with his son, Ayaan

Squadron Leader Ishan Mishra

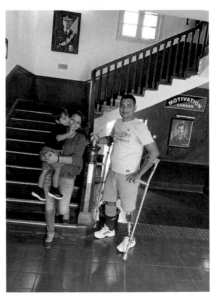

Squadron Leader Ishan Mishra with his wife, Squadron Leader Shalika Sharma, and son, Ayaan

Major Vibhuti Shankar Dhoundiyal with his wife, Nitika Kaul Dhoundiyal

Major Vibhuti Shankar Dhoundiyal at a forward Army base

Major Vibhuti Shankar Dhoundiyal's mother, Saroj, and wife, Nitika, receiving his Shaurya Chakra from the President of India

Nitika keeps this picture of Major Vibhuti and her in
the back of her phone

Lance Naik Karmdeo Oraon receiving his Shaurya Chakra from President Ram Nath Kovind

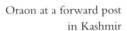

Oraon at a forward post in Kashmir

Lance Naik Sandeep Singh's son, Abhinav, with officers of 4 Para at his father's funeral

Lance Naik Sandeep Singh

Defence Minister Rajnath Singh shares a warm moment with Lance Naik Sandeep Singh's son, Abhinav

Lance Naik Sandeep Singh

Lance Naik Sandeep Singh's wife, Gurpreet, receiving his Shaurya Chakra from the President of India

Captain (now Commodore) Sachin Sequeira receiving his Shaurya
Chakra from President Ram Nath Kovind

Commander Bipin Panikar with his family

Commander Bipin Panikar poses in front of his
Sea King helicopter

Major Konjengbam Bijendra Singh with his wife, Jenipher, and daughter, Jasmine

Major Konjengbam Bijendra Singh receiving his Shaurya Chakra from President Ram Nath Kovind

Chief Petty Officer Veer Singh and Commander Ashok Kumar
in the Arabian Sea

Commander Ashok Kumar

Chief Petty Officer Veer Singh with his family

At Karalkot, things were getting worse as the ferocity of the attack intensified each minute. The post commander, Havildar Jitendra Singh, was somehow able to establish radio contact with his commanding officer and communicate the nature and gravity of the furious attack that had completely pinned down the men holding out against it.

'*Saab, yahan halat theek nahin hain. Dushman ne humko gher rakha hai, par hum jawabi karyawahi kar rahe hain* [The enemy has surrounded us, but we are taking retaliatory action],' Havildar Jitendra told Colonel Debashis over the radio.

'Karalkot Post was under a very heavy barrage of rocket and mortar fire from a Pakistan Army post,' says Sepoy Karmdeo. 'We were also subjected to automatic fire from the three other squads that had crossed the LoC and taken positions on nearby heights. It was difficult to pinpoint the directions from where the fire was coming.'

The five infiltrators were now 100 metres away and closing in on the bunkers of Karalkot Post. As bullets from the Pakistani support squads ricocheted off his bunker, Sepoy Karmdeo waited, watching the advancing figures closely.

They were 70 metres away.

As they closed in, the infiltrators became more visible. They were gesturing to each other, using tactical sign language typical of a special operations unit, a clear sign of some level of military-style training. From what Sepoy Karmdeo could make out, it seemed the infiltrators were perhaps under the impression that the furious fire assault launched minutes ago from all directions had in all likelihood paralyzed the men holding the post and maybe even killed a few of them.

Now, 60 metres.

Soon, 50 metres.

The five infiltrators stopped for a moment. After a quick gesture to each other, they opened up their assault rifles, firing directly at Sepoy Karmdeo's machine gun nest, the bullets smashing into the sandbags piled up in front of the bunker as a protective barrier. But the Indian soldier did not return fire. Not yet.

Taking deep breaths and cautiously watching their every step, Sepoy Karmdeo's position was now peppered by the five blazing Kalashnikovs right ahead, adding to the enormous volume of fire already pouring in from the other Pakistani squads. But he had decided to wait.

In the midst of the deafening clatter, another realization dawned on the solitary Indian soldier with his LMG and box of grenades. While the other bunkers at Karalkot Post were also under fire, it was unlikely that they knew about the infiltrators now just 30 metres from Sepoy Karmdeo's position. The sequence of events had moved so quickly that there was no time for an emergency communication. And the deafening chaos surrounding the bunker now made it impossible to communicate the situation clearly. And anyway, the infiltrators had just stepped even closer, the barrels of their Kalashnikovs flashing from just 20 metres away.

'For that moment, I needed to be oblivious to what was going on behind me at the post, or of any counter action being taken by our side to hit back,' says Sepoy Karmdeo. 'It was a moment for panic, but we know what panic can do in such situations.'

Closing in, 15 metres.

In a sudden move, two of the five infiltrators peeled away from the group and took positions on a mountain flank off the left overlooking Sepoy Karmdeo's position. It was clearly a move intended to split his focus and engage him from another direction. The three infiltrators firing from the trail ahead knew what they had to do.

'I wanted them to get closer. I could see the three terrorists firing at my post from barely 15 metres. And then, in the blink of an eye, they darted towards my post while the two men on the heights started firing rockets from a rocket-propelled grenade launcher and also turned a Pika belt-fed machine gun at my position,' says Sepoy Karmdeo.

Now, 10 metres.

With total focus on the three infiltrators now just a few steps away from his bunker, Sepoy Karmdeo's hand tightened around the pistol grip of his machine gun. He remembers skipping into a rare moment of total clarity, not uncommon with front-line troops in defensive close engagement situations. A difficult-to-describe lucidity where survival instinct and emotional attachments give way to a sudden, startlingly clear immediate picture.

'For me that moment of total clarity was that I wasn't going to allow these terrorists to storm the post on my watch at any cost,' says Sepoy Karmdeo. 'I was sitting on that desolate hill for a purpose. They would have to do it over my dead body. *Aur mujhe marne ki koi jaldi nahi thi* [And I was in no hurry to die].'

As the Indian soldier had not fired a single bullet yet, the three advancing infiltrators appeared certain that they were on the path of least resistance and would soon be celebrating inside an overrun Indian bunker. If the unremitting hail of fire hadn't torn the occupant's body to shreds already, they would have the chance to separate his head from his torso and return with the setting sun across the LoC. They began their final stealthy steps towards the bunker.

It was at this point, with the infiltrators less than 10 metres from his position, that Sepoy Karmdeo decided it was time to respond.

'I had been itching to do it the moment I spotted them but kept waiting as I knew I may only have one chance,' says Sepoy Karmdeo. 'I opened fire with my LMG, hitting two of the infiltrators at close range even as they continued to get cover fire from the two infiltrators who had separated from them minutes earlier to take positions looking down on my position. The two I shot dropped to the ground instantly.'

It was at this point that Sepoy Karmdeo was able to get his clearest view of the infiltrators. Dressed in black battle fatigues, they were wearing Kevlar body armour and helmet-mounted optical devices.

'*Jaise filmon mein dikhate hain* [Just like in the movies],' he recalls. 'They were equipped like special operations soldiers, not like the usual terrorists you see. Our input was totally correct—this appeared to be a BAT action by Pakistan.'

And as the two infiltrators lay motionless on the mountainside a few metres from the bunker, Sepoy Karmdeo once again saw the combat daggers tucked into their belts, left visibly unholstered.

But this was far from over. Only two men had apparently been dropped. There was a third infiltrator on the path ahead, two more on the mountain flank to the left, and three more squads of infiltrators in different positions who were still firing at the Karalkot Post.

'I was encountering something like this for the first time in my army career, although I have been involved in gunfights before,' says Sepoy Karmdeo. 'After I shot the two terrorists, the third one retreated and started running zigzag towards the mountain bend where all five of them had come from. I think I got him too but couldn't be sure at the time. Worse, when I scanned the path to ensure that the two infiltrators I had shot were dead, I noticed they were still moving. *Woh haath-paer hila rahe the* [They were moving their limbs].'

The Kevlar body armour the infiltrators were wearing had done its job. Not only were the two men not dead, they were not even badly injured. In a flash, they got to their feet and tumbled behind a boulder just 15 metres from the Indian machine gun position. With the rock now covering them, they resumed their attack, firing quick Kalashnikov bursts at Sepoy Karmdeo's bunker. The terrorists were following a simple but effective pattern in the close-quarter fight to pin down the Indian sepoy, by taking turns to take shots at him and providing cover fire to each other.

This was now a significantly more perilous situation. If the advancing infiltrators had earlier assumed the huge volume of fire had killed or incapacitated the Indian bunker's occupants, Sepoy Karmdeo had now signalled with his retaliatory fire that he was alive, pushing the terrorists into a stealthier attack mode.

That was how quickly things had changed. And the training and equipment given to the terrorists had made all the difference. In a matter of seconds, from being sprawled on the mountainside and practically assumed neutralized, the advantage was now fully back with them. The implications of this new dynamic hit Sepoy Karmdeo instantly. With a rock for cover and some breathing space, the infiltrators could summon more Pakistani squad members from the mountain flanks for a final assault on the Karalkot bunkers and overrun them. There was no option left, and the Indian soldier, his breath now coming in wintry wisps in the dying light, knew what needed to be done.

As the Kalashnikov rounds thudded into the sandbags that wreathed his bunker, Sepoy Karmdeo crept out of his post, armed with only an INSAS assault rifle. Positioning himself to the left side of his bunker and now almost fully exposed, he returned fire at the two infiltrators, emptying two full magazines of ammunition. It had been a daring move, but as the terrorists realized where the fresh fire was coming from, and now training their weapons directly at him and sending bullets whizzing past his head, Sepoy Karmdeo, on his elbows, dragged himself back into the bunker.

The LMG and assault rifle were now practically useless against the hiding terrorists. Sepoy Karmdeo looked over at the wooden ammo box containing hand grenades.

Meanwhile, an Indian Army post just north of Karalkot had been activated. The trail that disappeared behind the mountainside ahead of Karalkot led to a series of LoC-hugging posts held by the 8 Bihar battalion's Delta Company. Receiving urgent orders from his commanding officer at the Kaiyan Bowl, the Giani Post commander, twenty-four-year-old Captain Talisunep Longkumer, was placed on standby to rush much-needed reinforcements as quickly as possible to Karalkot.

But there was a problem, and it wasn't a small one as it would later emerge. The raiding Pakistani squads had placed ambush teams on all three mountain routes leading to the Karalkot Post, including the one from Captain Talisunep's Giani Post. The young officer had his orders, and he needed to figure out as quickly as possible a way to rush his troops to help Karalkot fight off the Pakistani assault.

Back at Karalkot Post, Sepoy Karmdeo was ready to use his grenades. But just as he picked one up from the box, a Kalashnikov round fired by one of the infiltrators found its way into the bunker and hit the Indian soldier squarely in the forehead, knocking him violently to the ground.

'I was down for a few seconds, and then staring at the bunker ceiling,' says Sepoy Karmdeo. 'I could move my eyes. Could still hear the firing. I moved my fingers. I was still alive.'

The 7.62 mm rifle round had impacted the Indian soldier on the steel plate of his bulletproof headgear. An inch below, it would have hit him straight in the face, killing him instantly. It was a providential escape, and Sepoy Karmdeo remembers thinking that the patka had done precisely what it was designed to do—give attackers a few less square inches to hit. Square inches that made all the difference in such fearsome close combat.

But as bullets continued to rain down on the bunker, Sepoy Karmdeo's patience turned into absolute fury.

'There was no blood. I felt no pain. I was alive. The firing was so intense from their side that I didn't even realize that a bullet had hit me on the forehead. I only felt a big *jhatka* [jolt] and fell. I decided to go after them with all my might. This firefight had gone on for longer than it should have, and I had to end it no matter what,' recalls Sepoy Karmdeo.

Certain now that there was nearly no chance of eliminating the terrorists from inside his bunker, the sepoy did something the infiltrators probably didn't expect.

The box of grenades in his hands, Sepoy Karmdeo crept out of his bunker into the fury of the incoming automatic fire once again. Taking position a few metres to the right of his bunker, he quickly flung all ten grenades in the direction of the two terrorists hiding behind the rock. Then he dived back into his bunker, hearing the grenades detonate in bright fiery thuds.

'I was not able to take them on with my LMG. The effort with the rifle also failed. The grenades were the only option. It worked. The only thing on my mind was that there was grave danger to the lives of my comrades if these terrorists slipped past me. I would not have let that happen at any cost,' Sepoy Karmdeo says.

The grenades had exploded at the intended mark, but the proceedings of that evening had made it clear that no assumptions could be made. Whatever the condition of the two terrorists behind the rock, Sepoy Karmdeo would only be able to check personally by going there. And at that point, it was out of the question—his post was still taking intermittent fire.

He looked out to the left for the two terrorists who were covering the manoeuvres of the 'dead' pair from the height, but there was no trace of them. Firing from that direction had stopped. The two appeared to have unexpectedly melted away into the forest behind them, the first solid indication that Sepoy Karmdeo's grenades had done their work. With the attack squad dead, the cover fire served no purpose. It was possible that they would attack from another direction, but for the moment, they had retreated into the darkness.

'Those two on the mountain flank were most likely Pakistani SSG commandos, who were not supposed to make contact but only provide cover fire to the three terrorists from a position of relative safety,' says Sepoy Karmdeo.

It had been twenty minutes since the first bullets flew, with the grenades bringing a blanket of silence back on the post by 4.50 p.m.

Back at the battalion headquarters operations room, Colonel Debashis's unwavering focus was on obtaining latest inputs on the overwhelming attack on the Karalkot Post. He was receiving a steady supply of information from three neighbouring locations in the area that had an unimpeded view of the Karalkot Post. It was about 4.45 p.m. when the firefight involving Oraon was in its closing stages.

'The picture was hazy, but I had managed to glean from the other posts that at least three men were trying to storm the post from where Karmdeo was standing guard and five men had positioned themselves between Karalkot and Giani to block the closest reinforcements,' says the commanding officer.

In minutes, it would be completely dark at Karalkot Post. The echoes of firing had cascaded away, allowing back the sound of the breeze through the pines, the air now tinged with gun smoke. There was no question of Sepoy Karmdeo lowering his guard at this time. He remained in position, fully aware from his training that the threat of terrorist squads mounting a second wave of attack was more than just possible.

It was last light at 5.30 p.m. when the unit's commanding officer ordered Captain Talisunep to depart from the Giani Post along with a seven-man quick reaction team (QRT) armed with multi-grenade launchers (MGLs), LMGs and Kalashnikovs, and rush to Karalkot in the cover afforded by darkness.

The unremitting severity of the Pakistani attack on Karalkot Post wasn't entirely over. The BAT action by infiltration squads may have temporarily been hit, but the post was now the target of heavy shelling and firing from Pakistan Army posts across the LoC. This time, the picture was being beamed live to the battalion headquarters. Specialized artillery observation equipment deployed by a neighbouring battalion at a height overlooking Karalkot was transmitting video feeds to the headquarter operations room. The real-time feeds were the first solid inputs illustrating the severity of the attack.

'Troop commander Havildar Jitendra Singh's description of the post having been surrounded by the enemy was corroborated by the video feeds being transmitted by the thermal imaging intensification observation equipment (TIIOE) deployed at the neighbouring battalion's Key Post,' says Colonel Debashis. 'The equipment can see up to 4 km at night. From my headquarters, finally I knew *kahan kya harkat ho rahi hai* [what movement was taking place where]. I could make out how our boys were moving within the post and what the enemy was up to outside. The squads attacking the post consisted of fifteen to sixteen men, including the ones who engaged Karmdeo.'

The images transmitted confirmed what Sepoy Karmdeo had personally seen as he shot the infiltrators. The raiding squads had all the trappings of a military team. The target chosen, Karalkot, was a remote and vulnerable post. The sure-footedness of the intruders showed that the Pakistani team had clearly carried out thorough reconnaissance of the area before the attack. Pakistani squads had positioned themselves to encircle and cut off the post and only one team attempted to storm it by making direct contact even as the rest launched coordinated assaults from stand-off distances. Military-style tactics.

Even the route taken by the infiltration squad that made direct contact with Sepoy Karmdeo was a surprise choice, intended to catch sentries off guard. Terrorist infiltrators were least likely to take that particular route to mount an assault as it was frequently used for administrative tasks such as transporting rations and other stores to forward posts scattered further up in the mountains. The route was also frequented by specialized teams dispatched to construct and repair bunkers, rotation of soldiers and evacuation of casualties. It was the last route that terrorist infiltrators would be expected to use.

And that's precisely what they did.

'Every method employed by the attackers was a clear indication that this was a well-planned operation,' Colonel Debashis says. '*Aisa nahin tha ki woh aise hi utth kar aa gaye wahan* [It was not as if they were there in the area by happenstance]. They must have carried out close reconnaissance days before the attack because the routes within a dense jungle are hard to tell from a distance. The terrain is such that they must have come closer undetected at some stage.'

The Pakistani teams positioned to intercept reinforcements attempting to reach Karalkot from nearby posts was another tell-tale element of military planning. On his way to Karalkot from Giani Post in the darkness, Captain Talisunep was expecting stiff resistance. Naugam was the young officer's second posting after he was commissioned into the unit in June 2016. That night was his fourth major operation along the LoC.

En route to Karalkot Post, the young officer spoke to his men. By now they had heard about the heavy attack and were raring to reach the location and join the fight. In a short radio message from Karalkot, troop commander Havildar Jitendra relayed that not an inch of his post had been spared by the devastating volleys of incoming fire from mortars, rocket-propelled grenade launchers, LMGs, Pika machine guns and other automatic weapons. The bunkers were almost completely destroyed. Captain Talisunep's QRT was speeding towards Karalkot in the nick of time.

'The boys in my QRT were highly trained and among the best in the company,' he says. 'We had been out on operations earlier too. We conduct drills to respond to different scenarios almost on a daily basis. Every man knew his job, what weapon he would carry and how he would move with the squad.'

As Captain Talisunep and his men manoeuvred down the snow-covered slope as fast as they could to answer Havildar Jitendra's desperate call for backup, the latter crept relentlessly between the scattered bunkers at Karalkot Post, personally reassuring each of the dozen men under his command, including Sepoy Karmdeo, that reinforcements were on their way, motivating them to give their all to defend the post.

Apart from Sepoy Karmdeo and Havildar Jitendra, the men holding Karalkot Post included three other soldiers from 8 Bihar, four men from the Border Security Force (BSF troops are co-located with the Indian Army in forward areas like Naugam) and three soldiers from an air defence (AD) unit. Each of the twelve men had a critical role to play that desolately cold night after the infiltration by the BAT team had been rebuffed.

The two AD soldiers used their ageing but highly effective Soviet origin Zu–23–2B guns to target the Pakistan Army posts that were providing cover fire to the infiltration squad. The other troops at Karalkot fired their medium machine guns (MMGs), LMGs, under-barrel grenade launchers and Kalashnikovs in retaliation.

'*Uss din karo ya maro wali baat thi* [It was a do-or-die situation that day],' says Havildar Jitendra. '*Aamne-saamne ki ladai thi* [We were in an eyeball-to-eyeball confrontation with the attackers]. The scale of the attack was overwhelming, and I had never seen anything like it in my twenty-one-year army service. I was able to locate their positions with inputs from the higher headquarters that were getting live feeds. We were concentrating our fire on those areas.'

The aftermath was turning out to be much less of a one-way affair. Karalkot was now getting critical support from other Indian Army posts in the area which were not only targeting the Pakistan Army posts with heavy weapons, but also firing at the likely locations of the retreating Pakistani squads that were estimated to be at distances of 100 to 200 metres from the nearly overrun post. But the men of Karalkot were still pinned down in their damaged bunkers, with shells still crashing into the ground around them.

The fearsome and sudden attack had become a full-blown crossfire across the LoC, with tracer rounds from both sides peppering the darkness with points of red light. How long would this go on for? What was the endgame now? Havildar Jitendra and the men under his command were prepared to fight to the last man but knew that only the timely arrival of reinforcements could save the post. Each shell that impacted was damaging the bunkers little by little. A handful of well-aimed shells would kill them all instantly.

Hurrying on foot, Captain Talisunep's team was now approaching the Pakistani squad that had been positioned between Karalkot and Giani posts to fight off any reinforcements. Pakistani shells hit the ground not far from them, sending showers of loose earth at the QRT team as it trudged down the mountainside in the darkness towards Karalkot.

One of the artillery observation posts had relayed imagery of the terrorist squad lying in wait for Captain Talisunep's QRT along with coordinates of their precise location. Now within minutes of that location, the officer issued final instructions to his men not to engage the terrorists until they were within a range of 150 metres, the range at which the 40 mm multi-grenade launcher, the most potent weapon the QRT was armed with that night, could be used in a precision role to strike a target at night in fully hostile conditions.

Since Captain Talisunep's QRT was moving down the mountainside, it was approaching the terrorist ambush from higher ground, a precious advantage in the circumstances.

'We finally stopped, took position, and the moment we opened up the multi-grenade launcher on them, the five men just fled,' says Captain Talisunep. 'They even left some of their weapons behind. It was evident they were not expecting us to be there. In my assessment, their operation was well-planned but not well-executed. Frankly, I was expecting a fight to the finish from them.'

It took the Captain's QRT an hour to reach Karalkot Post located 1200 metres downhill from Giani Post as the men were cautiously led to their destination by the officer whose top priority was to keep them out of harm's way.

'We were moving into the unknown in the midst of heavy shelling and automatic fire that was hampering our advance. I will not be stating the truth if I say there was absolutely no fear in my mind. I was concerned about the safety of my troops and taking all possible precautions on the way to Karalkot where we were needed. *Mere ko kuch nahi hoga syndrome khatarnak saabit ho sakta hai* [The nothing-will-happen-to-me syndrome can prove to be dangerous],' says Captain Talisunep.

By 6.30 p.m., when the reinforcements from Giani Post arrived at Karalkot, the intensity of fire had dwindled. Havildar Jitendra, still energized, was able to direct accurate fire at the two remaining infiltration squads, which were now making rapid manouevres to evade the fire coming from Karalkot. The precision of the fire directed at them was owed to a steady stream of real-time inputs picked up by Indian thermal imagers, relayed straight to gunnery positions from the battalion headquarters.

As company commander of 8 Bihar's Charlie Company that manned Karalkot too, Captain Talisunep immediately took charge. The arrival of the reinforcements led by an officer, their own company commander, immediately boosted the morale of the dozen men at the post. With twenty minutes of aggressive retaliatory fire under the captain's leadership, the two remaining Pakistani squads, most likely composed of the SSG commandos and terrorists, abandoned their mission and quickly retreated across the LoC. The exchange of fire finally ended at around 8.30 p.m., two hours after the backup reached the post, four hours after the first shot was fired that day.

With the greatest of care, Captain Talisunep and Havildar Jitendra crept between the bunkers to assess the damage and check on the dozen men. They still needed to be careful. The Pakistan Army posts would still be watching closely, and it was well within the realm of possibility that a few rocket-propelled grenades could be fired if a human target presented itself.

'I wasn't aware of Karmdeo's kills or how he staved off the attack on his position until later that night,' says Captain Talisunep. 'I learnt of his exploits while I was checking on the men, asking them about their well-being, the condition of their weapons and the ammunition they were left with. I got to know that Karmdeo had killed at least two terrorists and their bodies were lying outside the post.'

The captain told the men to stay vigilant through the night as the Pakistan Army could send squads to retrieve the bodies of the two terrorists and possibly launch fresh attacks. As he communed with his men, the officer knew it was a miracle that each one of them was alive.

'You have done a splendid job and made the unit proud. But there is no room for complacency. Do not forget the enemy can return with a vengeance,' he warned his men.

The maximum state of alert continued the following day. A failed high-energy assault of the kind that had been thwarted the previous evening meant that the Pakistan Army would try again at some point. The men of 8 Bihar also busied themselves decoding the assault.

The unit never did recover evidence to establish that the attacking squads consisted of Pakistan Army SSG commandos and regular troops, but Colonel Debashis and other officers of 8 Bihar, who studied the operation in minute detail, were fully convinced of their involvement and certain that it was a military operation. Every aspect of it, from start to finish, screamed commando assault.

'The way the attacks were planned, coordinated and executed was a dead giveaway of SSG involvement,' says Colonel Debashis. 'The men who made contact with Karmdeo could have been terrorists. The others most certainly included Pakistan Army personnel who cut off the post, provided close support with a variety of automatic weapons and vanished when the mission failed. They didn't come close enough for the obvious reason that if they were caught or killed, their involvement would stand exposed.'

The centrepiece of the assault was clearly an infiltration by the Pakistani raiding squads, but this wasn't an infiltration attempt in the general sense of the phrase associated with LoC operations. Terrorists usually infiltrate across the LoC to join terror cells deeper inside Jammu and Kashmir and replenish force levels of terror groups operating there. The 29 December infiltrators had no intention to remain in J&K.

'Their aim was to capture Karalkot Post, and if possible, return with the heads of a few of the boys,' says one of the soldiers who defended the post that night. 'All the terrorists were wearing bulletproof headgear. Have you heard of terrorists wearing such gear?'

In such a situation, it would always be near impossible to get a fix on the exact composition of the four Pakistani infiltration teams that mounted the assaults on Karalkot. But what there is total clarity about is Sepoy Karmdeo's actions.

'He showed extraordinary courage and composure even when his attackers were barely ten metres away,' says his commanding officer. 'He killed them and halted their advance. This changed everything. Had he frozen for some reason— and believe me it can happen to the best in such heavy-fire scenarios—the Pakistanis would have stormed the post. And remember, at this time, other men at the post were not aware of this group.'

In the morning following the incident, Captain Talisunep's QRT crept close to the rock behind which the two terrorists had taken cover. As expected, the grenades flung by Sepoy Karmdeo hadn't given them a chance to escape. Their bodies, clad in clear, military-supplied fatigues and vests, lay in the muddy snow.

'We found the daggers in their belts, and plastic bags in their rucksacks,' says Captain Talisunep. 'They had come with the intention of chopping off heads and taking them back as trophies. The fight would have been over long before reinforcements reached if it were not for Sepoy Karmdeo. And the mutilation of men has an unspeakable effect. It instils an anger that cannot be described.'

Recoveries made from the two terrorists killed included AK-47 assault rifles, a dozen magazines, grenades, improvised explosive devices, 9mm Chinese pistols, navigation equipment and incendiary devices.

'They came with the intention of burning down the post, killing us and returning with our severed heads,' says Sepoy Karmdeo. 'Why else were they carrying the incendiary devices and daggers? Had I become defensive that evening, the story may have been vastly different, and I may not have been the one telling it.'

The body of the third terrorist was never recovered, but the unit believes that Sepoy Karmdeo's fire in all likelihood killed him. Search parties found copious amounts of blood on a trail down the mountain path. It is possible that he (or his body) was picked up by the retreating Pakistani squads later that evening.

What happened during those two hours at Karalkot Post is now the stuff of Bihar Regiment's legends.

'Havildar Jitendra kept rallying his men to fight when things looked very bleak. The inputs he gave us over the radio after the telephone lines were cut off were critical and helped us with our initial planning. He also coordinated the movement of his company commander who was bringing reinforcements,' says Colonel Debashis.

Forty-one-year-old Havildar Jitendra is eagerly looking forward to upholding 8 Bihar's motto *Himmat hi jeet hai*

[Courage is victory] on foreign soil. The battalion has been selected to deploy as a UN Peacekeeping force in volatile South Sudan in 2022.

Six months after the defence of Karalkot, Sepoy Karmdeo Oraon retired from the Indian Army as a lance naik, returning to his village outside Ranchi in Jharkhand to begin the next chapter of his life as a farmer along with his wife and three children. He was eighteen when he joined the Army in 2002 and had never been in such a close-range firefight in his sixteen years of service. After a life on the front lines, he was ready for a new start in his fields.

On Republic Day 2020, the government announced Shaurya Chakra, India's third-highest peacetime gallantry medal, for the soldier. His company commander Captain Tenisulap Longkumer was awarded a Commendation Card by the Army chief for his indispensable role in the operation.

While the retired soldier has his hands full now with the ginger, tomatoes, beans and chillies that he lovingly cultivates on a 10 acre farm, the defence of Karalkot Post is never very far from his thoughts.

'There were some nerve-wracking moments. *Mujhe yakeen tha ki agar meine unko khatam nahin kiya toh woh mujhe bhi maarenge aur mere saathiyon ko bhi* [I was sure that if I didn't finish them off, they would kill my comrades and me]. It was a matter of my unit's honour. I trusted myself, I trusted my training and felt an instant rush of strength and confidence to take them on. I was shouting the Bihar Regiment's war cry "*Jai Bajrang Bali*" and targeting them,' he says.

He also realizes, with a smile, how closely death passed him by that evening.

'The first few seconds matter most. If you are able to stay on top of things during those crucial moments, chances are you will be triumphant. If not, you may be going home in a coffin.

The right training and discipline make all the difference. I was fully trained to do what I did, and so were the others holding the post,' he says.

Very little about the Indian Army's training regimen ever emerges in the public sphere, other than familiar images of fitness training and obstacle courses. While physical fitness is enormously important, the events of 29 December 2018 demonstrate the potency of mental conditioning and strength imparted to military personnel. A well-trained squad succeeded in fighting off a relentless commando-style wave of attacks without suffering a single casualty may boil down to a few strokes of happenstance, but is a huge measure of training.

The families of soldiers, however, cannot be trained to insulate themselves from tormenting thoughts about the perils and uncertainties their men unhesitatingly embrace as a military way of life. Only a day before the attack on Karalkot Post, Sepoy Karmdeo had managed to place a call to his wife.

'I reminded him that he was nearing his retirement, and that we, his family, were expecting him to return to our village in one piece,' says Priti. Nearly all conversations would end with earnest appeals not to take risks and to think of the family.

'I told her I was fine and there was no reason to get stressed. What else could I have said to reassure her?' says Sepoy Karmdeo. '*Duty toh karni hi hai aur achhe se karni hai* [I have to perform my duty and perform it well]. I told her that my superiors often tell other soldiers to carry out their duties like I do. She said the only thing that mattered to her was that I stayed safe. Neither she nor I had an inkling of what would unfold the next day. That's life. Isn't it?'

A full forty-eight hours would transpire after the Karalkot incident before Priti received a call from her husband. It was New Year's Eve.

'Families have a way of getting an inkling about what is going on but telling Priti about what happened at the post was out of the question as I did not want my family to get worked up and start imagining the worst,' says Sepoy Karmdeo.

What he did not know was that Priti was already aware of the Karalkot incident, courtesy her brother, Naik Somra Oraon, who happened to be in the same infantry unit as her husband but deployed in a different post.

'I got a ten-minute slot to make my call to Priti. There was no mobile network in the area. I was making small talk when she cut me short and began questioning me about the Karalkot operation. My brother-in-law had passed on the information that I wanted to keep from her. "*Jijaji ne aatankwadiyon ko maar giraya operation mein* [Brother-in-law killed terrorists in the operation]," Somra had told her,' says Sepoy Karmdeo.

Priti's question also brought a measure of relief. If she already knew, then he didn't have to endure the pain of seeing her jolted by the information. But Priti was relentless during that phone call, demanding that she be briefed with all details. In loving whispers, Sepoy Karmdeo shared a few nuggets.

'I told her the terrorists came to kill us but ended up dead themselves. I killed them. *Yeh sunn kar woh bahut khush hui* [She was delighted to hear that]. *Maine Priti se kaha ki agar meri duty ke dauran kuch ho jaata toh meri badnami hoti* [I told Priti if something untoward had happened under my watch, my honour would have been tarnished],' he says.

Priti still asks her husband about the Karalkot incident, each conversation bringing out fresh layers in the story. Hearing him tell it is a form of catharsis for her, a symbol somewhere that her anxious, earnest pleas for Sepoy Karmdeo to return to her in one piece had been obeyed by a dutiful husband.

'Whenever I was on sentry duty, I would tell myself there is a reason I am sitting here, far away from my home and family. That reason is my duty and I have to make myself count. When I learnt that there was a possibility of an attack in my area, my readiness was based on the premise that my post was the likely target. I was forever alert. I knew someone had my back and I had theirs,' says Sepoy Karmdeo.

President Ram Nath Kovind awarded him Shaurya Chakra at a ceremony held at Rashtrapati Bhavan in November 2021. The investiture ceremony at which the decoration was conferred on him was delayed because of the COVID-19 pandemic.

In February 2021, with both sides honouring it at least till the time this book went to print, India and Pakistan renewed their 2003 ceasefire on the LOC. How long it will last and how many more Karalkot-type incidents lie ahead is best answered by the retributive cycles that define the infiltration-heavy sectors of the LoC.

'I would get goosebumps watching TV and hearing about the daring exploits of soldiers being awarded gallantry medals at the Rashtrapati Bhavan. It felt surreal to be on that stage, standing in front of the President of India. Hopefully, soldiers from my unit watched me and thought, "If Karmdeo can reach there, so can we,"' he says.

His Shaurya Chakra citation speaks of his 'stupendous gallant actions, acute presence of mind, focused aggression and willingness to make the supreme sacrifice in pursuance of the operational task'.

The soldier may have made a new life in the fields, but his connection with the Bihar Regiment won't ever be severed. Not just because those ties never evaporate, but because Sepoy Karmdeo's two sons, aged eighteen and sixteen, are hoping to enlist and join their father's unit—8 Bihar.

'Nothing would bring me more joy than my children donning the uniform that I once did. I mean it, nothing. It's not an easy way of life, but I can't think of anything more honourable than it. The best part is that Priti agrees,' says the soldier. 'The overwhelming feeling of belonging to an army unit and the *josh* to uphold its undying traditions and ethos is something I hope my children can experience.'

As he waits for that day, Sepoy Karmdeo's life is as far as it can possibly be from the LoC. Gone are the familiar echoes of automatic weapons, the ominous whizzing whistle of shells as they career in both directions across the frontier. Gone is the ever-clinging feeling that sudden and certain death is always just an inch this way or that. Gone is the terrifying need for decisions to end life or have yours ended instead.

'On that patch I killed, on this patch I grow. Little has changed, really. I was a proud soldier then. I am a proud farmer now.'

7

'Whatever We Do, It Has to Be Now'

Lance Naik Sandeep Singh

'*Saab, bahut chhota baccha hai, bahut din se shakal nahi dekhi hai* [Sir, I have a very small child and I haven't seen him for a long time].'

Lance Naik Sandeep Singh was wearing a white vest, black combat trousers and what he hoped was his most lovable grin. It was September 2018, and at 12,000 feet in the Tangdhar sector of north Kashmir, it was anything but warm. But the thirty-year-old soldier had just finished a two-hour workout, and he had no intention of hiding the results of his toil behind clothing.

He had spent two weeks the previous month with his five-year-old son, Abhinav, and wife, Gurpreet, in his village, Kotla Khurd, a few kilometres outside Amritsar. It was the longest leave he had been granted in eleven years in the Army. It had been a restful, idyllic fortnight, spent mostly playing with his little son and showing him selfies of the breathtaking Kashmir landscape he had been deployed to. Lance Naik Sandeep had been grateful for the long break. But now back with his unit, the 4 Para Special Forces, in a forward area close to the Line of Control (LoC), he missed his family more than ever.

Thankfully, unlike Lance Naik Sandeep's earlier years in the Army, video calls were now a welcome salve for homesickness, even though these were nowhere near the smells and sounds of home. But high up in the Shamshabari mountains, a mobile signal is a dear but stubbornly elusive friend. And that's why the soldier now stood at the foot of the bed of his squad commander, Captain Gurjeet Singh Saini, a young Special Forces officer who had joined the 4 Para a few years before.

'Mobile network is scarce in the higher reaches of Tangdhar,' recalls Captain Gurjeet. 'There are barely a few pockets where you can make a voice call, maybe one or two points where signal strength is just enough for a very shaky video call. In our unit, we would go maybe once a week to make these calls. But that September, Sandeep would come to me three to four times a week, saying, *Saab, chalte hain* [Sir, can we go and try?]. How does one explain this soldier–family bond?'

Men from 4 Para had been forward-deployed from their unit base elsewhere in Jammu and Kashmir's Kupwara district to a 'staging base' in Tangdhar, a small camp situated close to an area of expected activity. And in Tangdhar, which sits on the LoC, there is only one kind of activity the Indian Army deploys its Special Forces to deal with: terrorist infiltration.

The officer leant back in his bunk, watching the soldier for a moment. He knew it was going to be futile trying to convince Lance Naik Sandeep that they should wait a couple of days, since they had made their calls just two days earlier.

Climbing out of his bunk and throwing on a jacket, Captain Gurjeet and Lance Naik Sandeep set out from their tiny Himalayan forward base nestled in a mountain pass. They didn't need a map to find their way around in that terrain. Remembering features and trails in the mountains was a standard requirement for soldiers in the area. After a twenty-minute trek up to a favoured 'signal point', the two men took turns to make calls home. They had to take turns because 'signal point' was literally that—a spot a few metres across. Lance Naik Sandeep, of course, went first.

It was usually Gurpreet who answered, but that morning, to Sandeep's even greater delight, it was little Abhinav. The call lasted just over six minutes. And then, as it usually happened with 'signal point', it was impossible to reconnect.

'*Mera ho gaya, aap karlo, saab* [I have finished. Sir, you go ahead],' Lance Naik Sandeep said, waving to Captain Gurjeet a short distance away.

'*Bacche ki shakal dekh li* [Were you able to see your child]?'

'*Haan, saab, bacche ne hi phone uthaya aaj* [Yes, sir, the child picked up the phone]!' said Lance Naik Sandeep, handing over his mobile phone to Captain Gurjeet.

Displayed on the phone was a screenshot Lance Naik Sandeep had taken from the video call. In the top right was a stamp-sized image of the soldier beaming into the phone, a perfect blue sky behind him. The rest of the screen was filled by a chubby little boy wearing a blue *patka*, his eyes wide and mouth open mid-sentence.

'*Bahut naughty shakal hai bacche ki* [He looks very naughty],' said Captain Gurjeet, returning the phone to Lance Naik Sandeep.

'*Naughty toh hai hi . . . Aapko ghar call nahi karni saab* [He is indeed naughty . . . Don't you want to call home sir]?'

'*Nahi, phir aayenge kissi aur din* [No, we'll come another day].'

The two men trekked down the mountainside to their staging base in silence, Lance Naik Sandeep immersed in the call he had just made. Captain Gurjeet slapped the soldier's back fondly.

'*Fit lag rahe ho, Sandeep, workout theek thaak kar rahe ho* [You look fit, Sandeep, seems you have been taking your workout seriously].'

'*Saab, fauji munda hoon, body banani hai, maintain karni hai, woh impression jo hai para wale bande ka, woh rehna chahiye* [Since I am a soldier, I have to maintain my body and keep up the good impression people have of the para forces].'

Lance Naik Sandeep didn't lose an opportunity to exude the commando look. A few days earlier at Kupwara, Captain Gurjeet had bumped into Lance Naik Sandeep returning from the unit's wet canteen with two large bags. Asked what he was ferrying with so much enthusiasm, the soldier sheepishly opened the bags. They were mostly filled with bags of dry fruits. But nestled underneath was a strip of Streax hair colour for a deep-brown tinge.

'Till those few weeks, my interaction with Sandeep had been very limited,' says Captain Gurjeet. 'Before we were deployed at our staging base, there were multiple inputs about infiltration attempts in the Tangdhar area. However, none of these were concrete enough to warrant deployment. But as a para unit, we rapidly prepared ourselves, selecting the team that would be sent forward once a specific input came through. It was at a final briefing of this team in Kupwara that I was taken aback to see Sandeep.'

Lance Naik Sandeep, who joined the Army in 2007, had been a mechanical transport (MT) driver before joining the 4 Para Special Forces in the same role. He would spend years transporting commandos and weapons between their bases. But with exposure to operations and training within the unit, he was soon convinced that he must volunteer as a scout—a high-risk commando position that forms the eyes and ears of a Special Forces squad in an operational area. If driving military vehicles in a hostile and demanding environment wasn't perilous enough, the role of a scout was literally in the line of fire.

'I was a little confused about how a guy from MT could suddenly become a scout,' says Captain Gurjeet. 'Being a scout requires youth and physical fitness. You are the eyes and ears of your squad. What you do impacts everyone else. You walk in the front and provide the information necessary to complete an operation. It is not a joke. What settled my doubts and concerns was when he told me he had volunteered to be a scout. Now remember the Special Forces are 100 per cent voluntary. Nobody can be forced to join the Special Forces. And within it, if you volunteer to be a scout, it says a lot about you. It is a dangerous thing to volunteer for. He had put in enough service and seen a lot of action from close quarters, so I was confident about Sandeep.'

This thought would remain at the back of Captain Gurjeet's mind for a few days as he contemplated the mission ahead. Much was being placed on his young shoulders, and he knew he had the unit's formidable recent legacy to uphold. It was this very unit, the 4 Para, that had conducted the September 2016 surgical strikes* on terror launchpads in Pakistan-occupied Kashmir, an operation in which 4 Para commandos had managed to eliminate nearly forty terrorists and return safely without a single casualty to their own. In the storm of public attention following the announcement of the operation, the reputation of 4 Para, already hallowed within the forces, reached legendary status. The Special Forces work in secrecy, necessarily away from the public glare. But the stupendousness of the 2016 operation meant that the unit would forever, going forward, have soaring standards to match.

'When the standby team was being assembled, Lance Naik Sandeep could have easily remained silent,' recalls Captain Gurjeet. 'Or if he was asked, he could have simply said, "*Nahi, saab*, I'm from MT, I prefer not to come for this operation." But he was fully ready and willing. That spoke to me about his self-belief and professionalism. It was also his first scouting mission after coming from MT.'

---

* The only first-hand account of the 2016 surgical strikes, by the officer who led the operation, is a chapter in *India's Most Fearless 1*.

With Captain Gurjeet as the standby team's leader, the team waited for its orders, using the time to train and prepare for what would be a much higher altitude operation. Over the next three weeks, the inputs varied widely, making it persistently unclear if an infiltration would or would not happen in the Tangdhar sector.

On 19 September, the team finally received an intelligence input that was detailed enough to trigger the much-awaited forward staging to Tangdhar. Since the team was ready in most respects, it was only a question of loading their weapons and gear and rolling out. The team of nine men (one and a half squads) with Lance Naik Sandeep as scout, his buddy Lance Naik Surendra Singh as second scout and Captain Gurjeet as team leader departed the unit base at 11 p.m. on foot. The movement of Special Forces is masked to the maximum extent in forward areas in order to deceive powerful human intelligence assets that terrorist groups maintain in the area. If terror groups receive word about the arrival of Special Forces in an area, they are able to switch tactics, methods and sometimes even the composition of infiltration parties.

'There were no proper tracks leading from our base to the staging area, so we had to make the trail ourselves in the dark,' says Captain Gurjeet. 'Our lights were off as we made our way forward. We used our night-vision devices to navigate the very steep climb to a high-altitude, boulder-strewn terrain.'

With Lance Naik Sandeep out in front, his priority was to get the team to the staging area before sunrise.

'Sandeep got us there before first light, by 4 a.m.,' says Captain Gurjeet. 'This was his first mission, and he was proving his physical capabilities as a scout.'

At the staging base in that small mountain pass in Tangdhar, the intelligence input abruptly ran cold. It was something the team was prepared for, but it also meant they had no choice but to wait.

On the night of 20 September, Lance Naik Sandeep, his buddy scout and the team leader stepped out of the staging camp for some air after supper. The moon was bright enough to cast shadows of the mountains and of the three figures who now stood on the gentle grassy slope. Captain Gurjeet was looking closely at a tablet device with a map displayed on it. He pulled and zoomed across different parts of the screen in silence. The men knew where they were, but the conflicting intelligence inputs, including the one that had just been retracted, meant they could be setting off in any of the three or four directions up the mountains of Tangdhar.

Captain Gurjeet could tell that Lance Naik Sandeep was restless that night.

'*Jaldi input aajaye to achha hai, saab* [Sir, it will be good if we get the input quickly],' he said. His team knew what the scout was feeling. A familiar, enormously ironic discomposure typical in Special Forces units deployed on an operation. They would remain restless until the mission began properly, along with everything that came with it.

Captain Gurjeet remembered the words of his esteemed senior in 4 Para, who had led the surgical strike mission less than two years earlier. Asked about his mental state as his squads awaited final orders to roll out from Uri into PoK for their assault, Major 'Mike Tango', who went on to be decorated with the Kirti Chakra for the mission, had said, 'For us, there is infinitely more disturbance in calm than in an actual firefight. Once "contact" is made and bullets begin to fly, that's when calm truly returns.'*

---

* See *India's Most Fearless 1*.

Every Special Forces man understood the essence of those lines that captured precisely what the men of Captain Gurjeet's squad felt that night as they turned in.

As always, the men expended their anxious energy training and working out at the staging base. They couldn't go far from the site, lest they be spotted and reported by the eyes and ears of the enemy. So they had to make do with what they had—tables, chairs or each other for a rigorous group workout. There was nothing else they could do but wait for that order with a direction to head out in.

It was in this cloud of hair-trigger anticipation that the next morning, 20 September, Lance Naik Sandeep had woken up his team leader, requesting a trek to 'signal point' to phone his family. This was a welcome distraction from the numbing drudgery of the commando's wait. The rest of the day had passed by even more slowly.

The next morning, Lance Naik Sandeep appeared even more restless than usual. Once again, Captain Gurjeet knew why. The squad in Tangdhar would likely be 'deinducted' from the forward base back to Kupwara if a concrete infiltration input didn't come in the next forty-eight hours. This was a high possibility, given just how many inputs had run cold over the last few weeks.

Before turning in that night, Captain Gurjeet went to check on Lance Naik Sandeep. The soldier was busy neatening up his bunk. It was a familiar sight. He had a compulsive obsession with tidiness, something that gave his hearty, jovial personality a studious, measured side.

'*Kal kuchh milega, saab* [We should get something tomorrow],' Lance Naik Sandeep said to his team leader. '*Woh feeling aa rahi hai, ki kucch tagdi input aayegi* [I get the feeling that we will get a major input].'

Early the next morning, noticing the particularly crisp sunshine, Lance Naik Sandeep stepped outside, stretching and rubbing the sleep from his eyes in the kind of rejuvenating air only found in those mountains. His hair dishevelled, he pulled out his phone and took a picture of himself. At 8.15 a.m., he sent it to Gurpreet.

'*Bahut oonche pahad hain* [These mountains are very high].'

The soldier had a separate mobile phone just to talk to his family. When he got it, he had told Gurpreet, '*Jadu wee time mile, mein tenu phone karanga, phone apne kol hee rakh* [Whenever I get time, I will call you, keep your phone with you always].'

At Kotla Khurd village Gurpreet saw the message immediately. Texts from her husband had a separate notification tone.

She beamed at the picture and the message. He loved showing her the landscape that was now his second home. Gurpreet's phone was filled with such pictures, of the man she had fallen in love with at her cousin's wedding in 2011. She was nineteen, he was twenty-three and four years into Army service. They would marry the following year, and their son Abhinav would arrive the year after, in August 2013.

'*Aap risk kyu le rahe ho, mobile rehne do abhi* [Why are you taking a risk, leave the mobile alone], focus and be safe,' she replied.

'*Abhi kaam pe jayenge thodi der mein* [I will soon be on duty].'

'*Zyada fit lag rahe ho aap* [You are looking nice and fit].'

He couldn't continue the conversation. Something had just come in.

Early in the morning on 22 September, in Awantipur, about 100 km away from the staging base as the crow flies, an Indian Air Force Heron drone took off on a surveillance flight. A pair of Israel-built unmanned aircraft operating from the base south-east of Srinagar was being constantly used over days in the hope that conflicting inputs about infiltration plans from Pakistan-occupied Kashmir in any of the LoC sectors could be nailed down with unshakeable visual intelligence.

The Heron's flightpath that morning took it over the Kashmir valley, west over the Kupwara sector, and then a sharp turn south parallel to the LoC. As it flew along the LoC, the drone's sensors scanned large swathes of mountainous terrain on both sides of the line, the live video stream being watched closely by imagery analysts in an operations centre in Srinagar. At 8.04 a.m., the drone found what it had been sent out to look for. Two tiny dark figures stood out against the rest of the terrain on a desolate ridge in the Shamshabari mountains. The drone operators at Awantipur were quickly signalled to put the Heron in a tight circuit, to keep that frame firmly in the view of the drone's cameras. For a whole minute the camera zoomed slowly, attempting to get a clearer image. But as it did so, and while the analysts watched, the figures moved a short distance. And then they abruptly disappeared in the shadow of a rock feature.

Formatted and encrypted, it was relayed in minutes via secure communication channels to the 4 Para base in Kupwara and onward to Captain Gurjeet and his team at Tangdhar, where it was more than sufficient to trigger an immediate roll-out.

Lance Naik Sandeep scanned the Heron's images. Obsessed with maps and charts, part of his training, he immediately recognized the location from a set of hill features captured within the camera's frame.

The climb this time was even more steep, and it would involve scaling one rock face after another to save time. Out front once again, Lance Naik Sandeep led the way, providing a clear path to the other eight men to follow. After scaling one particular rock face in Tangdhar's Retnar area, the scout felt his silent mobile phone vibrate in his pocket. *An active mobile signal!* Instinctively he first looked in every direction, a commando habit. He fished out the phone. A pending message had delivered. But the real notification was that the phone had picked up a tiny strand of unexpected mobile signal. Quickly he dialled Gurpreet.

She picked up on the second ring.

'Found a lucky mobile signal, thought I would call and tell you I'm leaving for some work, I will call you tomorrow.'

'Okay, *apna khayal rakho* [take care].'

Gurpreet sighed and hung up. She knew what getting a phone call through meant to her husband, so there was no way he would want to end a call if he didn't really have to. Abhinav had been pestering his mother to try calling his father. 'You'll have to wait,' Gurpreet told him after the ten second call, 'your father is busy.'

Mobile phone back in his pocket, TAR-21 rifle back in ready position, Lance Naik Sandeep resumed his scout duties.

'The input we got was that some movement was seen across some passes along the LoC, so we immediately deployed forward and began an initial search. We reached the ridgeline by afternoon because, again, the climb was very steep,' recalls Captain Gurjeet.

At over 12,500 feet, the air perceptibly thinner, the sun was beating down sharply on the ridgeline. To the east, the mountain descended sharply into a small snow-blown valley, and then endless green dappled hills rolled across the LoC. They were now close to a location in the mountains where the dark figures spotted by the drone earlier that day could reasonably have reached. If their destination was the Kashmir Valley, then there weren't too many different paths they could take.

The timing of the squad's arrival in the Retnar area of Tangdhar to intercept two terrorists—either Pakistani nationals, or Pakistan-armed—couldn't have been more ironic. At 3.01 p.m. that day, Pakistan's prime minister, Imran

Khan, had publicly lashed out at the Indian government for cancelling a scheduled meeting between the foreign ministers of both countries on the sidelines of the UN General Assembly in New York City the following week. While Khan bristled with indignation, India's reasons were clear: first, the abduction of three policemen in Jammu and Kashmir's Shopian; and second, in a move that displayed a flagrant disregard for Indian sentiments, Pakistan had officially, and provocatively, issued a postage stamp with the face of Burhan Wani, a Hizbul Mujahideen terrorist killed by security forces in 2016.

It was an incredible repeat of a similar provocation that had been made two years earlier. On 21 September 2016, speaking at the UN General Assembly just three days after the terror attack in Uri, Pakistan's then prime minister, Nawaz Sharif, would take the stage and exalt terrorist Burhan Wani. A little over a week after Sharif's speech, men from 4 Para conducted the surgical strikes.

Two years later at Tangdhar, Captain Gurjeet's squad had no orders to cross the LoC, but the relentless cycle of history between the two countries would become starkly apparent in the days that followed.

Diplomatic channels lit up over the fresh crossfire, and Prime Minister Khan made a grand display of anger and despair that his peace gesture had been declined by India. Unplugged from the news whirl, on a remote mountainside in north Kashmir, the Indian commando team prepared to make contact with Pakistan's newest exports from across the LoC.

Spread out but held together by their scout and team leader, the nine commandos began an initial search, a careful surveillance of the area for tell-tale signs either of the presence of the infiltrators or of their having passed that way. Forty minutes into the initial search, Lance Naik Sandeep raised his hand, signalling the squad to stop in its tracks. Whispering, he motioned Captain Gurjeet to move towards him. All the men, armed with Tavor TAR-21 assault rifles, held their weapons in firing position as their team leader stepped towards the scout.

'Sandeep was pointing at a patch of ground which had what looked like some footprints,' says Captain Gurjeet. 'Because of a light drizzle that day, it was difficult to verify if those really were footprints or just some scattered mud. But Sandeep seemed certain that it was a track and insisted we follow it.'

The squad moved as quietly as possible behind Lance Naik Sandeep as he climbed up the rocky mountain slope. They were now around 100 metres from where the scout had sighted the footprints when Lance Naik Sandeep once again raised his hand to signal another tell-tale find to the commando squad. This time he looked back, nodding and smiling.

'Sandeep had identified the footprints correctly. What he had now found was some food wrappers, aluminium foil and fruit peels,' remembers Captain Gurjeet. 'This was Sandeep's crucial confirmation of the input we had received earlier. It also meant we needed to be even more cautious as we continued our search. The infiltrators were breathing the same air as us on that mountaintop.'

The same air.

The painfully slow sequence of events was over, and things were unfolding fast now as the 4 Para squad continued its climb. Four minutes later, Lance Naik Sandeep stopped the squad for the third time. This time it wasn't for footprints or food wrappers. He had spotted the infiltrators.

'*Banda dikh raha hai* [I can see someone],' Lance Naik Sandeep whispered in an urgent hushed tone from out front.

'*Kitna dur hai* [How far is he]?' Captain Gurjeet whispered back.

'*Bees metre* [Twenty metres].'

The same air.

'Sandeep was out front and could see him, but I did not have a direct view of the infiltrator because in that terrain boulders and nooks provided natural hideouts,' says Captain Gurjeet. 'Sandeep carefully gestured to me to come towards him and also conveyed that we should not yet open fire. I asked Sandeep to wait and cautiously moved ahead till I could see the infiltrator for myself. And I now saw what Sandeep had seen. A sliver of a black jacket was visible behind a boulder. The path to that location was across a very narrow crag with deep gorges on both sides.'

Captain Gurjeet signalled to the rest of the squad to hold their positions. It had to be ensured that the commandos weren't being lured into a trap. They waited, hoping for some movement or activity—anything that gave away a little more about the man wearing the black jacket or those with him.

'*Saab, hum wait nahi kar sakte* [Sir, we cannot wait],' Lance Naik Sandeep whispered to his team leader. '*Jo karna hai, abhi karna hai. Andhera ho jayega toh khel khatam* [We need to act right now, otherwise it will become too dark and we will lose the game].'

Captain Gurjeet knew he was right.

'Darkness would make things easy for the terrorists and difficult for us. I agreed with Sandeep, we needed to wrap up the operation as quickly as possible.'

With whatever planning was possible in such a close engagement, the nimble-footed scout moved forward along the crag, his team leader a few steps behind. The gorges on both sides fell steeply down a jagged cliff with rocky outcrops.

'I was a little nervous about Sandeep, since he did not have real experience in this kind of terrain,' recalls Captain Gurjeet. 'But everything he had done that day was already of a very high calibre, so there was absolutely no reason to doubt his abilities. He was sure-footed and calm. And this helped the team keep its focus steady.'

Half-way across the crag towards the hideout, a burst of fire flashed, hitting the ridge a few feet in front of Lance Naik Sandeep. The 'black jacket' had now stood up and opened fire with his AK-47 at the approaching Indian squad. Lance Naik Sandeep immediately sprang forward, letting loose a long burst of 5.56 mm rounds from his TAR-21, 'dropping' the black jacket instantly. On his elbows, he turned quickly to signal the rest of the squad to stop, and that he had managed to drop the first terrorist.

Just as he turned back to face the hideout, a grenade came flying from behind the boulder, exploding against a jagged edge on the crag. Before Lance Naik Sandeep could flatten himself, shrapnel flew into his chest and neck, injuring him severely. For a few seconds, he lay there motionless.

The grenade thrower—the second terrorist—now opened a blaze of AK-47 fire at the rest of the squad as they stood exposed on the crag, but Captain Gurjeet and the squad's second scout, Lance Naik Surendra Singh, buddy soldier to Lance Naik Sandeep, returned fire, forcing the second terrorist to remain behind the boulder that served as his hideout.

'Sandeep had neutralized the first guy in a very close firefight, just about ten to fifteen metres,' says Captain Gurjeet. 'Everything happened in a matter of a few seconds.'

During the exchange of fire, Lance Naik Surendra noticed the lead scout moving. Lance Naik Sandeep, bleeding profusely, had revived himself from the grenade blast, and was now crawling along the crag towards the hideout. Making the final few metres on his elbows as bullets flew between the hideout and the rest of the squad, Lance Naik Sandeep then leapt to his feet as he turned the corner behind the boulder.

'He was so close, he initially grappled with the terrorist in hand-to-hand combat. Then pulling himself loose, he shot the second terrorist from literally point-blank range, but sustained bullet injuries himself,' says one of the squad members. 'As he fell, his assault rifle came loose, rolled and fell into the gorge. He then turned towards us for a brief second and screamed, *Ek aur banda hai* [There is one more fellow]!'

There was a third terrorist.

'The third guy was in the hideout, and we didn't expect that,' says Captain Gurjeet. 'We could not see who or what was inside. Even the initial surveillance had only seen two terrorists. Sandeep had also said, "*Do hi bande honge, do hi bande ki movement dikh rahi hain* [I have seen only two]." And the hideout looked very small. So, we didn't expect a third guy inside.'

Lance Naik Surendra immediately fell flat on his stomach and began crawling towards his buddy, grievously injured on the other side of the crag near the hideout. When Captain Gurjeet motioned him to stop, he turned to say, '*Saab usko goli lagi hai, usko iss taraf kheench lete hai* [Sir, he has been hit by a bullet, let us pull him to our side].'

Injured but conscious, Lance Naik Sandeep heard his buddy's words and noticed Lance Naik Surendra crawling across the crag towards him.

'*Meri fikar mat karo . . . Bas inko na jaane dena* [Don't bother about me . . . just don't let that man go]!' he screamed.

Lance Naik Sandeep had been hit on his body by a grenade shrapnel and at least one 7.62 mm rifle bullet. Nobody in the squad expected him to do what he did next.

Unarmed, he rose once again to his feet with the last ounce of his strength and charged at the third terrorist in the hideout, but he was met with a burst of fire that hit his helmet, violently throwing him backwards and into the deep gorge where his rifle had fallen.

'It happened right in front of my eyes,' says Captain Gurjeet. 'It took me a moment to register what had happened. It was a moment of shock for everyone. We quickly took our positions. It was still not confirmed what kind of condition Sandeep was in. And there was a third terrorist still in the hideout.'

Keeping four men from the squad on the ridgeline, Captain Gurjeet along with Lance Naik Surendra and two other commandos descended into the perilous gorge to look for Sandeep.

'I hoped and prayed that he may have just fallen a short distance away and could be saved,' says Lance Naik Surendra. 'As we were climbing down the gorge, the third terrorist opened fire on us because we were down in a nallah and he was at a dominating height. This was the most difficult part. Every time we tried to get closer to Sandeep, he would fire at us.'

'I remember thinking as we were climbing down, how rapidly things can change in an operation like this where in a flash the priority shifts from taking a life to saving a life,' says Captain Gurjeet.

In the hail of fire from up at the hideout, one 7.62 mm round tore into Lance Naik Surendra's thigh, a flesh wound that wasn't enough to debilitate the commando. Provided cover fire by the four commandos still on the crag above, Captain Gurjeet and the other three finally managed to reach Lance Naik Sandeep.

'When we saw his body, I said another prayer,' says Lance Naik Surendra. 'I prayed that he would only be injured. *Jo bhi hai, hum fix kara denge* [Whatever the injury, we will take care of it].'

'But Sandeep was gone, we had lost him,' says Captain Gurjeet. 'The fall had been very intense. The gorge was full of boulders, and Sandeep had fallen over sixty metres. His body had taken a grenade hit, many Kalashnikov rounds and a sixty-metre fall. It was only that last thing that killed him though. He fought till the end.'

Injured by the third terrorist, Lance Naik Surendra volunteered to remain with his buddy soldier's body to secure it. It was 6 p.m. and the sun was about to set. There was one terrorist still in a dominating position in his hideout.

As Captain Gurjeet and the other two commandos climbed back up towards the crag, the 4 Para unit base had been updated about the sequence of events. Three more commando squads from the unit—eighteen men, including Captain Gurjeet's team commander—arrived on site shortly thereafter to surround the hideout and ensure the third terrorist wouldn't escape in the darkness.

'With the reinforcements, we established surveillance points to monitor the third terrorist. We needed to be careful not to remain in the same place, or else he would have had a killing zone,' remembers Captain Gurjeet.

Over four squads of the 4 Para Special Forces remained deployed overnight on that desolate mountain. The loss of Lance Naik Sandeep, the first such operational loss the unit had suffered, had galvanized the men, but also made them supremely aware that more men could drop if they didn't take every last precaution in eliminating the third terrorist. There was also the possibility that the terrorist had summoned his own reinforcements via radio, so no chances could be taken. The surveillance points provided a wide, but tight net around the deadly hideout.

The caution would mean the hideout couldn't be cleared the next day either. Scouts from the squads would venture close to the hideout and return. The third terrorist was inside, but not firing at the commando squads. This could either have been a trap or he was injured and buying time to recuperate for a final blaze. Either way, the unit had decided it would take no more fatalities in that operation, no matter how long it took to get the third terrorist.

On the morning of 24 September, the team commander decided that the operation could not be allowed to stretch any further. A scout was tasked with firing a pair of incendiary devices into the hideout.

'The third terrorist was injured but not killed. We didn't know what was going on in his mind. He came out of his hideout, probably knowing that he had no escape, and opened a burst of fire that narrowly missed my team commander and his scout, who were making their way towards the hideout for a final clearing mission. They fired back, taking cover. When the terrorist crept out a little later, one of the men at a surveillance point managed to hit him,' says a member of one of the squads.

For forty-five minutes, the commando squads conducted a meticulous search on the mountain to make sure there was no fourth, fifth or sixth terrorist waiting for an opportunity to strike. A Heron in the air provided a sweep of the area, confirming no further suspicious presence or movement. In the Srinagar operations room, analysts would receive images of the commandos as they wrapped up the mission and began their return.

All twenty-six men climbed down the gorge to accompany Lance Naik Sandeep's body down the mountainside to the Tangdhar staging area. An Army Dhruv helicopter picked up the soldier's body and flew it straight to Srinagar where the 92 Base Hospital would officially declare Lance Naik Sandeep Singh dead. This would pave the way for numb ceremonials.

'It was the first time the unit had suffered an op casualty,' says Captain Gurjeet. 'Our unit had been blessed with never having had such a tragedy. It felt personal for everyone in the unit. Everyone felt like they had lost their own family member.'

At the 4 Para Special Forces unit base in Kupwara, the usual raucous camaraderie had given way to a grieving, but galvanized silence. When the initial operational debrief concluded, there was nothing to do but train endlessly for such missions in a hostile high-altitude terrain.

The team commander, who had narrowly dodged the third terrorist's bullet a few hours earlier, ended the briefing with an exhortation to the men.

'This is what we are here for. These things will happen in the future as well. We should be ready for it. We must train more to ensure we don't lose another man. Our morale should always be high. Sandeep died for us. We must pay him back by training even more fiercely every day. The only way to overcome any feelings of doubt, and to keep Sandeep's memory alive, is to train for such missions and to overcome anything we face.'

After a wreath-laying ceremony in Srinagar's Badami Bagh cantonment, Lance Naik Sandeep's body was flown by helicopter to Kotla Khurd village, where images of a grieving Gurpreet and a stoic Abhinav would be beamed by television cameras across the country.

'A good soldier was lost. Usually when you lose someone like this, there is something to blame. But in this case, I don't know. I still go over the operation minute by minute, wondering if something different could have been done, whether I could have approached it differently, but there are no clear answers,' says Captain Gurjeet.

If the young officer had doubts about his performance, the Army didn't. His role in the operation, despite just two years of combat experience, would be widely commended by his seniors. The Army concluded that his 'tactical acumen, intelligence generation and source handling' had been impeccable. The Army would also observe that despite frictions imposed by terrain, climate, lack of cover and a limited number of troops at the operation site, Captain Gurjeet successfully led his squad to eliminate the first two terrorists. The message from the leadership was clear—the young officer had demonstrated every quality of a fine Special Forces warrior.

While every other soldier in the squad would similarly be commended, the Army made it a point to recognize Lance Naik Surendra's 'nerves of steel', standing guard over the mortal remains of his buddy while braving a hail of bullets from a terrorist holding a position of enormous advantage.

Captain Gurjeet couldn't travel to Kotla Khurd with Lance Naik Sandeep's flag-draped casket. It was important for him to remain with his squad as they dealt with the aftermath of the operation and readied themselves mentally for whatever came their way next.

While Special Forces units are immensely tight-knit and familial, the jolt of losing Lance Naik Sandeep was visible as his body was consigned to flames. Not only was the 4 Para's then commanding officer present, but two of his immediate predecessors also attended Lance Naik Sandeep's last rites and grieved with his family.

One of the former 4 Para commanding officers who attended noted, 'To demonstrate the reach of our nation's capability in ensuring that the last line of defence is never breached or exploited by our neighbour, it is men like him with the capacity of a thousand hearts who operate along and ahead of the LoC to deny the enemy that space to hurt our nation. He was one of the tigers I led, who gave me the largeness to roar from the pits of my cave.'

Two men from Lance Naik Sandeep's earlier squad were permitted to attend his funeral. One of them says, 'If Sandeep had not spotted those footprints and that trail, and correctly identified them, we would have walked on ahead unclear about the presence of terrorists nearby. We would not have been alive today. It was his astuteness as a scout that gave us that crucial information before the encounter. His scouting skills saved us. He took all the risks to keep us juniors safe like an elder brother.'

On Independence Day 2019, Lance Naik Sandeep Singh would be decorated with a posthumous Shaurya Chakra, India's third-highest peacetime gallantry medal.

The 4 Para's current commanding officer, a commando who had operated alongside Lance Naik Sandeep on numerous operations, will never forget the soldier.

'He lived his life for the *paltan*. And left this world for his paltan. He will be unforgettable to us as the *joshila Khalsa* [bold and courageous Sikh], whose constant refrain was, "*Ohh, saab ji, tension di koi lod ni, sabb ho jao gaa* [Sir, there is no need to be tense, everything will be done]." His pet dialogue, I can never forget was, "*Sahab, kaam koi bhi karaa lo, chhutti time ton bhejj deyo* [Give me any amount of work but send me home for a holiday]." Devoted to the fight and devoted to his family. He lived, he died, and now he lives again through this book,' says the commanding officer of 4 Para.

As he was consigned to flames, an image would go viral across the country. Little Abhinav, his face serious, in a checked, black-and-white shirt, cracking a full salute, his mother by his side.

'He always told me, "*Officer banayenge Abhinav nu* [We will make Abhinav an officer]." I feel even more lonely now, as Abhinav is studying in a hostel. Every evening Sandeep's parents and I speak about him,' says Gurpreet.

Each day, she scrolls through her most prized chat window where her husband beams at her from a never-ending stream of images. The photos over the years capturing the soldier's transformation as a commando.

Gurpreet smiles at that last photograph from the staging base in Tangdhar.

'He really took care of his fitness,' she recalls. 'He used to tell me constantly *ki fitness par dhyan doh and theek raho* [be fit and be healthy]. A month before whenever he was supposed to come home on leave, I would sometimes go on walks to improve my fitness. I couldn't tell if it worked because he was always so happy to see me.'

Gurpreet now hopes to fulfil Lance Naik Sandeep's dream for their son.

When Abhinav made that final salute, he was wearing the same blue patka that he had worn in that last video call to his father.

8

'The Seas Will Break Your Ship'

Captain Sachin Reuben Sequeira

16 March 2021
Heera Oil Field
Arabian Sea

'Return to your bunks immediately.'

Dilip Kumar looked quizzically at the foreman standing guard at a heavy door that led out on to the deck of the P-305—the large accommodation barge* that for both men, along with 259 others, was home for weeks on end out in an oil-rich patch of ocean south-west of the bustling western metropolis.

'Very heavy wind and big waves, it's not safe on the deck.'

That wasn't a big deal, Dilip thought. The men on board weren't unused to the deck being closed, but it was an unusually cool night with a steady breeze that had blown through every opening of the barge, bringing some welcome respite to what was otherwise an existence that toggled between fierce, unrelenting air conditioning and sticky salty humidity. A walk on the deck on such a cool night was the best possible way to wind down after a day of labour.

---

* A large, flat-bottomed vessel with accommodation for personnel working on nearby offshore platforms. The barge is unpowered but held in place by a series of heavy anchors. Personnel are ferried to and from the rigs either by boat or helicopter.

The 261 men on board the P-305 all worked at the giant Oil and Natural Gas Corporation (ONGC) oil rig that towered 200 metres out of the sea. Dilip had spent a typical day as one of the many welders working on the upkeep of an endless network of pipes that made up the heart of the rig. Barred from any deck time, he and his mates walked back down the steps towards their bunks. Half-way down the flight of stairs, one of the men caught a glimpse of the sea outside.

'The waves were easily nine metres high and crashed into the side of the barge,' he recalls. 'And in the distance, I could see the lights on the rig just as it began to rain.'

This wasn't unexpected weather. Barge P-305, along with three other barges and a tug boat had all received a weather alert two days earlier about a deep depression in the Arabian Sea that had gorged on warm coastal air, whipped itself into cyclonic strength and had been christened Tauktae. On the day when Dilip and his fellow workers were making their way back down to their bunks, Tauktae had strengthened into a very severe cyclonic storm.

From the bottom of the stairs, Dilip turned back up towards the foreman, who was watching them from the deck door.

'We're moving around a little bit. Are all the anchors holding steady?' Dilip asked.

The foreman shot a quick glance out through the thick pane of glass on the heavy door that separated him from a deck that was now being lashed with heavy rain falling at a sharp angle, almost horizontally. He stared back down into the stairwell at the men who were waiting for an answer.

'I don't know, but I hear six of the anchors have snapped.'

Barge P-305 had eight anchors.

16 March 2021
Naval Dockyard, Mumbai

Well past midnight, 70 nautical miles (129 km; 1 nm at sea equals 1.85 km on land) away on the mainland, Captain Sachin Reuben Sequeira walked hurriedly through a corridor on the upper deck of INS *Kochi*, the over 7500-tonne Indian Navy destroyer under his command. Six years old, 163 metres long and formidably armed, the warship had returned to her dock the previous day after weeks of sailing across the Arabian Sea, delivering hundreds of tonnes of COVID relief supplies to Persian Gulf countries, and on the return leg had brought back oxygen cylinders* to Mangaluru on India's west coast.

The ship was at her berth, but the full crew—250 men— was on board that night. Rough sea swells rolling into the harbour as a result of the gathering storm meant that warships docked there needed to be on scramble alert to sail out if the weather deteriorated beyond a certain limit. Captain Sequeira was rushing to the bridge of his ship to get a full view of what things were looking like.

The officers and men on the bridge were at their stations, already ordered by their commanding officer to be prepared to move at very short notice. The ship may have been docked, but things were far less than comfortable for the crew, because INS *Kochi* was berthed next to—literally rubbing shoulders with—her two sister ships, INS *Kolkata* in the middle and INS *Chennai* alongside the actual dock. This wasn't ideal even in calm weather. And that night, it was a dangerous risk the crew of all three ships had to take, thanks to the well-known congestion in Mumbai harbour.

---

* This was during India's second COVID-19 wave, one marked by severe shortages of medical oxygen.

'So, there were three of us, three massive ships closely berthed alongside,' says Captain Sequeira. 'When weather goes bad, the basin takes a lot of swell and the ships tend to move a lot, scratching and rubbing each other. Double berthing is not uncommon because of limited space. But when you do that, your ropes and bollards are not meant to take so much stress. And here we were with three warships on one berth, that's nearly 23,000 tonnes held together by ropes. The crew of INS *Chennai* complained that there was a lot of strain, and her ropes might just tear apart. We were on tenterhooks that night.'

Briefing the officers and sailors on night shift on the bridge and reminding them that the ship was to be ready to move out at very short notice, Captain Sequeira retired to his cabin below a deck that was being lashed more fiercely with each passing minute.

At 8.30 a.m. the following day, the rain now ruthless, an emergency message from the Western Fleet office flashed on the ship's communication system, ordering INS *Kochi* to prepare for sailing out towards a location where an unspecified but dangerous 'situation' was evolving in the Arabian Sea.

'No further inputs were available on what the situation was,' says Captain Sequeira. 'In the next sixty minutes, there were two more calls from the fleet office saying that something was happening and a barge seemed to be in distress and may require some sort of assistance.'

By 10 a.m., the orders became definite, but the crew of INS *Kochi* still didn't have a clear picture of just how bad things were beginning to get at the Heera Oil Field.

'The conditions were quite bad because Tauktae was about 100 nautical miles south-west of Mumbai,' says Captain Sequeira. 'The port had shut down completely. There was no movement on the Mumbai Port Trust side. Ships outside from the previous night were already in distress with some dragging anchors and not under control. In such conditions, harbours generally don't allow you to move in and out to minimize the possibility of damage due to collision.'

But INS *Kochi* had to get out of the harbour, and fast.

The lake-like calmness of the harbour on normal days was shattered by a swell that now rose 3 metres, churned by winds gusting at speeds of 35 knots. The warship needed to get out before things got worse at the dockyard. Even the slightest deterioration in weather could potentially lead to the heavily-armed warships smashing against each other, risking the prohibitively expensive vessels and their crews.

INS *Kochi* had just been assigned a mission at sea. But the first big challenge was to safely get the destroyer out of the harbour. With the spiralling outer arms of Tauktae now heaving coastal waters into a boiling churn, the ship was about to commence it's most dangerous exit from its berth.

'When the port is not operating and winds are that high, it becomes extremely hard to leave the harbour,' says Captain Sequeira. 'Prudence tells you not to try any stunts because the risks involved are huge. But there was an SOS out at sea. And it was grave enough for us to have to take every risk possible to move.'

'Can you do it, Sequeira?' asked a voice from the fleet office on the ship's comms.

'We will do it. We absolutely will,' replied the commanding officer before ordering his men to unmoor and sail out.

As the crew got busy with the symphony of tasks and manoeuvres required to detach their ship from its berth and point it out of the harbour, Captain Sequeira glanced around at the young officers and sailors on the bridge. It was late in the morning, but the weather was a deep, foreboding grey.

'The safety of my men and my ship is my responsibility,' says Captain Sequeira. 'I was the captain, and the buck stopped with me. Those things were weighing on my mind, all the more so because we weren't sure what was out there. You only hear of cyclones and how people try to dodge them. You don't hear of people going *into* cyclones at sea. Even for a 7500 tonne sturdy warship like ours, we knew this was going to be a day requiring our fullest.'

One of the newer ships in the Western Fleet, INS *Kochi* was in excellent condition, with the crew having just 'worked up' the vessel after its first scheduled refit.

Now standing on the ship's deck to cast her off, Captain Sequeira remembers the rapidly changing sight outside.

'Nothing could be seen,' he says. 'Visibility was so bad that I could not see the front part of my ship from the bridge.'

On a good day, the warship could have cast off and manoeuvred itself out of the harbour without help. But on the morning of 17 May, every conceivable impediment to safe passage was ringing an alarm bell.

'Most of us take pride in our manoeuvring skills and usually use the powerful and agile engines to manoeuvre the ship out of harbour,' says Captain Sequeira. 'But this was out of the question that morning as we had no control. We got three tugs to pull us out of our berth. After that, it was entirely up to us.'

The crew of INS *Kochi* gave their vessel a massive burst of power to charge out of Mumbai harbour.

'This was risky because we didn't have enough speed, and the elements could take charge,' says one of the crew members on the bridge that morning. 'Even in normal conditions, if winds reach a speed of 15 knots or more, it can become tricky. The winds start pushing you one way or the other, and you don't have power as yet to pull her out. And here we are talking of a wind speed of 35 knots, which is off the charts.'

With the ship's four Ukrainian-built Zorya-Mashproekt DT-95 gas turbines now roaring at near maximum power, Captain Sequeira estimated that the powerful winds produced by Tauktae were blowing in precisely from the direction in which the ship was headed.

'I had no choice but to push full power and charge into the wind,' says Captain Sequeira. 'I had to make sure that I didn't bang into the jetty, berths and walls that flanked the harbour. The winds were coming right at us.'

As the ship sailed out in the extreme weather, a tourist on the coast captured the destroyer's silhouette disappearing into a firmament of grey. Tauktae's rain was coming down in copious torrents now.

'I took cover behind a radar antenna and ducked below it to look ahead,' says Captain Sequeira. 'I told my navigator to just stand behind me and hold the mic next to his face and just repeat what I was saying. I was looking from below the radar. It was hard to even stand there. We somehow pulled the ship out, turned it, gave it a burst of power and charged out.'

It may have seemed difficult then, but the INS *Kochi* crew had just completed the easiest part of their mission. Once out of the harbour, there was still ship traffic to look out for, especially since the cyclonic winds were likely to have thrown smaller merchant ships off their course and caused them to 'drag' anchor.

'What we essentially did was blind piloting,' says a sailor who was assisting with navigation duty that morning. 'That meant piloting the ship without any visual inputs and relying only on our radars and other electronic sensors to safely navigate the ship out of the harbour because the visibility was very bad.'

'We realized that the wind was so powerful, and the swell was so strong that we simply couldn't sail straight,' says another sailor on radar duty. 'We were actually going about 25–30 degrees off our intended course. We had the ship in a zigzag manoeuvre to maintain this narrow path.'

On a good day, Captain Sequeira would have issued orders and attended to other tasks on board his ship. But with his vessel headed into the heart of Tauktae, he knew there was no question of stepping back.

Manoeuvring around buoys was also critical.

Moored with heavy anchors and chains, large floating buoys help ships navigate safely through a channel, but they were anything but helpful that morning. Brightly coloured to enhance their visibility, the overwhelming weather had even blurred the buoys out. Breaking free from their moorings, the buoys with their chains could severely damage a ship's propellers.

'One nick from a metal object can cause enormous damage because the shafts are moving at about 100 rpm (revolutions per minute). Here we are talking about massive cylinders. If my ship were to get damaged, I would have to return to the dock and then it would take forever. It would also involve huge costs,' says Captain Sequeira. 'The buoys outline the channel, and in normal conditions, there is enough space for a ship to move. But in stormy conditions runaway buoys can pose a great danger. We were relying on our eyes to pick them up because it was quite likely that the radar wouldn't detect them in that bleak and worsening weather.'

Radar operators tend to optimize the parameters of the detection system during stormy passage to pick up bigger vessels to prevent collisions at sea. Echoes coming from fishing trawlers, smaller boats, buoys and the like tend to get lost as the main focus is on clutter reduction. 'The smaller boats and buoys go off the picture as you want to see less clutter. You have to play a very careful game on your radar settings to detect the valid echoes,' he says.

The only way to keep an eye on what was ahead of and around the ship was to deploy more men to lookout positions on the deck.

'In such conditions you come back to your basics, which is eyesight, hearing, monitoring every possible input inside the ship, outside the ship, radio, anybody seeing something—everybody has to be on the ball,' says Captain Sequeira.

Finally, out of Mumbai harbour after a tense ninety minutes of white-knuckled navigation, INS *Kochi* began to encounter a more vicious aspect of Tauktae, with Sea State 7, identified by waves up to 30 feet high.

'Once we were out at sea, it was rougher than anticipated, with the waves picking up and a massive swell coming in,' says a sailor who manned one of the lookout positions. 'You could not stand exposed on the deck. There was no question. The first thing we did as we came out of the harbour was to go and batten down the hatches to ensure there was no flooding of the ship. Our ships are designed to be watertight, but the situation was perilous and we couldn't take any chances.'

Captain Sequeira ordered all men on the deck back inside the ship.

'As soon as we were in open water, I ordered everyone inside,' he says. 'These huge waves were breaking over our fo'c'sle, the forward part of the ship, sweeping across and coming over two decks high and almost hitting the bridge. I was on the bridge and could see the towering walls of water smacking us.'

Late in the afternoon, an emergency update flashed on board INS *Kochi* informing the crew that barge P-305 was now adrift. A frantic call from on board the barge had finally been relayed to the Western Fleet.

The P-305's last two anchors had snapped. The barge was now like a piece of cardboard being tossed around by the monstrous waves that were rising up to 40 feet.

'Our information was that the barge had taken in water and was moving without control,' says Captain Sequeira. 'There were 261 people on board, we were told, but there was no direct communication between us and the barge crew. We checked all parameters and decided to increase speed towards the location of the barge. P-305 was drifting fast and was about seventy nautical miles away.'

The P-305 was now being battered by wall-sized waves. No longer moored to the seabed, the barge had been flung by a particularly large swell towards the oil rig, colliding with a piece of machinery, before spinning away, its hull damaged and now taking even more water. On board, there was total panic.

Dilip and a group of his mates had descended to the lowest deck of the barge to help clear out the water ingress, though this soon proved to be futile. Sea water had begun to gush into the barge through a gaping hole torn in the hull by the brief collision with the rig. And the enormous waves were now sending huge amounts of water down all open vents and hatches into the lower decks of the vessel.

Things rapidly worsened when the men on P-305, now convinced they needed to abandon ship, found that most of the twenty-four life rafts attached to the sides of their barge were damaged in the swell, with many torn into useless shreds by razor-sharp barnacles that encrusted the sides of the vessel.

Over 50 nautical miles out, INS *Kochi* was also getting rocked like never before by one of the strongest cyclones ever to churn the Arabian Sea.

'We realized that we were rolling about 35–40 degrees at times, and as we were tossed around, things inside the warship started falling all over the place,' says Captain Sequeira. 'It was difficult for one to even stand. We normally stand at 3–4 degrees of rolling. People start getting sick between 8–10 degrees. Most can't stand at 35–40 degrees. I remember taking a moment to wonder, can I handle her or not? If you get seas on the side, the waves breaking on the side, she will tend to roll. If you get the waves from the front, from where you are headed, you slam into the waves and then you come out. So, either way, you choose what damage you want to take.'

The commanding officer remembered the words of a mentor from his days as a cadet:

'If you go into the seas, seas will try to break your ship.'

Forty of the 250 men on board were new personnel who hadn't spent much time out at sea in rough weather, and quickly began to experience the effects of a violently rolling and lurching ship. Young men in their twenties on their first tenure in the open ocean. But under the care of the more experienced men, the affected young sailors were back on their feet. They would never be that sick again.

But INS *Kochi* was taking a true beating that afternoon.

'The sea was so rough that it was now pushing us back with a strength of about four knots,' says Captain Sequeira. 'So, let's say if I was using engine power to give me what is normally twelve knots, I was only getting about eight knots. My effective power was getting struck down by almost 30 per cent.'

The crew was confident of their warship. This was a superbly sturdy vessel with solid, indigenously built bones. But this was a sea the crew had never encountered before. Not even the most experienced men on board.

'She was getting slammed badly, and it put a lot of stress on her,' says a senior sailor. 'Our ships are built to take a certain amount of beating. But we had to be mindful that we were subjecting Kochi to a lot of stress. How much could she take? You are exposing your machinery to a lot of beating, which is not normal. All we could do was try our best to see how we could minimize this roll and pitch motion of the ship.'

As barge P-305 continued to drift and take in more water, INS *Kochi* continued to get inputs from the shore about its last known position. Dilip and a small group of men were now huddled in the radio control room on the barge, desperately trying to send out more messages.

'At around 2.30 p.m., we got a call and we could hear a guy from P-305 calling us on Channel 16, the common calling channel for all merchant vessels,' says a sailor on INS *Kochi* manning comms in the operations room. 'He got to know we were coming; he must have been in touch with his people. He was a radio operator. We asked him where the barge was now, and he gave us some coordinates. We realized that the barge had drifted further north and was now north-west of us.'

The mission had been a proverbial race against time from the beginning. The radio call and fresh coordinates brought the first realization on board INS *Kochi* that the mission could fail badly. The barge, with 261 men on board, was being violently tossed around. How would an over 7500 tonne warship be able to safely manoeuvre anywhere close to it? How would it rescue anyone at all? The ship hadn't even reached the drifting, sinking barge, but it already seemed like an extremely difficult and dangerous mission.

'As we turned, the ship got slammed right in the beam, sending us rolling well over forty degrees,' says Captain Sequeira. 'That was very risky. We were finding it hard to maintain course and the seas were tossing the warship around. If I could barely stand on my feet, I could only imagine the impact on my machinery, my radar, my equipment. The basics would go for a toss. And that would have risked the whole ship. So, we were doing the desperate zigzag manoeuvre again to somehow reach the waters where the distressed barge said it was. And this position itself was changing dramatically by the minute.'

Another call from the P-305 crackled through on Channel 16. It was Dilip.

'I remember his voice very clearly,' says the sailor on INS *Kochi* who received the call. 'I could now make out there was enormous desperation in the voice. We got inputs that the barge had taken in water, and it would go down. And in their mind, there was full panic that they were going to die before we reached them. They said everybody was up, on the part of the barge that was out of water, and said, "*Jaldi aao, jaldi aao* [Hurry, come quickly]." I told them to have faith that we would reach them soon and would not spare any effort to get there as quickly as possible.'

The P-305 was now tilted at an angle and sliding slowly into the water. With over 100 men jumping into the sea, the other 161 perched themselves on the end of the barge that was sticking out of the water.

'Now that we knew the barge was sinking, it was plainly life and death,' says Captain Sequeira. 'As we were approaching, we kept telling them over Channel 16 that we were coming, *aa rahe hain*.'

But it was impossible to go any faster. There was a limit to how much power the ship could be cranked up to.

'We had all the four gas turbines running right from the start,' says a sailor from INS *Kochi*'s engine room. 'In fact, we never stopped the engines at all. As you push more power, you get more impact on the ship. We had to trade off between how much speed we could achieve and how much beating we were willing to subject the ship to. The higher the power, the greater the beating. So, there was also an increasing strain on the propulsion system.'

At 4 p.m., five hours after INS *Kochi* had set sail from Mumbai, the naval vessel finally reached the general location of the sinking barge, slowing down when it spotted the P-305 from just under two nautical miles away. The barge was leaning at a steepening angle into the aggressive swell.

'Using binoculars, we saw that the remaining on board the barge were all clustered in the part that was protruding out of the water,' says Captain Sequeira. 'Over Channel 16, they said they had their life jackets on and pleaded they be rescued at the earliest. In my mind, that was the moment of truth.'

One of the lookout sailors tasked with assessing the approach says, 'Their accommodation block was in the aft structure. The barge was hit in the front, so the front part was now below the water. There was one huge crane-like structure that was sticking out.'

'As I looked out at the barge, it was quickly confirmed that the barge was huge, almost as big as my ship,' says Captain Sequeira. 'And I am nearly 7500 tonnes. There is no way I can take my ship anywhere close to the barge and let's not forget, I can't fully control my ship. At one moment I am here and at another moment, I am there. The angry sea is just tossing me around. Those guys were getting panicky, asking us to reach quickly but at that point there was little we could do. Like I said, moment of truth.'

If this had been a routine rescue of a distressed ship in fair weather, the crew of INS *Kochi* would have lowered lifeboats to bring the men on the P-305 to safety. But with the conditions now worsening to Sea State 8 with waves over 45 feet high, anything lowered into the sea would simply be swallowed. No boat would have remained afloat in that swell.

The next possibility was the warship's life rafts, emergency twenty-man rafts reserved for the ship's own crew in the extreme event that they needed to abandon the vessel. These had a better chance of surviving that maniacal sea. But how would the crew get those rafts out to the men marooned on a rapidly sinking P-305?

'Whatever we threw into the sea at that point would be eaten up by the sea. And I was not prepared to send divers into the water either. Nobody could swim in that water,' says Captain Sequeira.

The crew of INS *Kochi* then conducted a sweep for other vessels in the area, quickly latching on to an offshore support vessel (OSV) that operated at the Heera Oil Field to support and service barges. Fitted with bow-thrusters, OSVs move at a slower speed and are more manoeuvrable, unlike warships that rely on brute power to roar through the water in aggressive forward motion.

'We asked the OSV if it could approach the barge and transfer the life rafts,' says Captain Sequeira. 'The guy who responded said it was not possible at all. So, we were in a very difficult situation. We were less than a nautical mile away from the sinking barge and kept telling the men to hold on.'

Just before 5 p.m., INS *Kochi*'s comms room could make out that there was an abrupt spike in the desperation of the voices reaching them from the barge.

'There was total panic now, and the men on the barge clearly felt that it was going under,' says one of the sailors who was responding to the desperate calls. 'It's not easy to calm somebody whose life is on edge. We were there for an hour. We also felt that the situation may only worsen. We were in Sea State 8 and the sea was deteriorating further.'

Armed with fourteen perfectly good life rafts, Captain Sequeira was determined to get them to the men on P-305. But the rafts needed to be released into the water. And given how violently their ship was being buffeted, that in itself was a death wish.

'These life rafts are meant to operate automatically when they hit water, by pressure release,' says Captain Sequeira. 'They're supposed to open on their own. But in this case, I decided to send five of my men to the upper deck to release the rafts. At this point the ship was still being tossed around badly, and at any instant, there was the possibility of these guys getting knocked into the rough seas. One wave comes and they slip and go, that's it. I will never see them again. But we took the chance. There was no other way. We lowered fourteen life rafts and hoped that they would get somewhere close to the barge.'

When the men returned below deck, the commanding officer instantly knew that this had failed too. The men revealed that as the life rafts went down, they were all ruptured, torn and got lost in the sea.

At 5.30 p.m., the comms room on INS *Kochi* received a call from the barge, strangely calm and therefore even more disturbing, informing that the remaining men were abandoning the P-305 and jumping into the sea.

'It was a very gentle voice, without any panic,' says the sailor who responded. 'It was very unsettling. It was the voice of someone who had totally given up. There were many men on that barge who did not know how to swim.'

Minutes later, one of the sailors on lookout on the upper deck of INS *Kochi* shouted through the ship intercom to the bridge that he had spotted groups of men in life jackets from the barge in the water not far from the ship.

'So, the men were now in the water, which changed things,' says Captain Sequeira. 'But we still couldn't go near them as our warship could hit them and knock them dead. There was literally nothing else we could do at this point.'

It was then that they thought of a final last resort.

Scramble nets.

These were cargo nets that could be slung down the side of the ship into the water, giving the men in the water the chance to somehow clamber aboard the destroyer.

'You roll it down, the guy can climb or hold on to it, just average fitness is good enough,' says Captain Sequeira. 'We said let's try the scramble nets. That was the only thing we could think of. But again, the problem was the same. How do we get close enough to them so that they can reach the nets and climb up? The sea was still tossing *Kochi* around. The men in the water were also getting tossed around everywhere.'

Desperate now to close the gap between his big destroyer and the men bobbing desperately in the sea, the commanding officer of INS *Kochi* began a process of manoeuvring his ship with a series of power stops and starts. It would be the most delicate navigation he had ever done.

'We saw them coming in a certain direction, so we weren't really moving in that direction but manoeuvring in a way with massive power surges and stopping and trying to see how we can get anywhere close to them,' says Captain Sequeira.

Four teams of men from INS *Kochi* were now positioned on the decks to handle the four scramble nets, one giant net and three smaller ones.

'Frankly, at that point nobody believed it would work as we had to get the ship close to these small groups of survivors when we ourselves were not able to control how we were moving,' says a sailor on one of the scramble net deck teams. 'But the way we were manoeuvring helped and we finally came closer to the survivors. We had to be very careful as a large ship. One small move and our hull could kill everyone in the water.'

An agonizing hour of painfully delicate manoeuvring ensued as dusk fell over the Arabian Sea. Just before 8 p.m., the deck team manning the big scramble net saw something that it was least expecting.

An exhausted survivor had reached the scramble net and was now slowly clambering up the side of INS *Kochi*.

'It was just one guy, but it was a huge thing for us,' says the sailor who spotted the first survivor. 'We suddenly realized this was working. A few minutes ago, we were not even able to stand on the deck. And now we had got one of the survivors on board. So, we just kept doing what we were doing.'

'Even in normal conditions, climbing the net is difficult,' says Captain Sequeira. 'Even one or two metres of up and down motion can make it very difficult for a person to climb. It sounds simple but it isn't. The rope in the net is quite thick and has wooden beams in it. One of them can hit your head and break it open.'

The men of INS *Kochi* had thus far seen how ruthless the sea could be. In a twist right after the first rescue, they began to witness what they regarded as the other side of the ocean's dual nature.

'The sea abruptly calmed down a bit,' says Captain Sequeira. 'Suddenly it wasn't that bad. The swell had come down to five to six metres from the earlier eight to nine metres. We were now able to manage the rescue slightly better.'

With more survivors from the barge managing to reach the scramble nets and hoist themselves to safety, the rescue settled into a hopeful rhythm.

The sea, which had brutalized the barge, appeared to be willing to make up for it in at least some of the cases.

'There was this one survivor who could not grab the net. He drifted in the current and ended up behind our ship. But a powerful wave threw him right on to the ship's deck. It was a miracle,' says Captain Sequeira.

By 9 p.m., INS *Kochi* had rescued forty-five men from the P-305. In the darkness lit up by the ship's floodlights, the crew watched the barge finally sink beneath the waves. The stray sounds of groans and whimpers from the sea kept the warship's crew on full alert. With 216 men still theoretically out there in the sea, the night would afford no break to the rescue crews. In fact, it would provide an opportunity for individual acts of heroism.

'I saw my anti-submarine warfare officer, Lieutenant Commander R.K. Manu, struggling to balance himself on the warship's deck,' says Captain Sequeira. 'He peered down the starboard side and was gesturing to a group of middle-aged offshore workers to climb up the scramble net. These men were fatigued after being in water for hours, hopeless and gripped by the fear of imminent death. They could not climb the net. They could get to the net, but they just could not climb. That's when Manu secured himself with a rope and climbed down the net to get these survivors to safety. He held the survivors by their collars and pulled them up.'

The sea fell ominously silent, with no further survivors visible or audible. By 11 p.m., INS *Kochi* received a call from another OSV a few kilometres away in the area saying it had spotted more survivors in the water.

By 5 a.m. on 18 May, INS *Kochi* had rescued 115 persons from the sea. Right around this time, before first light, things were stirring at a separate location back on shore.

INS Shikra Naval Air Station Colaba, Mumbai

A part of the main hangar roof had blown away in Cyclone Tauktae's powerful winds, with rain flooding the insides of the hangar where Sea King Mk.42B helicopters of the Harpoons squadron were parked.

Commander Bipin Panikar was up while it was still dark. He had received orders from the Western Naval Command late the previous night to fly out on a search-and-rescue (SAR) mission at first light to the Heera Oil Field, where INS *Kochi* had managed to rescue a number of survivors from the sunken barge.

Like they had with INS *Kochi* at the Mumbai dockyard, Tauktae's winds were doing everything they could to keep the navy's Sea King helicopters firmly on the ground.

'We were on the clock, but there was a real issue,' says Commander Panikar. 'There's a wind envelope in which you can take off and fly. The Sea King has an automatic blade folding system. Wind speeds have to be less than 45 knots for the blades to spread. If the wind speeds are more than that, not only will the blades not spread, but there could be damage to the helicopter too. And then we can forget about flying.'

That was the first problem.

'Secondly, during very high winds, if you ask a chopper guy to engage rotors, when the rotors start turning at low rpm, there is a huge chance of the blades striking the body of the aircraft,' says Commander Panikar. 'It's a big aircraft and the blades are big too. The first thing was to get the chopper started.'

The pilot's predicament was unprecedented. The Indian Navy's trusty old Sea Kings had proven worthy of launch and flight in very poor weather before. But Tauktae had presented new limits to what the machines could be forced to go up against.

At 5.30 a.m., the squadron duty officer called Commander Panikar to inform him that there was no way a Sea King could even be wheeled out of its hangar—the blades were banging against each other even inside the hangar, he said. Not launching a helicopter mission wasn't an option that morning, given the situation with barge P-305. And so, with the squadron's commanding officer in tow, Commander Panikar walked across INS *Shikra*'s helipad to the Sea King hangar.

'The Sea King is a very robust aircraft but the winds were 45–50 knots, just on the margins of its operating capabilities,' says Commander Panikar. 'We needed to act fast because I should have been airborne by that time. I knew I would not be able to take off from the standard take-off position close to the sea. That was not possible as the chopper would encounter more wind than is considered safe. So, I picked a spot between two hangars for lower wind impact.'

With some difficulty, the big hulking helicopter was wheeled to a strip of asphalt between two large hangars. Climbing into the cockpit with his co-pilot, Commander Panikar carefully started the first of the two engines.

'The wind was still too strong and the main blades started rattling with each other,' says Commander Panikar, 'So we had to put one of our technical guys on top of the aircraft, where he held the blades. He was a brave guy. The blades were earlier colliding with each other. Once you start one engine, it starts all the drives, and they activate the blade fold system through hydraulics. Normally, you wouldn't spread wings or engage rotors in these conditions. The aircraft can take much more once it's airborne. The most important part was the rotor engagement.'

After a measure of struggle, the Sea King was finally running its rotors at full power. What was usually a routine helicopter launch sequence had turned out to be an hour-long battle with Tauktae's winds.

'The entire air station, crew and commanding officer had gathered at the take-off area and it felt as if I was going out for batting in a cricket match,' says Commander Panikar. 'Some guys told me not to go far out in the sea if the conditions were too bad. If it's not looking possible, come back, they said. In aviation, you don't chase the weather. I knew the weather picture, it was moving northwards and I was trying to chase the weather. This was not normal. Ask any aviator, he will try to steer a course which is opposite to such weather conditions.'

As with INS *Kochi* a day earlier, the Sea King's mission that day was literally to fly into trouble.

'I was to be that guy who went there, understood the weather, the situation and tried to rescue whoever he could. I was to come back and brief the other guys on the situation so that subsequent launches could happen,' says Commander Panikar.

The commander had flown Sea King missions during the milder Cyclone Ockhi in 2017, but the moment he got airborne from INS *Shikra* and headed into Tauktae, he knew this was something else altogether.

'The abnormal movement of the control stick made me realize we were up against a daunting task of having to factor in wind effects on the helicopter,' he says. 'The stick was shaking. When the winds are strong and changing direction very rapidly, you have to continuously move the stick to nullify that wind effect. There was a lot of stick movement.'

Banking over the grey Arabian Sea, the Sea King headed past Prong's lighthouse on the southernmost point of Mumbai, four miles from INS *Shikra*. There were no other aircraft in the sky that morning thanks to Tauktae, affording rare permission to Commander Panikar from Mumbai air traffic control (ATC) to fly wherever he wished.

'"Nobody is flying, and we are heading into bad weather"—that's the first thought that crossed my mind and it was a bit unsettling,' says Commander Panikar. 'But we also knew we had to reach the rescue site at the earliest and expand the scope of the SAR before it was too late. When I looked out at the sea and the weather, it looked really terrible. We had to fly ninety to hundred nautical miles to reach the SAR location. Dark patches of low-level clouds at 200–300 feet were visible, and my radar was showing me a lot of red, warning me about the weather I was wilfully flying towards.'

The Sea King's navigator piped in.

'Do you really want to fly into this?' he asked. 'It looks very bad.'

'Let's try and skirt those clouds,' said Commander Panikar. 'And the moment we feel it is not doable at all we will turn back. Let's do some assessment so that we give a "sitrep" to the base at least.'

Cruising at 1000 feet, the Sea King descended to 500 feet. Almost immediately, inside the cockpit, it felt like day had turned to night.

'We were totally and suddenly engulfed in clouds,' says Commander Panikar. 'That hit all of us in the aircraft—my co-pilot, our navigator and my aircrew diver Prahlad. Each of us thought the exact same thing. That this was like night flying.'

At 500 feet, and with the pilots flying the Sea King on instrument readings rather than outside visibility, things took an even more surreal turn.

'There was sudden lightning all around,' says Commander Panikar. 'The lightning lit up the insides of the cockpit. And then it would be dark again, so I switched on the cockpit lights.'

At 500 feet over a surging sea, the pilots were forced to trust their instruments. Things in the cockpit took a hit with pressure instruments that provided crucial airspeed and altitude data becoming unreliable.

'The weather was making them go wonky,' says Commander Panikar. 'One electronic instrument that was still working was the radio altimeter (radalt) which was telling me the exact height from the sea surface. I turned a course forty-five degrees away from my destination to get away from the dark clouds.'

The pilots flew a course that took them in and out of the low, dark cloud deck, the helicopter shuddering with each repeated dive into the clouds. The crew exchanged glances with each jolt, agreeing that this was one sturdy helicopter they were flying.

'Every two or three minutes we got such bad jolts that we actually asked each other if everything was okay,' says Commander Panikar. 'There was crazy wind, rain and this thick cloud deck we were flying through. The pressure instruments were giving us incorrect and unreliable data, so we had to fly cautiously. For instance, my airspeed reading showed sixty knots when my ground speed was only thirty knots. That cyclone was really testing us that day.'

Pilots are trained to trust their instruments when visibility goes to zero or all else fails. The crew of the Sea King were flying without visibility and reliable instruments just 500 feet from the ocean surface. The risk of controlled flight into the sea couldn't possibly have been higher.

It was the helicopter's sole non-pressure instrument that kept things on even keel.

'The radalt came to my rescue,' says Commander Panikar. 'It transmits a radio beam down, it hits the ground or sea surface and comes back. I was relying on it. There are so many instances of controlled flight into terrain in bad weather. When you are flying and visibility is not good, you feel you are at 1000 feet and are comfortable and then suddenly you are in the water. To avoid that, it was very important for me to know at what height I was flying. These things were weighing on my mind.'

Like INS *Kochi* on its voyage towards the Heera Oil Field, the Sea King was being flown in a zigzag flight path to avoid the worst of the bad weather. Since this was a vanguard mission, the pilots were carefully recording their flightpath in order to share it with other Sea King crews who would fly subsequent missions later in the day.

Ninety minutes later, the Sea King arrived at its target position, coordinates that had been shared by the Indian Navy's maritime operations centre.

'We were at 200 feet and could see nothing in the sea,' says Commander Panikar. 'I was thinking, we've come ninety nautical miles and there's nothing here and nobody to rescue.'

After an uncomfortable and dangerous flight over the Arabian Sea, there was disappointment and anxiety in the cockpit as it hovered at 200 feet.

'We wondered if we had come to the wrong position. We checked the coordinates again and it was clear we were at the position given to us. Visibility ahead was not even one nautical mile. I tried calling the ships in the area, including INS *Kochi*, over the radio frequency for the scene of action, but there was no response. It was imperative for the ships to respond to me because I had been tasked with dropping body bags on their decks. And we couldn't stay airborne indefinitely.'

The Sea King's navigator started scanning the area again on radar, desperate to locate something—anything—before it was time for the Sea King, forced by fuel endurance, to swivel around and head back to base.

'We needed to find something very urgently,' says Commander Panikar. 'I was circling around in an environment that was rapidly changing, the winds, the clouds. All of us in that cockpit knew it could lead to disorientation. About eight minutes into the latest loop of low-level flight, my observer spotted something on the radar.'

But it was 30 nautical miles out.

'I was constantly concerned about losing endurance,' says Commander Panikar. 'I asked my observer if he was sure. He said he was. With every passing minute, we were losing the ability to stay airborne longer. I was concerned about having enough fuel to return. How much time will I take to return? Thirty nautical miles meant another fifteen minutes of transit time. The observer was very confident that he had picked up something. I was praying he hadn't picked up some merchant vessels.'

The helicopter flew low, but it was still in a thick envelope of clouds. As the Sea King approached the coordinates identified by the navigator, its radar started picking up a sudden burst of contacts. Commander Panikar prayed once again that it wasn't a pod of whales or dolphins that had been spotted. As much as he loved animals, he wasn't here on a sightseeing sortie. He pitched the Sea King forward so it could descend through the clouds.

And there they were.

'When we broke cloud, we saw a large number of people floating in the sea,' says Commander Panikar. 'We came down to 150 feet for a clearer picture. It was a sea of survivors in orange jackets, and we could also see INS *Kochi* and other ships conducting their rescue operation at some distance.'

It was 9 a.m., and there were a lot of men to be rescued from the sea. The Sea King descended further. And as they got nearer to the sea surface, the true horror of the picture became apparent.

'Many of them didn't seem to be alive,' says Commander Panikar. 'But we didn't have time to process the tragedy. We had to find those who were alive and get them out of the water. We were now keeping a hawk's eye on any movement in the water.'

Hovering gently above the surging sea surface, the crew of the Sea King carefully scanned the cluster of orange below them. The co-pilot quickly spotted one man struggling to keep his head above the water, barely alive.

'Normally you have an automatic hover system which you engage and the helicopter tries to maintain its altitude with respect to the sea which is crucial for such rescue missions,' says Commander Panikar. 'But that was out of the question because of the swell of the sea. And that meant we had to do the hover manually. Hovering over sea is harder than hovering over land because of lack of visual reference. A manual hover is difficult in such situations, besides the swell was tossing the survivors around. There I was trying to position myself over the guy, and in a flash, the swell displaced him. Next, I would find him fifteen to twenty metres behind me. All this kept happening. And all this when wind speeds were touching fifty knots.'

With time rapidly running out, and wind speeds only picking up, Commander Panikar asked master chief aviation (flight diver) II Prahlad to get into the water and bring the survivor up.

'I told Prahlad not to disconnect from his harness under any circumstances,' says Commander Panikar. 'If he disconnected to pick someone up, I could lose him in the choppy sea.'

It would take twenty minutes to winch up the first survivor.

Remaining at that dangerously low altitude, the Sea King began to hunt for more survivors. As it did, INS *Kochi* came into view once again, reminding the pilots about their secondary task. In a careful manoeuvre that had its own share of challenges, the Sea King delivered body bags to INS *Kochi* and the other ships rescuing men from the P-305.

'After a second rescue, we were about to turn back,' says Commander Panikar. 'We were running very close to the required fuel levels for the return flight. While we were on our way back, we spotted a guy folding his hands and shouting for help in the sea. This time we were hovering at thirty feet. That was the height of the waves in the area. It was a surreal sight from the cockpit.'

For this third rescue, diver Prahlad decided he had to disconnect from his harness as the survivor was totally exhausted.

'We were very low on fuel but I had seen this guy, and we knew we couldn't leave him behind,' says Commander Panikar. 'And the other two survivors we had rescued urgently needed medical support. They were in very bad shape, and I felt they could die in the aircraft. I had seen that happening before in an earlier mission.'

Winched up along with Prahlad, the Sea King rose above the cloud and flew at maximum speed back to the INS *Shikra* air base.

'We were dangerously low on fuel when we landed,' says Commander Panikar. 'It was important for me to reach back and brief the other crews on the mission and the shortest route. The briefing room was set up next to the helipad to save time.'

The next Sea King missions began immediately and continued through the day, contributing to a string of additional rescues from the Heera Oil Field site.

Diver Prahlad accompanied other Sea King missions that day, rescuing a total of twenty-eight survivors, including three who were on the verge of drowning and rescued during the first mission.

Commander Panikar flew more sorties himself, rescuing a dozen more marooned persons from another barge. Sea Kings from INS *Shikra* rescued thirty-four survivors in all.

Operating an aircraft to the extreme of its limits is an art pilots can learn only when they fly missions like this . . . In normal day-to-day flying, pilots can't push aircraft to the extreme because if something goes wrong, they will be held accountable.

By noon on 18 May, ten more survivors were rescued by INS *Kochi*. Another sixty-one were rescued by other Indian Navy ships, the Sea King helicopters and OSVs.

That evening, INS *Kochi* called off its search and set course back for Mumbai. On board, along with the 125 rescued men, were the bodies of seven of their mates who had drowned.

'We were in touch with Sea King choppers right through the rescue missions,' says Captain Sequeira. 'The warships and the helicopters worked in tandem to carry out the SAR. We saw people floating in life jackets but found that many of them were dead. We reached Mumbai on the morning of 19 May, delivered the survivors and the bodies of the dead and then returned to the Heera Oil Field area the same day. In the second round, we found only bodies and no survivors.'

While Captain Sequeira was decorated with a Shaurya Chakra, Commander Panikar received a Nao Sena Medal for gallantry. In many ways, both officers came away from Tauktae with similar experiences.

Both faced crushing challenges to get their missions started.

Both were forced to deal with the possible mortality of their own men.

Both were forced to think out of the box while a life-and-death clock ticked ominously.

Both also came away with an uncannily similar lesson from their respective missions: that humans are capable of achieving much more than they believe they can.

Captain Sequeira says, 'Everybody on my ship was worried about what will happen. Not only to the men on the barge but also to us. What would our fate be? How will this end? But we made it. At the end of the day, you have to give it your best shot no matter what the odds are. You really have to try to make some sort of a difference. If you just keep sitting and thinking, "What do I do and how is this going to play out?", you are not likely to achieve anything. When we left the Mumbai harbour on 17 May, even I was thinking of what exactly I was going to do there. There were no answers then. But my philosophy seems to have changed a bit: at least try, do something, it might just work.'

The warship captain's gallantry citation reads, 'The successful and daring execution of the SAR operation under unprecedented stress and extreme rough weather highlights the extraordinary leadership, professionalism and fortitude of the officer. This brave act of leadership and courage was in keeping with the ethos of the Navy and in service of the nation in times of peril and adversity. For his extraordinary bravery, courageous leadership, exemplary grit and determination, in the face of extremely challenging conditions, the officer is recommended for the award of Shaurya Chakra.'

INS *Kochi*'s anti–submarine warfare officer, Lieutenant Commander Manu, who went into the water down the side of his ship to pull exhausted survivors from the sea, was decorated with a Nao Sena Medal for gallantry. His citation reads, 'He displayed extraordinary leadership skills and courage with complete disregard to his personal safety during the SAR operation undertaken by the ship, during Cyclone Tauktae, resulting in the saving of 125 lives. Through personal example, the officer led his team of men during the rescue mission for 36 hrs at a stretch, under extremely adverse weather conditions.'

Sea King pilot Commander Bipin Panikar's gallantry citation reads, 'As the first pilot and Captain of the aircraft, the exceptional courage, bravery and fortitude displayed by him in the face of extremely dangerous, hazardous and unforgiving weather conditions resulted in the successful rescue of three lives of sunken Barge P 305. For utmost exceptional courage, fortitude, skill and display of valour during the SAR operation of survivors of sunken barge P305, Cdr Bipin Panikar is very recommended for the award of Nao Sena Medal (Gallantry).'

And finally, commando diver Prahlad, who saved twenty-eight lives, was also decorated with a Nao Sena Medal for gallantry. His citation reads, 'Prahlad, with absolute disregard to his own safety and life, undertook these unparalleled rescue missions single-handedly in extremely hazardous and hostile sea state. It is his commendable swimming skills and years of experience as a flight diver that saved the lives of 28 personnel from a near-death situation. The exceptional bravery, initiative and nerve displayed by him merits recognition and he is strongly recommended for the award of Nao Sena Medal (Gallantry).'

Dilip the welder from barge P-305 survived and was rescued.

9

'This Time Holi Will Be with Blood'

Major Konjengbam Bijendra Singh

Dibong village
Manipur
March 1999

The eight-year-old boy usually slept soundly, the breeze gently blowing through this verdant village near the Assam border a reassuring lullaby. But that night, a loud midnight knock on the front door of the small mud house had made Konjengbam Bijendra Singh sit up, rubbing his eyes. To his side, his two siblings were still asleep nearly four hours after he had tucked them in. The children had gone to bed earlier than usual that night so they could be up early to celebrate Yaosang, the five-day Manipuri equivalent of Holi, a festival to usher in spring starting on a full-moon day.

And like in Holi, the children would play with colours.

Bijendra heard hushed, anxious voices in the Meitei language as his parents shuffled out of bed. Then he saw the shadow of his father, Konjengbam Binod Kumar, a part-time teacher in a local government school, stumble half-awake to the door. Bijendra stepped out of his bed and squatted furtively near the door of the room, so he could see what was happening.

As soon as his father unbolted the door, three men pushed their way into the house. They had assault rifles slung around their shoulders. One of the men wielded a pistol of some kind.

'Serve us dinner, we're hungry like animals,' said one of the men in a rough tone as he looked around the tiny dwelling.

Bijendra's mother, Konjengbam Tilotama Devi, now shuffled into view, walking up to her husband as he faced the three men. His father turned around briefly to check on the room in which the three children were supposed to be asleep. He saw three sleepy but wide-awake faces peering back at him from the shadows of the bedroom. He gestured to them to return to bed immediately, but Bijendra and his brother and sister stayed where they were, transfixed by the late-night invasion.

After a few seconds of inaudible conversation, Bijendra's mother proceeded towards a corner of the main room that served as the kitchen. Turning on a kerosene stove, she prepared a quick meal of leftover rice and pork curry from the night's dinner, serving it in bowls to the three men who were now sitting on the floor, their weapons leaning against a wall in the dimly lit room.

It wasn't the first time Bijendra and his siblings had had their sleep interrupted this way. Armed insurgents were a common sight during those decades in Manipur, knocking at doors in village homes for a meal, shelter or to hide from security forces. Amid a rising tide of militancy in the North-eastern state, armed groups frequently extorted from innocent families that had nothing to do with the insurgency. To villagers like young Bijendra and his family, the sound of those three men gorging noisily on the rice and pork was still a gentler aspect in an insurgency that was otherwise drenched in blood.

'We should sleep now,' Bijendra said to his siblings, the three of them still watching as their parents sat down with their uninvited guests. 'We have to be up early for Yaosang.'

Back into bed, Bijendra remained awake, still listening. The smell of the rice and pork had wafted into the children's room, triggering a pang of hunger in the boy. But he knew there was no way he was going to see if he could get a bowl of his own. He lay in bed, waiting for the narrow triangle of light to go off, so he could relax and fall back asleep. Then he heard their voices again.

'Thank you for the food,' said one of the men. 'We are likely to be back tomorrow. And the day after that. Cook extra so there's enough. There should be more rice and curry next time.'

Then they left, and Bijendra heard the front door being bolted. His parents didn't say a word as they cleaned up, switched off the light and went back to their room. As he waited for sleep to overcome him, Bijendra was surprised by the spasm of rage he felt. This wasn't the first time he had seen armed men arrive at their house in the darkness and demand food or shelter. But it was the first time he hadn't heard his parents talk about it after the men left. Their silence numbed the boy. Only eight years old, he felt a tide of anger over whether his parents were so worn out by the unpredictability that hovered over the safety of their home with three little children, that they simply had nothing left to say.

It was with that resentment that Konjengbam Bijendra Singh fell into the deepest sleep he ever remembered.

* * *

Assam Rifles base
West Manipur
March 2019

'Are you sure you want to launch the operation on Holi?'

Colonel Rajkumar Bishnoi, commanding officer of the 23 Assam Rifles unit, was talking to his company commander.

Now twenty-eight, Major Konjengbam Bijendra Singh found himself in Manipur on the eve of another Yaosang.

'I have no doubt in my mind, sir,' Major Bijendra said. 'Haopu and his men will be least expecting the Assam Rifles to come after them on Holi. I have handpicked my best men, trained them hard.'

'So, *khoon se Holi khelne ja rahe ho* [So, you will be playing Holi with blood]?' the commanding officer said with a grin.

Holi was six days away, on 21 March.

Major Bijendra smiled. The very same words had been used by a soldier on the team a few hours earlier when plans were being finalized.

Khoon se khelenge Holi.

It wasn't a facetious comment. Major Bijendra, whose job it was to lead his company of men and their charged emotions, knew that the blood of innocent villagers was already being spilled in villages and the hunt was on for one of the principal insurgents responsible for local terror and kidnappings in that part of Manipur. Their target was Haopu Khongsai, the self-styled commander-in-chief of the Liberation Tigers of Tribals (LTT), an armed Kuki group.

The hunting ground was a vast one. Major Bijendra's area of responsibility (AoR) covered the expanse between the Barak and Makru rivers and was infested with various small militant groups owing allegiance to a handful of larger insurgent outfits, including the two primary factions of the National Socialist Council of Nagalim (NSCN), Zeliangrong United Front (ZUF), United Tribal Liberation Army (UTLA) and Haopu's LTT.

Major Bijendra's company had been on Haopu's tail for over a year. And on that March afternoon in 2019, months of often frustrating intelligence collection and analysis had been distilled down into a pattern of Haopu's movements, crucially narrowed down to a jungle stronghold 75 km from the company operating base (COB) at Kamai.

'We are very close, sir,' Major Bijendra said, pointing to an area on the map that pinpointed the jungle stronghold.

'If the intel fits, go for it,' said his commanding officer. 'But I don't need to tell you. They'll have innocents with them for cover. Don't come back with any innocent's *khoon* [blood] on you.'

The intelligence Major Bijendra was armed with was as precise and actionable as it was possible to obtain in the circumstances. It captured details of when and which village Haopu and his militant group were in, where they went next, who led them, what weapons they carried and the uniforms they wore.

'We shouldn't delay, sir,' Major Bijendra said. He knew he was as close as he could get to getting a militant who had been in his crosshairs since October 2018 following a spate of killings and kidnappings of villagers in the Kamai area. This was just months after the young officer, fresh on deputation from the Corps of Army Air Defence, had assumed command of 23 Assam Rifles' Alpha Company. In each encounter, Haopu's intricate network of informers had managed to ensure he escaped before the Assam Rifles arrived. And after each escape, Haopu would send a message by cranking up the violence and kidnappings. Villages would be crippled by fear every time Haopu managed to escape. They knew he would be back soon to announce his presence with blood.

The intelligence Major Bijendra now had even detailed when and at which house the militants showed up unannounced for a meal or shelter, very much like the late-night visits to his family home two decades earlier. Nothing had changed. Things had, in fact, become worse.

His commanding officer's go-ahead itself was a breakthrough. Major Bijendra had accumulated and waded through piles of intelligence data for almost six months before approaching his superiors to get the green light for the operation he was planning. All previous attempts to get approval for hunting the militant from the Assam Rifles leadership had failed. His superiors had ordered Major Bijendra to revisit and fine-tune the intelligence. They told him that it simply wasn't enough to avoid either collateral damage or major casualties to the Assam Rifles.

Weeks before the day his commanding officer finally approved the mission to hunt down Haopu, Major Bijendra had failed to convince his seniors at a security conference chaired at Khongsang, another 23 Assam Rifles company operating base, by Brigadier Ravroop Singh, the commander of Indian Army's 59 Mountain Brigade.

At the conference in early February 2019, Major Bijendra made a comprehensive presentation on the security situation in his area and detailed it with the intelligence he had gathered on the militants and their activities, the fourteen-man squad he had hand-picked and readied for the mission and a broad description of how and where they planned to ambush Haopu and his band of militants. He had displayed a sense of impatience, even exasperation.

In a testament to just how meticulous planning, checks and balances are almost always in place in the Army, Major Bijendra's pitch hit a wall. The brigadier and the commanding officer, while impressed by the major's unsparing approach, single-mindedness and vigour, still declined approval. A disappointed but disciplined Major Bijendra was ordered to keep preparing for the operation, further verify the leads he had gathered, make sure there were no loose ends and wait for authorization.

There was no time to be despondent. Days after the security conference, Major Bijendra, along with a few Manipuri members of his squad, disguised themselves as villagers to carry out reconnaissance of their area of interest to obtain first-hand information about the terrain, routes and possible vantage points for the planned mission. At the time, the soldiers weren't fully aware of the purpose of the reconnaissance missions they had been part of, though they vaguely knew that something big was afoot. Their company commander had dropped perhaps the biggest hint a few months earlier.

'No Holi holiday this time,' he had told them. 'You can all take leave after that.'

As it turned out, the reconnaissance missions gave the Alpha Company precisely the inputs it needed to fill in the blanks in the operation plan. Coupled with large amounts of intelligence that poured in subsequently, the overall accuracy of Major Bijendra's existing assessment stood confirmed.

By early March, he was convinced that there were big risks in keeping the operation on hold for too long. And with some crucial finishing touches that he asked for from his informers in the target area, he had the final operational plan that checked all the boxes in his commanding officer's requirement.

As frustrating as the process was, Major Bijendra knew that intelligence can be a tricky beast at the best of times when tackling militancy. There's no shortage of incidents, both big and small, where flawed intelligence has resulted in things going horribly and tragically wrong.

Colonel Bishnoi was clear. He knew that no operational plan could be 100 per cent foolproof. But he knew he had worked the young officer to the bone, building a mission blueprint that was close to actionable as it was possible under the circumstances. It was one of the sharpest pieces of intelligence he had seen for a high-level militant. He was impressed, but he knew he also needed to be apprehensive. Even the most well-constructed missions had a nasty habit of going south.

'KB, I am fine with your Holi plan,' Colonel Bishnoi said. 'You have been at it for months and I trust your judgement. Go ahead and get those guys.'

The commanding officer then departed from the Alpha Company base to head back to the 23 Assam Rifles headquarters in Tamenglong in the Naga Hills of Manipur.

The boss had left. His approval was in.

'Finally,' Major Bijendra said aloud to himself in the operations room of his base. Looking around at the maps and charts that had finally won him approval to proceed, he went to prepare his men.

There were loud cheers from the barracks as Major Bijendra broke the news to them. Every single soldier at the Kamai company operating base knew the name of Khaikhohao Khongsai, alias Haopu, the ruthless and slippery commander-in-chief of the LTT, and his trigger-happy cadres who had brazenly opened fire at the base at least twice in the past six months.

The Alpha Company's hunt for Haopu began with the daylight abduction of two employees of a private company associated with the construction of a crucial Indian Railways project in the North-east, the 111-km Jiribam–Imphal rail line. The Rs 12,265 crore project, expected to be completed by December 2023, is intended to significantly improve accessibility to Manipur and involves the construction of forty-seven tunnels and 156 bridges, including the world's tallest pier bridge that will rise 141 metres over the Ijei River. India plans to further extend the railway line to Moreh on the Myanmar border to link up with the Trans-Asian Railway Network in line with its Act East Policy to make the North-east a gateway to Southeast Asian countries.

Extortion and abduction by militants like Haopu had slowed down the Jiribam–Imphal rail line project in the preceding years, throwing a shadow over the intended benefits to local communities in remote parts of Manipur and its neighbouring states.

When news of the abductions filtered in on the Assam Rifles intelligence network, Major Bijendra had been particularly enraged. As a student, it would take him around twelve hours to travel from his village in Jiribam district to Jawahar Navodaya Vidyalaya in Manipur's capital Imphal by bus. The railway line would now allow children from his village to cover the distance in just over two hours. Haopu and his militant group were specifically targeting development projects because they knew development meant prosperity, movement of communities and a loss of territory to manipulate. To a young Army officer who had struggled to break barriers of access to wear the uniform, a more sinister, cynical, self-defeating set of actions couldn't be imagined.

Images from his childhood in Dibong would flash frequently in his mind as he got to work on the hunt for Haopu. It was men like these, Major Bijendra thought with a familiar pang of resentment, who pushed their way into people's homes, demanded pork and rice, and then actively destroyed the hopes and dreams of those very families.

Bijendra's father had worked as a government school teacher in the 1990s, but lost his job as the situation deteriorated in the area. Through that decade he drove lorries along the dangerous highways of Manipur to support his young family. There were no jobs, and there were no choices.

The internecine warfare between militant groups had destroyed decades of development in Manipur and its sister states in the North-east.

It saddened, infuriated and galvanized Bijendra. As he and his men broke bread together that night, they knew Haopu was but one of several such men who paralysed the North-east and its people. But to their tiny paramilitary company, he was the face they needed to hunt. That was their bit in the larger fight for peace and tranquillity in one of the most beautiful corners of the country.

'*Iss baar Holi thodi alag hogi* [This time it will be a different Holi],' Major Bijendra said as the men ate together. '*LTT ke saath khelenge. Yaad rakhna, sab ki nazar humare operation par hogi* [We will be playing Holi with the LTT. Remember, all eyes will be on how we conduct our operation].'

At sunrise the next day, 16 March, Major Bijendra ordered his squad to the operations room at the company base. While the soldiers knew that Haopu was their quarry, this would be the first time the soldiers would be given the full picture of what they were up against. The maps on the military easels made it immediately clear to every man in the room that the plan was to hunt Haopu and his men down in their very backyard, on their turf. Major Bijendra didn't need to explain how dangerous this was.

'We depart at first light on 19 March,' said Major Bijendra. 'Carry rations to sustain ourselves for at least a week. No other tasks or duties except this operation now.'

He sensed questions in the silence of the operations room.

'The intel is airtight,' he said. 'I'm vouching for it personally.'

Not that the men needed convincing—they had been waiting for this mission for six months—but Major Bijendra knew they were now committing themselves to a mission that each man knew could be his last.

'I am not exaggerating when I say I can visualize where Haopu is and what his men are doing right now,' he said. 'The militants won't know what hit them. This is the operation you and I have been waiting for.'

Being a Manipuri, it had helped Major Bijendra build a strong rapport with locals in his area of responsibility, as well as cultivate a fairly solid network of informants, who he often turned to for leads in the constantly shifting cat-and-mouse world of anti–militancy operations. On the night of 18 March, he called them for an update on the latest developments in and around Longphailum village near Nungba town where intelligence had picked up significant militant movements in the preceding weeks.

The Alpha Company squad planned to set up its ambush in a jungle not too far from Longphailum seventy-two hours later.

But being a Manipuri had a deeply dangerous side. One that radiated outward from the company operating base to Major Bijendra's home village and the village of every Manipuri soldier in the squad. Both he and his men would often receive phone calls from militant groups, warning them against conducting operations unless they wanted to see their families harmed.

'Doesn't your mother still live in Dibong?'

'Isn't 4698 the number of your brother's motorcycle?'

'Don't you want to see them ever again? Aren't you afraid of the consequences?'

Threat calls were common, but it wasn't easy to dismiss them. Militants went to great lengths to gather information about the families of security forces. If not to actively harm them, then to play mind games with them over the phone. Mind games that could have a telling effect, especially on younger soldiers new in the force and freshly away from their families.

Major Bijendra had trained himself not to be rattled by the calls. Sometimes they would mention things about families that nobody could have possibly known unless they were physically present near them. That was the extent of the network and the lengths to which militants like Haopu often went to intimidate the men who were now hunting him.

Growing up during the militancy, Major Bijendra was largely inured to the atmosphere of threat. But he would never forget how close those men came to his family. Their weapons casually leaning against that mud wall as they ordered his parents around in their own home. The sound of boots crunching the gravel and bullets whistling through the air and hitting their home's front wall on more than one occasion only to be anxiously, quietly prised out and discarded at first light with an iron spike by his sleepless father.

As he got older, the resentment grew, churned by a sense of helplessness over not being able to do anything about it. It was in this brooding phase that a teenaged Bijendra was returning to his boarding school in Imphal after spending the summer vacation with his family in Dibong in 2004.

As the bus rumbled down the Imphal–Jiribam highway, Bijendra noticed a band of armed men on the road ahead, using oil drums to block the way. When the bus stopped, the men ordered every passenger out with their hands up. Over the next few minutes, each passenger was robbed of their money and belongings at gunpoint. From Bijendra, they took the little money his father had given him for the journey and a bag of pickle and home treats his mother had packed for him to enjoy in the hostel dormitory with his friends.

Such looting of passengers was a frequent occurrence in those dark days. But what happened on that highway would fan a Manipuri boy's indignation into an unremitting rage. He would never forget the faces of those militants who grabbed his belongings. At his hostel that night, especially homesick and alone, Bijendra decided he would 'do something'. His friends would tease him, wondering why he had taken a commonplace highway robbery so much to heart. What they didn't know at the time was that the incident had made a quiet, unusually focused teenager out of Bijendra.

Seven years later, Bijendra had grown into a confident young man. His commitment to 'doing something' would remain unwavering, but he was confused like so many young adults about precisely what to do. As he waited for an epiphany, he enrolled for an engineering degree at the North Eastern Regional Institute of Science and Technology (NERIST) in Arunachal Pradesh right after graduating from school. But before classes could start, a chance meeting with a cousin in the elite National Security Guard (NSG) finally made Bijendra's path clear.

He quickly withdrew his college admission deposit from NERIST and used it to pay for a crash course before appearing for the Services Selection Board (SSB) interview. With an anxious family firmly behind him from distant Dibong, Bijendra saw to it that he was admitted into the hallowed campus of the Indian Military Academy (IMA) in Dehradun.

A year later, in December 2012, Lieutenant Konjengbam Bijendra Singh was commissioned into the Corps of Army Air Defence. For his parents, who had arrived from Manipur for the ceremony, the moment couldn't have been prouder. Bijendra would be only the second man from their village to be commissioned into the Army. If there was any anxiety about their son's career choice, they didn't let it show on that day, only hugging him and wishing him a safe, peaceful journey in uniform likely to be far away from them.

And now, seven years later and two ranks senior, Major Bijendra was back in his home state as part of the Assam Rifles. In fact, the Alpha Company base was less than 50 km from his village near the Assam border.

At dinner with the men, Major Bijendra heard his phone vibrate in a low thrum on the Sunmica table. He knew who it was even before he looked.

'You haven't seen your texts, everything okay?'

It was Jenipher, Major Bijendra's girlfriend in Imphal. The young officer had created a shadow account on Instagram to keep track of militant propaganda and pictures sometimes posted by younger cadres. Joining conversations on the app, he and Jenipher had begun talking. She was in her final semester of a BSc zoology course at the GP Women's College in Imphal. After due diligence from both sides, the two had met offline, their Instagram affection blossoming into a real-world relationship. Not that he didn't trust her, but Major Bijendra made it a point never to discuss his work in any detail with his loved ones. If they ever asked, he would simply say it was for their own safety.

'Sorry, Jen, was a little tied up with some planning work. Everything okay?'

'That's fine, but please don't ignore my texts, it's not easy for me.'

'Sorry, love. Also, Jen, I may be a little offline for the next few days, so if messages don't deliver or if I don't answer, don't worry. I'll call you soon.'

It had been two years since their relationship had begun. Jenipher's early insistence on details had given way to acceptance that this was how it needed to be. She understood that her Army boyfriend's reluctance to speak about his work was out of concern, and not based on trust issues of any kind. She and Major Bijendra's family were simply better off not knowing.

'OK, please text me whenever you get a signal.'

Major Bijendra knew he wanted to marry Jenipher. He had decided he would pop the question after the mission was over. It would also give him the opportunity to take some leave and spend time with her.

But for the next five days, the officer knew he would need to be laser-focused on his mission.

Glancing over at the men who were still eating, Major Bijendra knew he didn't need to worry about their abilities.

He and these men had been on multiple missions together in the lush jungles of Manipur, where they had forged deep one-on-one relationships to create a cohesive team that was supremely disciplined, well-trained and fierce.

One of the men held up a leg of chicken.

'Mission *ke baad*, this is them,' he said with a smirk.

After dinner, with less than forty-eight hours left for the squad to move to the ambush site 75 km away, the men conducted a final check of weapons and ammunition, bullet-proof gear, night-vision devices, communication equipment, field rations and first-aid kits.

Before turning in for the night, Major Bijendra dialled one of his informants located not far from the target site.

'No change. All normal,' said a hushed voice, before disconnecting.

* * *

Kamai COB
19 March 2019

Fully kitted out for the mission, the squad was on parade at the designated staging area of the company base at 4 a.m. as ordered, the sky still dark and pouring a steady drizzle.

The men split into two teams with their equipment and the soldiers were about to climb into the two Tata 407 pick-up trucks when Major Bijendra signalled to them to stop for a quick final briefing, more of a ritual before any mission he led. The men knew what their company commander was about to say.

'We play to our strengths, we fight as a team, we make sure there is no collateral damage and we come back victorious. We have done it before, and we will do it again.'

With a hoot of approval, the men bundled into the trucks, their company commander in the front seat of the first. The vehicles would ferry them until just ahead of Nungba, 50 km away. The remainder of the 25 km journey to the ambush point would be a trudge through a jumble of jungle routes.

As the pick-ups rumbled over hilly terrain at moderate speeds, Major Bijendra's mind was occupied with three dominant concerns. First, he needed to make sure the squad didn't squander the element of surprise. Second, the squad needed to make contact with the militants at the earliest. And third, all fourteen men needed to make it back alive and if possible unhurt. It was a tall order, but anything less would have meant second thoughts about the sharpness of the operation plan.

As planned, the 407s dropped the soldiers a few kilometres ahead of Nungba from where, with heavy bags, AK-47 rifles and light machine guns (LMGs) on their backs, they started their journey on foot to the ambush site. Led by two scout soldiers who were part of the reconnaissance missions in the previous weeks, the Alpha Company men trekked through rough and rolling tracks in the hilly jungles, moving as stealthily as they could. It wasn't, by any measure, a casual march. Each man had his weapon unlocked and ready, moving in a single file with extreme caution as militants were known to have observation posts and small hideouts in the woods.

'We were there to surprise them and not the other way round,' says Warrant Officer Shivram, the second-in-command for this mission. 'Hence the caution. The immediate goal was to reach the ambush site in time to pitch a few small tents and set up a small base before it got dark. We weren't sure how long we'd be there.'

Fifty-four years old at the time, Shivram was the oldest man in the squad. With maximum exposure to combat, he was a soldier whose experience the squad depended on. He had operated against the Liberation Tigers of Tamil Eelam (LTTE) in the late 1980s as part of the Indian Peace Keeping Force (IPKF) in Sri Lanka and also operated in Jammu and Kashmir as well as other North-eastern states in his three-decade military career.

'If I could fight and survive the LTTE, then I could definitely hold my own against the LTT under KB Saab's command,' says Shivram.

Slicing through jungle vines and bridging boggy swamps churned by the rain, the squad steadily inched towards the ambush zone, making the final approach as surreptitiously as possible, their postures now crouched. In the failing light, the men arrived at their destination, a small hilltop looking down on a swathe of jungle and a network of narrow dirt tracks. It was here that Major Bijendra ordered the men to establish their temporary base. It was from here that they would lie in wait for Haopu and the other militants.

By 8 p.m., under driving rain that spattered the orange mud of the hill, the tents were up. One of the men had sliced down some banana tree leaves enroute to keep over their heads in the downpour. Deep orange rivulets flowed down the hillside.

Khoon ki Holi.

The squad was again split into two teams. The first, including Major Bijendra and Shivram, took concealed positions along an arc on the hilltop to keep an eye on the main track below, a small stretch of which lay hidden from the base camp's view because of the way the hill jutted out.

Rifleman K.D. Burman manned the LMG position, the powerful weapon with a very useful rate of fire for the vagaries of jungle warfare, where targets often melded into the foliage.

The second team pitched pup tents using jungle bamboo a short distance behind, its crucial task to provide backup and ensure sufficient quantities of ammunition, food and water. The men had arrived equipped to stay for a week. If the mission stretched beyond that, the men of Alpha Company would need to abort and leave empty-handed.

'We were carrying more ammunition and rations than anything else. No metal support for the tents, using bamboo instead. A 4.5 kg tent weighed only 1.5 kg without the support gear. The planning was that detailed,' says one of the soldiers.

If jungle warfare is about fighting an often unseen enemy who has harnessed a wealth of hiding places and camouflage, it is equally about survival and endurance in a setting that is almost always unforgiving. Training at the Indian Army's jungle warfare schools dwelt deeply on living off the land to conserve rations.

And so, on that hill, pairs of soldiers would be dispatched into the woods, variously bringing back wild sweet potatoes, banana stems and berries. A dried fish pickle the men carried as a compulsory ration added a spicy, protein-rich tang to forest-given chow. Five men were capable of finishing a kilogram of rice in a single meal. It needed to be stretched.

'The dried fish achar was among the staple items we carried during all our missions, apart from Maggi noodles, dry fruits, protein bars and some other high-calorie items. The pickle never disappointed, it could make anything taste good. While we were carrying rations, wild treats were common as the food had to be conserved to cater for an extended mission,' says Rifleman Burman.

Snakes are a recommended food item on jungle missions, given the numbers in which they're encountered in the deep, rain-drenched woods. They're considered nutritious and easy to prepare over a simple campfire. Strangely, Major Bijendra and his squad found no snakes on the hill or nearby.

'You need to adapt and improvise to accomplish the mission. Use the terrain to your advantage. Staying out in jungles for long and operating in those conditions had become second nature to us,' points out another soldier from the squad.

Under the dense canopy of the forest, the soldiers settled into their positions, harvesting rainwater using their raincoats and keeping a watchful eye on possible movements in the undergrowth below. All this while they battled an expected battalion of leeches, mosquitoes and numerous other creepy crawlies that make Manipur's forests some of the richest and most splendid in the country.

'The leeches don't matter much when you are on the move. But leech attachments can be very irksome when your mission involves lying in wait for days,' says Shivram. 'We spent a good amount of time flicking them away,' he says.

Up on the arc in his own tent, Major Bijendra bunked down for the night. Four soldiers at separate lookouts would remain awake through the night on watch. As he wound down, he pulled out his phone for the first time since they had got out of their pick-up trucks earlier in the day. A single message from Jenipher flashed on the lock screen.

'Just be safe and come back, that's all.'

While there was a single bar of mobile signal, he thought it best not to reply immediately. Switching the phone off, he tossed it into his rucksack and lay back to sleep. Pictures from the day washed over him. The jungles and terrain of Manipur had instantly reminded him of Vietnam war films like *Platoon*, which he had seen in school.

Treacherous and stunning, he thought, as he drifted into an exhausted sleep.

Another day passed on that hill with no sign of any movement on the rain-spattered dirt tracks below. All through, Major Bijendra remained in contact with his informants on a second mobile, a primitive old push-button phone with no data or Internet. The informants steadily confirmed that Haopu and the other militants were still at Longphailum village and didn't appear to be suspicious about any imminent action. One of the informants provided a crucial tip, the kind the squad was depending on.

'They will cross the patch of jungle you are in anytime now. Don't take your eyes off the track.'

Major Bijendra mostly spoke directly to his informants. But on this mission, he had assigned the important responsibility to two Manipuri soldiers brought along for the specific purpose of staying in touch and updating the rest of the squad.

The concrete tip-off put the squad on full alert, with every man at his station and with his weapon. But nothing happened on 20 March. After hours in combat mode, the men exhaled and returned to their ambush posts. Every man knew that the next day was Holi.

'There was no compulsion that we had to strike on Holi, but symbols are very important to us, and we knew it was important to KB Saab,' says Shivram. 'The only fear was that sometimes you returned empty-handed after putting in one hell of an effort. It had happened before with our squad. *Kuch nahi mila aur hum vaapas base ja kar agle operation ki tyaari shuru karte the* [We found nothing and returned to our base to prepare for the next operation]. And then we were back in the jungles after one or two months for another hunt. Holi or no Holi, we were just hoping that was not the case now.'

Holi arrived with a distinctly ironic lack of colour. A low fog and steady rain painting the otherwise verdant landscape all the many shades of grey. But if the weather wasn't going to be festive, the day would bring some crucial gifts to the men of Alpha Company in the form of the first direct evidence of the presence of Haopu and the other militants in Longphailum village. Early in the afternoon, as the sky cleared a little to bring a semblance of colour back to the forest, Major Bijendra and his men heard the echoing clatter of automatic gunfire from the direction of the village.

Informers conveyed to the squad that the gunfire—once in the afternoon and the second time later that night—was to celebrate the construction of Haopu's new home in the village.

As the gunfire continued into the night, Major Bijendra quickly assembled a five-man team, leading them down the hill and towards Longphailum village. The team stopped 3 km from the village, carefully avoiding any further advance.

'There was a lot of firing and blaring music. Haopu and his men were there for sure,' says one of the men.

The team remained on site near the village for an hour, conducting 'listening' drills and soaking in everything they could. The number of firearms, the stray hoots of laughter, the shouts. The militants didn't appear to be masking their presence in the village. But like all things in guerrilla warfare, this could mean two things. One, it could mean that Haopu and his men were clueless about the Assam Rifles squad lying in wait for them just a few kilometres away. Or they could be celebrating as a decoy to lull the Alpha Company men into complacency, only to either quietly escape or strike unexpectedly.

'Haopu's informer network was too solid to discount that second possibility,' says Shivram. 'So if we were already being careful, we needed to double our guard now.'

Holi had ended, but no blood had been spilt. Back at their hill camp by 11 p.m., Major Bijendra gathered the men of Alpha Company. He was convinced that the mission was about to reach its peak.

'*Tayyar raho, militants se contact hone wala hai*,' he said to them. '*Shayad kal hi. Holi ek din late manayenge* [Stay ready, we may make contact with them not later than tomorrow. We will celebrate Holi a day later].'

'We fully trusted our commander's instincts. If he was saying contact was imminent, it had to be,' Shivram says.

Their commander's sense of certainty infused fresh energy into the squad. There was still an hour of Holi left. And so, on that desolate hilltop, intoxicated by the prospect of the encounter finally in sight, the men decided on a small celebration.

Generous helpings of khichdi, the one-pot meal cooked with fistfuls of rice, dal and water followed, in a welcome break to the monotony thus far of Maggi noodles and forest produce. The dried fish pickle once again worked its magic.

'We had been eating Maggi and the jungle fare as our orders were to conserve food. Khichdi had never tasted as good before. I will say it had the makings of a princely meal for us,' says Rifleman A. Brijit Singh, the then thirty-five-year-old buddy soldier of the company commander. The battle buddy system followed by the Indian Army involves pairing soldiers in combat to watch over each other.

Their bellies full of rice, the men should have been exhausted that night. But not a single man slept. The moment Major Bijendra and his men had been waiting for was now less than fifteen hours away.

Jungle near Longphailum
22 March 2019

It had been pouring non-stop for three days, but the day after Holi brought with it crisp, glinting sunshine. Bereft of mist and rain clouds, the squad on the hilltop had its first sweeping view of the woods that stretched all the way towards Longphailum village. It wasn't just an omen. It was also literally better weather for the militants to move.

At 1 p.m., Major Bijendra used his binoculars to scan the dirt tracks that snaked their way into the foliage. As he panned, he stopped abruptly. In the distance, maybe 3 km away, he saw a giant JCB earthmover rumbling slowly through the undergrowth with what looked like six men in the excavator's big mouth bucket. It was near the area he had scouted the previous night with four other soldiers, after the first round of celebratory firing.

'It's them,' Singh called in a hushed tone audible to the men holding the arc on the hilltop. 'We will still wait for an airtight visual confirmation. Let them come as close as they can. No one will open fire till I order it.'

The possibility of local villagers accompanying any militants in the earthmover couldn't be ruled out. The true dilemmas of jungle warfare were now throbbing. The near impossibility of identifying targets until they were very close and a major risk to the team lying in wait. Not a sound emerged from the hilltop as the men of Alpha Company held their breaths, not a word more was spoken after Major Bijendra's last order not to open fire without his order.

A squad scout sitting on the arc then observed through his binoculars the JCB machine turning to the right and making its way back into the woods. The men they had spotted in its mouth bucket minutes ago, now mysteriously gone. Every man in the squad now either had a pair of eyes or a weapon pointed at the dirt track down from the hill. For twenty minutes, nothing moved, and there was no sign of the men from the JCB.

Then they appeared.

The faces were familiar. Each one of the men, a known LTT militant. The intelligence had been spot on. But where was Haopu, Major Bijendra asked himself as he searched from one face to the next.

By 1.30 p.m., the first five militants were within rifle range of every man in the squad. Except the last man.

Where the hell is Haopu?

The squad knew it couldn't wait longer. With the militants in range, it was imperative that they act quickly. Any closer and the militants would either spot the ambush site and escape or be in a better position to return fire.

'I was ready to pull the trigger on my AK–47 but held back as the company commander's instructions were unambiguous,' says Shivram. 'We were to open fire only on his command. I had waited three days for this moment, a few more minutes were fine by me.'

Their automatic weapons slung around their necks, the militants walked single file down the meandering track into the Alpha Company squad's 'kill zone'. Their advance neatly spaced, each man walking around 40 metres behind the one in front.

It was an obvious tactic militants deployed to keep casualties low in the event of an ambush by security forces or even by rival militant outfits. The tactic also provided militants further back in the line valuable time to slip away or take cover to fire back at the ambush team. Additionally, it keeps the ambush team in suspense about the exact number of men making the advance.

The distance between the first militant, carrying a Kalashnikov with a tripod, and the sixth man, who was still perplexingly not in view of the ambush party, appeared to be more than 200 metres.

'After I spotted the first militant on the track, the second man came into my view after twenty-five-odd seconds and then the others in the same time gap,' says Rifleman Brijit. 'We waited as I wanted to make sure that all of them were within the range of our weapons.'

The first militant crossed the blind spot on the track just below Major Bijendra's position and reappeared after a few seconds. The firing positions were barely 10 metres above the track. The first man was about to disappear behind the hill, but the sixth militant had still not appeared.

'*Saab, fire kholein nahi toh yeh nikal jayega.* [Let's open fire before the first man disappears],' the Major's buddy whispered directly into his ear, articulating the immediate concern of the squad.

Holding his breath, Major Bijendra, with his AK-47 aimed at the first man, waited two more seconds. Then he gave a hand signal to Shivram to ask the militants to surrender, a standard protocol during anti-militancy operations. It was a contentious combat rule, but needed to be followed, since the militants, for all their destructive ways, were Indian citizens with rights.

The call to surrender was the most dangerous element of an ambush. It meant that any squad lying in wait needed to voluntarily sacrifice its element of surprise in the hope that it had done everything necessary to pin down the militant into a 'no escape' situation. In encounters such as this one with most-wanted militants, the possibility of the targets dropping their weapons and raising their hands was next to nil.

As expected, once Shivram shouted to the militants to give themselves up, the militants responded with immediate bursts from their firearms. The silence of the forest quickly erupted in a fierce assault-rifle and light-machine-gun crossfire.

Major Bijendra fired shots at the first militant as the rest of the ambush squad engaged the remaining militants in a firefight. The first man tumbled down the hill after being hit but the shot wasn't fatal. He was definitely still alive.

Major Bijendra leapt out of his ambush position and scrambled down the hill, four soldiers from the squad following him in pursuit of the injured militant. The blind spot on the track offered the soldiers temporary cover as they emptied their Kalashnikov magazines in the most likely direction of the militant.

Quickly regrouping in the gun smoke, Major Bijendra made a quick assessment with his men, deciding to quit pursuing the injured militant any further, and instead train their sights on the other militants. Including the sixth, who by now would have stopped in his tracks and taken cover from a distance.

Haopu?

But climbing back up the hill and returning to the safety of his ambush position was no longer an option. Doing that would make him and the four men with him vulnerable to a well-aimed fire from the hiding militants. They would need to remain on the dirt track now, exposed and on the same level as the men who were likely to hunt them back.

'We will now confront them on the track. Let's hit them from an unexpected direction,' the officer told the four soldiers as they slammed fresh magazines into their assault rifles.

Like with much else in jungle warfare, decisions were frequently the result of a total lack of options.

'We trusted KB Saab's judgement. We knew he had a plan,' says Rifleman Brijit. 'And there wasn't a moment to waste.'

Flat on the ground, the men could hear bursts of fire whizzing overhead and towards the hilltop behind them. This was a stroke of luck. The militants were aiming up, not aware that five army men were on the dirt track and edging closer to them.

Major Bijendra and the team emerged from behind the blind spot on to the track in a dash-down-crawl-fire military move typical of close-combat warfare. The move involved quick sprints, throwing oneself down to the ground, crawling on one's elbows and firing a few shots. It allowed the men to close the gap between themselves and the militants, while still maintaining a firing posture.

'We didn't have a good view from the top. That was no longer the case after we approached them from below and directly took them on from barely a few metres. KB Saab had trained us for such situations,' says Rifleman Brijit.

The militants, especially No. 2 and No. 3, were now facing the full fury of the Alpha Company's assault weapons, both from the hilltop LMGs and the AK-47s now just metres away from them.

'From above, I could see KB Saab get very close to the militants, dangerously close,' says Shivram who focused his fire from up on the hilltop. 'I could tell that he wasn't planning on retreating. He simply did not stop crawling forward. It was a little unnerving to those of us who could see. But he was leading from the front and doing what we had come here for.'

As the rest of the Alpha Company squad provided cover fire, Major Bijendra made a final hair-raising dash towards the two militants within his reach, killing both with a spray of close-quarter rifle fire. Falling back to his elbows, Major Bijendra screamed for the squad to blaze their weapons into the forest, determined not to let No. 4, No. 5 and, crucially, No. 6 escape.

'Even from that distance I could read KB Saab's mind,' says Shivram. 'We had come this far. We had succeeded. But where was Haopu?'

Over the next four minutes, return fire from the militants tapered off, with only the Alpha Company squad still firing into the forest. After two more minutes of intermittent bursts, Major Bijendra asked his men to hold fire, the echoing clatter taking many seconds to be engulfed once again by the silence of the woods. He needed to use the lull—it if was a lull—to get his men back to the safety of the hilltop. Still careful not to present themselves as targets, the five men crawled back towards the hill, quickly scaling the slope in a crouched jog, single file, spaced 20 metres apart.

Up on the hilltop, Major Bijendra grabbed his binoculars once again to scan the woods and dirt track below. There was nothing. Not even signs that there had just been a gunfight. The only giveaways were a streak of blood on the dirt track where militant No. 1 had been hit, and then the bodies of No. 2 and No. 3. That night, a pair of scouts went down the hill to look for No. 1, but he was nowhere to be found. It was concluded that he managed to get some distance, but in all likelihood died of his wounds. Militants No.4 and No. 5 managed to flee the encounter site.

No. 6 didn't even come into view.

As his scouts retrieved the bodies of No. 2 and No. 3 from the track below, Major Bijendra called his informant at Longphailum village.

'We got two of them, maybe three.'

'Yes, the news has just filtered in.'

'Was the sixth man Haopu?'

'Yes, it was Haopu. He has not returned.'

The militant squad's tail, the man this mission aimed to eliminate, had made a clean getaway. Shivram and the other soldiers knew this was a delicate moment, but they knew they needed to stand with their commander as he processed the events of the day. No man said a word. It was Major Bijendra himself who broke the silence.

'Had I known for sure that Haopu was the last man, I would have waited for him to enter the kill zone, and allowed the first three or four guys to pass,' said Major Bijendra to the men.

'*Unke ghar mein ghus ke maara hai saab* [We have entered their territory and killed them],' Rifleman Brijit said. 'It was never going to be easy. We still scored at least two kills. Haopu now knows he cannot rest in his own backyard. We have stolen his sleep forever. His time will soon come.'

Now that the ambush site was known to the militants, the Alpha Company squad needed to move quickly. Packing up their tents and equipment in the darkness, the fifteen men began the 25 km trek back to the point where they would be collected the next morning by their vehicles.

On the long march back, Major Bijendra dug his phone out of his rucksack. Switching it on, the lock screen displayed a stack of messages from Jenipher. The last one simply read, 'Missing you, please tell me all is okay.'

This time he texted back: 'All okay. Back at base shortly. Will call.'

Then Major Bijendra dialled his commanding officer, who by this time had received the operation report.

'We didn't get Haopu, sir. He got away.'

'Never mind, very good show, KB. You got them in their own playground. Next time.'

'I'm sorry, sir. He was there and we didn't get him.'

'No time for sorry. Stay focused.'

But the escape of Haopu would continue to haunt Major Bijendra. There was nothing personal in the hunt for the individual. But his escape was a reminder of how difficult it was to eliminate those holding Manipur hostage to their terrifying ways.

By late morning on 23 March, the Alpha Company men were back at their operating base in Kamai. As they returned to their barracks to rest, Major Bijendra dialled his mother.

'Is everything okay?'

'I'm okay, just called to check on you.'

'Yes, please come and see us soon.'

'I will, very soon.'

And then, after a day of debriefings and post-mission stock-taking, just before he turned in for the night, Major Bijendra texted Jenipher again.

'I'm coming to see you.'

* * *

Ten months after the mission, in January 2020, it was announced that Major Konjengbam Bijendra Singh would be decorated with a Shaurya Chakra, India's third highest peacetime gallantry medal. The citation would credit Major Bijendra's 'conspicuous bravery and stout leadership in going beyond the call of duty in the face of grave and imminent danger to his men'.

A month after the Shaurya Chakra announcement, in February 2020 Bijendra and Jenipher were married in Imphal; their daughter Jasmine arrived in October.

Nearly a year later, while Major Bijendra was in Imphal with his family on leave, he received a call from Warrant Officer Shivram.

'*Haopu khatam ho gaya, KB Saab* [KB Sir, Haopu has met his end].'

The elusive LTT commander-in-chief, who had completely dropped off the map for over two and a half years since the Alpha Company encounter, had finally met his end. Haopu and two other LTT militants were eliminated by security forces in Maojang village in Manipur's Sadar Hills area. The slippery militant had managed to move large distances within the state, finding a safe haven in the Saikul area, a testament to his resources and ability to survive.

'We didn't get him, but we put a huge target on his back,' says Major Bijendra. 'My men are right in what they say— Haopu must have spent his final years constantly on edge, constantly running, never being able to rest in one place. Hopefully he felt something like what the people of Manipur felt thanks to the actions of outfits like his.'

Three months after the killing of Haopu, with the COVID-19 pandemic slowing down in the country, a long-postponed defence investiture ceremony was called at the Rashtrapati Bhawan in Delhi. Those whose names had been announced for decorations could finally receive their medals from the President of India.

As Major Bijendra, now thirty years old, walked down the maroon carpet to receive his Shaurya Chakra, twenty-six-year-old Jenipher took in the crowd's thunderous applause.

'It was an indescribable moment,' she says. 'But my heart equally went out to the brave women whose husbands were posthumously honoured for their heroism. The way these women held themselves together when the citations of their husbands were being read out gave me goosebumps. We in the army are a close-knit family. Like our pride, we share our grief too.'

Major Bijendra's Shaurya Chakra citation, read out at the Rashtrapati Bhavan ceremony, was televised live and watched by his mother, Konjengbam Tilotama Devi, who was babysitting the couple's thirteen-month-old daughter at a Delhi hotel. Her eyes welled up, thinking of what an extraordinary achievement this was for her son, who, as a teenager, struggled to arrange money to travel to Allahabad in 2008 for his SSB interview, the final hurdle before joining the armed forces.

'My heart was full,' says Konjengbam Tilotama Devi. 'Bijendra could rarely afford to buy lunch when he was undergoing coaching at a private academy in New Delhi ahead of the SSB interview. He would tell me how even a paratha served by a street hawker was a luxury thirteen years ago. And here he was on the television screen, looking proudly into the camera as the supreme commander of the armed forces was pinning the medal on him. What could be a greater moment for a mother? I only wish his father was alive to see this.'

Major Bijendra will never forget the hard times the family fell on after his father was forced to drive lorries to make ends meet.

'After I became an officer, I made sure my father stayed with me till he breathed his last a few years ago. I wish he was here to see this medal,' says Major Bijendra. 'I may be wearing the medal, but it belongs to each of the fourteen men who were under my direct command during the operation. We were a cohesive unit and in the driver's seat all along. The men followed the instructions they were given to a tee. We did well but for not getting Haopu. It took time for us to digest that. That file is now closed. We have moved on.'

Several men from the Alpha Company of 23 Assam Rifles also received honours for their roles in the March 2019 mission.

Warrant Officer Shivram was awarded the Director General Assam Rifles' (DGAR) commendation card; Rifleman K.D. Burman's contribution was recognized with a similar commendation by the Eastern Army commander; Rifleman Kazhingmei, the scout, got a commendation card from the division commander; and Singh's buddy, Rifleman Brijit, was awarded the governor's gold medal.

Militant activity in the Kamai area dropped drastically after the March 2019 operation.

'I left Kamai in December 2020. There was no firing incident in the area till then,' says Major Bijendra. 'The militants got the message that we had the means and the will to hunt them no matter where they hide.'

The frequency of militant activity may have reduced over the years thanks to persistent operations, community building and development work in the state. But militancy itself is far from over.

Just nine days before the award ceremony at the Rashtrapati Bhavan, the dangers that soldiers operating in Manipur face came terrifyingly to the fore once again. On 13 November 2021, a group of heavily armed militants ambushed an Assam Rifles convoy in broad daylight near the porous 398 km India–Myanmar border in Manipur's Churachandpur, killing five soldiers, including the commanding officer of 46 Assam Rifles, Colonel Viplav Tripathi, along with his wife and their eight-year-old son.

A crucial piece of India's modern military history is associated with the North-eastern state—India's first publicly acknowledged 'surgical strike' on foreign soil was launched from here in June 2015.

On 9 June 2015, a team from the 21 Para Special Forces infiltrated from Manipur* into Myanmar to hunt down the militants responsible for a brutal attack on Indian soldiers in Manipur's Chandel district just days earlier. The operation had been supervised by Lieutenant General Bipin Rawat, who at the time commanded the Army's 3 Corps, headquartered in Nagaland's Dimapur. The general, who rose to become chief of the army staff and then India's first chief of defence staff, was killed in a helicopter crash along with thirteen others near Coonoor in Tamil Nadu in December 2021.

Major Bijendra was posted out of Manipur at the time this book went to print. But he welcomes the opportunity to go back if the Army requires him to. As a decorated officer, his name and face are now well known across the landscape.

---

* See *India's Most Fearless 1*.

A source of pride, but also a source of danger for him and his loved ones.

'As a child, I saw militants intimidating simple, hard-working Manipuri people,' says Major Bijendra. '*Hero ban kar ghoomte the woh* [They used to roam around like heroes]. There has to be a breaking point where we say enough is enough. For Manipur. For India.'

10

'You Have Five Minutes on the Seabed'

CPO Veer Singh and Commander Ashok Kumar

25 March 2015
Arabian Sea
25 nautical miles off the Konkan coast

'It's been twelve minutes. Time's up. Initiate ascent, immediately.'

The dive supervisor's voice had acquired an urgent tone as he knelt by the edge of a Gemini boat, a tiny black speck far out in the Arabian Sea, off the coast of Karnataka.

'It's way too dangerous to remain there any more,' he said.

Master Chief Petty Officer (MCPO) N.S. Dahiya was speaking into a handset that sent his voice through a communication wire, nestled in a dive 'umbilical' that went deep into the sea to the two men it was his job to warn.

Sixty metres below the sea surface, two Indian Navy divers armed with 12-inch combat knives heard the call from the boat above through the cable that fed into their diving harnesses and headsets. The warning came again after ten seconds.

'Abort NOW! Do you read me? Initiate ascent without further delay.'

MCPO Dahiya was now nearly screaming over the whip of sea air. The two divers knew that warnings from the man in the boat were non-negotiable. Their lives were quite literally in his hands as they scoured the inky depths of the Arabian Sea.

But on that day in March 2015, the two men—both among the Navy's finest divers and at the very top of their game—had decided to push the limits.

In their full combat diving suits, Chief Petty Officer (CPO) Veer Singh and the officer leading the mission, Commander Ashok Kumar, were certain they were not prepared just yet to begin their ascent towards the surface.

'This is your second ascent warning, do not ignore this,' the dive supervisor called now, his voice softer but firm.

As the two divers descended further, they needed to be sure what they were looking at before they sent word up through the umbilical to justify not heeding a critical safety warning.

'I see the watch on her wrist,' CPO Veer said.

'I see her hand.'

Less than 2 metres away in the murk, the two divers had finally spotted what they were searching for—the pale, lifeless body of Lieutenant Kiran Shekhawat.

* * *

24 March 2015
INS Hansa Naval Air Station
Goa

The previous evening, twenty-seven-year-old Lieutenant Kiran had climbed into the observer's seat of an Indian Navy Dornier Do-228 maritime patrol aircraft at the INS Hansa Air Station in Goa. The aircraft, part of the Navy's most decorated unit, Indian Naval Air Squadron (INAS) 310, nicknamed the Cobras, was being flown that night by pilots Commander Nikhil Joshi and Sub Lieutenant Abhinav Nagori, the mission was a familiar, routine night mission over the Arabian Sea to track suspicious movements by potentially hostile vessels looking to land in the darkness.

The Dornier took off at 6.30 p.m., with the pilots steering it straight out over the Arabian Sea to begin the night surveillance mission. On board, Lieutenant Kiran got busy with her observation duties, keeping a watch through the plane's night sensors and maritime patrol radar for anything that needed to be red-flagged for either urgent action or follow-up the next day. Assigned a sector of the ocean to surveil, the plane flew a large circular path, tightening with each instance. Missions of this kind were designed to last up to five hours where necessary, giving the surveillance crew 'time on station' to get a proper fix on the ocean surface. But just over three hours after the mission began, the Dornier flew into major technical trouble. The pilots tried to keep the plane flying, relaying their position and situation over the talk-back.

Ground control at the INS Hansa base lost radar contact at 10.08 p.m., around the time the Dornier had crashed into the Arabian Sea.

Minutes later, an alert sounded at Mumbai's naval dockyard, where some of India's top combat divers had just finished dinner and were preparing to retire to their barracks. While details of the accident were still sketchy, the alert quickly triggered emergency protocols that saw eleven men from the Navy's elite Command Clearance Diving Team (CCDT)—including CPO Veer and Commander Ashok—on full readiness to roll out for a search-and-rescue (SAR) mission.

Well before midnight, the divers' team set sail south towards the Karwar coast on board the ocean-going tug INS *Matanga*, a 68-metre vessel that was deployed on a variety of emergency missions off the Konkan coast.

'We knew there was no time to waste,' says CPO Veer. 'Each one of us in that team knew that the essence of our job was to scramble against time and complete the mission. We couldn't wait to get there and begin our work.'

INS *Matanga*, one among a dozen vessels activated for the emergency search mission, was now speeding towards the crash area. Another vessel, INS *Makar*, a hydrographic survey vessel equipped with sonar equipment capable of gazing into the murky oceanic depths, was also on its way.

No one slept on the vessels that night. Not after the teams on the ships received word from the Western Naval Command control centre that the pilot of the Dornier, Commander Nikhil, had miraculously survived the crash. He had reportedly drifted nearly 20 km from where the plane hit the water and had been rescued by a fishing boat. How did the Indian Navy get to know this so quickly? The crew of the fishing boat had dialled a toll-free hotline that had been introduced after the 2008 26/11 Mumbai terror attacks. The pilot was soon picked up by a fast interceptor boat and rushed to naval hospital INHS Patanjali in Karwar, south of Goa.

'The news of the rescue made this an even more time-critical rescue mission,' says an officer who was at the Western Naval Command control centre at the time. 'If the pilot had been rescued from the sea surface, then we had to fully account for the possibility that the other two may have survived too. And may have been drifting.'

Other Dornier aircraft and Sea King helicopters were already flying missions in rotation both by night and the following day, scanning the sea surface as meticulously as possible in the hope of spotting bobbing heads. An alert was broadcast to fishing boats in the area, including the one that had rescued Commander Joshi, requesting them to keep a close eye out for Lieutenant Kiran and Sub Lieutenant Nagori in the hope that they had also, by some miracle, survived.

As the aircraft skimmed over the sea, hunting in tightening flight paths for the two missing officers, the surface ships went all out to locate the doomed Dornier. Criss-crossing each other in wide arcs over the Arabian Sea, a dozen ships worked uninterruptedly to triangulate and pin-point the crash site. Combining inputs from last detected location, the direction in which the aircraft was headed and last radar contact, the vessels quickly narrowed things down. But it wouldn't be until the morning of 25 March that something finally glinted on INS *Makar*'s side-scan sonar from the murky, heaving seabed 55 to 60 metres below.

The commanding officer of INS *Matanga*, Commander Nikhil Srivatsa, dropped anchor around 200 metres away from the coordinates given by INS *Makar* and the dive teams were launched on a pair of Gemini boats, along with the equipment they had carried from Mumbai.

'INS *Makar* had given the coordinates of the main chunk of the wreckage or what it called a large metallic object. But the debris was spread over a wide area. The skipper of INS *Matanga* anchored the ship at a safe distance to avoid any further accidental damage to the wreckage,' says a Navy officer who was involved in the operation.

The two Geminis were above the possible crash site by 10 a.m., and the first pair of divers was launched into the sea an hour later to confirm the exact location of the Dornier wreckage. The Navy follows a buddy system in which divers operate in pairs during such missions.

Before the first two divers slipped into the warm Arabian Sea on a particularly crisp, sunny day, a shot-line was lowered down from one of the Gemini boats to the seabed to calculate its precise depth as INS *Makar* had only presented a broad estimate. The depth turned out to be 60 metres. Every diver on those two boats immediately had the same thought.

60 metres.

What followed was a quick satellite phone call to the Western Naval Command headquarters in Mumbai. The chain of command had to be informed about the depth at which the divers would be required to operate and how the discovery of the wreckage had suddenly raised the stakes.

'Underwater visibility was unbelievably good that day. It was around twenty metres,' says CPO Veer. 'I have been part of many operations where I could barely see more than a few inches ahead of me. The first two divers were instructed not to descend beyond forty metres as from there, they could easily see a further twenty metres below, the depth at which the wreckage possibly lay. The operational constraints were weighing on our minds.'

The first two divers returned to the surface without sighting anything. Commander Ashok then ordered the two boats to a distance 50 metres further south of where the first two divers were launched into the water. From there, the second pair of divers plunged into the sea to look for the wreckage, holding a shot-line fastened to a 100 kg sinker earlier dropped into the sea. The shot-line allows divers to head straight to the intended location at the bottom of the sea without drifting.

Minutes into that second dive and from a depth of 40 metres, the two men sighted the Dornier sitting on the seabed around 20 metres below them and instantly communicated the critical discovery to their supervisor. The second dive team, having done its job of spotting the wreckage, was instructed not to descend any further and return to their Gemini immediately.

For all the technology involved in detecting aircraft wreckage at sea, finally sighting it is something of a magical process. Unlike an air crash on land, finding a crash site at sea is an exponentially more difficult proposition. Everything about an accident is loaded against those looking for where it happened. Consider this: when an aircraft crashes into the sea, it quickly sinks. Any floating parts or patches of tell-tale oil or fuel quickly drift from the point of the crash. Once the aircraft sinks below the surface, it may not always go down straight, its planar surfaces and angles twisting it in different directions, possibly at considerable distance from where it entered the water. The aircraft could sink to unmanageable depths depending on how deep the sea is at that point.* It is a common misconception that the seabed is one endlessly flat plain, when it is in fact not only full of dramatic terrain with mountains, trenches, valleys and crevasses, but also dynamic, in that the seabed constantly shifts with the currents. So theoretically, the place where aircraft debris settles after sinking could shift significantly with the shifting seabed.

'It's a difficult, moving target where nothing is in your favour, literally nothing,' says a sailor who served on INS *Makar* at the time the Dornier was detected. 'A very competent and committed search, combined with some favourable depth parameters allowed us to locate the wreckage quickly.'

With the wreckage finally sighted by human eyes, it was time for the decisive third dive. CPO Veer and Commander Ashok were already in their dive suits and in a Gemini boat with dive supervisor Dahiya when the second team had ascended.

---

* Air France Flight 447, a wide-body Airbus A330 airliner which crashed in June 2009 in the Atlantic Ocean took nearly two years to locate. The aircraft wreckage was found nearly 4000 metres deep. Malaysian Airlines Flight 370, which disappeared over the Indian Ocean in March 2014, has still not been located. In July 2016, an Indian Air Force Antonov An-32 aircraft went missing over the Bay of Bengal with twenty-nine people on board. It has not been located to date either.

The dive team had changed for this third descent. What hadn't changed was the depth at which the wreckage lay. Commander Ashok and CPO Veer were certain about one thing when they planned their descent, though. If someone had to take the risk to pull it off, it would have to be them. They had more diving experience than anyone else in the squad.

'It is not possible to measure risks involved in such operations. But it is reasonable to assume that someone with lesser experience may not be comfortable operating at depths they are not qualified for. Manoeuvring with a body isn't easy either. My foremost priority was to keep the mission incident-free,' says Commander Ashok.

Like so much in the military, 25 March 2015 involved a collision of emotions. On the one hand, things had been upbeat for the rescue teams. The Dornier's pilot had survived. And the aircraft debris had been located. On the other hand, with several hours of airborne search for the other two aviators drawing a blank, every sailor in the rescue team knew deep inside that a tragedy was unfolding.

'You have fifteen minutes,' said Dahiya as CPO Veer and Commander Ashok lowered themselves into the sea. Carefully descending into the murk, the two divers reached a depth of fifty metres in under three minutes. The location data they had been provided was spot on. Ten metres below them, through the murk lit vaguely by filtered sunlight, they saw it.

The twisted, mangled fuselage of the Dornier sat on a sloping seabed dune at 60 metres. But there was a problem. Stringent diving protocol normally does not allow Navy divers to descend to depths below 55 metres. The effectiveness of their unpressured diving sets diminishes significantly beyond 50 metres.

'Ten more metres may not sound like much, but with those constraints, it's all the distance in the world,' says CPO

Veer. 'But the wreckage was right there below us. We could see the whole thing, and we reported this to Dahiya.'

It was at this moment that the dive supervisor issued his first warning, asking the two men to terminate the mission and return to the surface. The instruction wasn't unreasonable. As per well-defined operational standards, the two divers were literally operating out of their depth with potentially dangerous consequences. Keeping the two divers safe and focused was Dahiya's chief responsibility. He had assessed risk and decided that a further 10-metre descent, along with an unpredictable amount of time that would be required at that depth, meant it was a clear no-no. Dahiya also knew he had a pair of very committed divers on his hands, including Commander Ashok who headed the squadron's salvage unit.

'Dahiya, we're proceeding with descent,' Commander Ashok said into the dive mask microphone. The dive supervisor knew he had to acknowledge.

The two divers gave each other a thumbs up as they began their final descent past 50 metres, approaching the wreckage as it rocked gently in the current. At 2.30 p.m., with the sun high, CPO Veer and Commander Ashok reached the broken Dornier. In their earpieces, the two divers received a second warning on their depth.

A risk had been taken, and it needed to pay off as quickly as possible. The two divers were far from oblivious to the double threat they faced—human limitation and the very real possibility of equipment failing since it had been taken beyond its prescribed parameters.

Both divers unsheathed their combat knives, steering clear of the sharp metal edges protruding from the mangled heap of the Dornier. They used their knives to cut the mess of wires and cords that had been ripped from the aircraft's innards to allow passage into the cabin and cockpit area. At every step, they relayed their position and what they were looking at to their dive supervisor. Up on the Gemini boat, Dahiya acknowledged.

It had taken the divers just over three minutes to reach the wreckage. Of the fifteen-minute window they were allowed, they now had under twelve minutes to search the wreckage and begin their ascent. Dahiya had already allowed the divers a depth risk. He knew he couldn't permit a 'bottom time'* risk, or what is also known as 'limiting line' in the Navy's safety manual.

The men, focused on the mission's execution, had not only breached their safe operating envelope but were now clearly flirting with danger in an alien environment by staying there longer—even if it was only for a minute or two. And the risk to their safety was mounting with every passing second.

'We knew that if we returned without retrieving Lieutenant Kiran's body, we would not be able to go back down the same day,' says CPO Veer. 'The safety manual does not permit back-to-back diving missions beyond a depth of forty-two metres. It prescribes a surface interval of six hours between two deep-sea dives.'

In love with the sea from an early age, CPO Veer had joined the Navy in July 1997 so he could spend as much time either in it or close to it. When the opportunity to train at the prestigious Diving School in Kochi presented itself, a young Veer hadn't thought twice.

With Dahiya providing a stopwatch update every thirty seconds, the two men had to rely on brute strength to pull apart the jammed cargo door on the port side of the aircraft in order to finally gain entry into the main cabin.

---

* Bottom time is calculated from the moment a diver descends from the surface till the point the diver initiates his/her ascent.

The two divers had taken crucial inputs on the structure of the Dornier aircraft and its design from two men. The first was Commander Srivatsa, an aviator who had himself served as an observer in the Cobras squadron in a previous role.

'It was a stroke of good luck that the commanding officer of INS *Matanga* had served in a Dornier squadron,' says Commander Ashok. 'With his inputs, I felt I knew the aircraft well. It was most critical to planning the mission, finding entry into the aircraft and locating Lieutenant Kiran's body.'

The second man with useful inputs was Petty Officer R.K. Singh, a sailor from the Navy's aviation branch with years of experience in a Dornier squadron. He was a close friend of CPO Veer's who had also served in the aviation wing before he earned the coveted diver badge.

'In my naval aviation days, I worked as an electrical technician on the Sea Harrier fighter aircraft,' says CPO Veer. 'But I had no clue about the Dornier. Apart from Commander Srivatsa, my friend also shared information on the plane, cockpit layout, observer's workstation, emergency exits, location of the black box, and the like.'

The inputs were critical for the mission.

CPO Veer now carefully slipped into the shattered cabin of the Dornier. It was dark inside, the wreckage closing out any sunlight filtering down to the surrounding depth. Stepping carefully forward through the murk, he switched on his underwater flashlight. The observer's seat in the Dornier is located right outside the main cockpit. He stepped towards it, twisting his body to avoid protrusions of jagged debris inside the aircraft's cabin.

'For some reason, at that point I remembered the words of one of my former commanding officers,' says CPO Veer. 'Whenever he addressed us he would say, "We are here for war and we are here to win." Those words rang in my ears when I was about to enter the wreckage. Every mission, to my mind, is akin to war and the only choice is to emerge victorious.'

The aircraft was totally destroyed, with no clear paths to exit.

That's when he saw Lieutenant Kiran's wrist, with her watch still on. With Dahiya reporting time in an ever-elevated tone, the two divers took their last few steps towards the observer's seat to free her body.

'It was a surreal sight. She looked peaceful,' says CPO Veer. 'Her unfastened seatbelt seemed to suggest that at some stage, she tried to get out of there. It's hard to imagine what the last moments would have been like.'

Both divers knew instantly what they were looking at— the first woman naval officer to be killed on duty.

'Extricating her body from the seat was very painful,' says CPO Veer. 'But there was no time to stop and think. Processing the tragedy would have to wait till later.'

'We had to use our knives again to clear more wires and cords to bring Lieutenant Kiran's body out from the cargo door. We manoeuvred with extreme caution as sharp metal parts could have not only damaged the body but also our diving gear,' he says.

Lieutenant Kiran had been part of the Navy's first ever all-woman marching contingent at the sixty-sixth Republic Day parade two months before the crash. Two years before, she had married fellow naval officer Lieutenant Vivek Singh Chokker. At the time of the crash, he was an instructor at the elite Indian Naval Academy in Ezhimala, Kerala. Operational postings had kept the young couple in different locations since their wedding, though both were finally to be posted in Kochi together later that year.

The two divers had been made aware of all these details as they made their way to the crash site the previous day.

Up on the Gemini boat, MCPO Dahiya hadn't received the customary acknowledgement from the divers of his time warnings for three whole minutes. The two men had been so focused on removing Lieutenant Kiran's body from the aircraft, they had forgotten to acknowledge the last six countdown warnings, driving Dahiya into a frenzy of worry over whether the rescuers would now need to be rescued themselves.

CPO Veer and Commander Ashok had been on the Arabian seabed for fourteen minutes. Counting their descent time of three minutes, the men were well past the fifteen-minute bottom time considered safe for a diving operation at that depth. This was no longer a calculated risk, Dahiya thought. This was life critical. And there was total silence from the depths. Sensing that he needed to be prepared for the worst, Dahiya put the dive teams in the two Geminis on standby, and if needed, the men would plunge down to 60 metres for a rescue.

Had the two divers, so immersed in their mission, slowly lost their faculties and drifted into a paralytic daze? Had the additional pressure slumped their bodies? Had they been incapacitated—alive, but unable to communicate? All possibilities crossed Dahiya's mind as he screamed for a reply through the umbilical.*

Deep-sea diving is fraught with danger.

Nitrogen narcosis during descent and decompression sickness on the way up are deadly conditions that can develop very fast in the underwater environment and have well-

---

* The surface-supplied diving umbilicals—a lifeline for divers— consist of a breathing gas hose, communications cable and a pneumofathometer or pneumo hose to monitor the operating depths. The divers were using umbilical cables measuring 75 metres in length that day, with their supervisor feeding the line to them as they went down.

documented debilitating effects on divers. Variously described as 'raptures of the deep' or the 'Martini effect' in the world of diving, the first condition refers to a dangerous altered state of consciousness triggered by breathing nitrogen under increased pressure, usually kicking in at depths of more than 40 metres. That's why the Navy's safety manual prescribes a limiting line for different depths.*

Nitrogen narcosis can cause disorientation, dizziness and vision trouble, significantly impairing a diver's ability to make quick and considered decisions in testing conditions. CPO Veer and Commander Ashok, with hundreds of diving hours between them, managed to evade nitrogen narcosis and its associated complications during their descent.

On the eighteenth minute, right before Dahiya had planned to set off emergency rescue protocols, a voice came in from 60 metres.

'We have her, Dahiya,' shouted Commander Ashok. 'We are about to initiate ascent. Please inform INS *Matanga* that we are coming up with Lieutenant Shekhawat's body.'

Dahiya and the eight men in two Gemini boats finally exhaled.

The two divers carried Lieutenant Kiran's body to the shot-line a few metres away from the wreckage before they began their ascent. Right before they set off for the surface, Commander Ashok sent up a crucial update.

'No sign of Nagori.'

But as they ascended, well past their time and depth safety margins, the threat of decompression sickness loomed even larger. The buoyancy of Lieutenant Kiran's body

---

* The atmospheric pressure at sea level is 14.7 pounds per square inch, or 1 atmosphere. Pressure mounts as a diver descends deeper into the sea, increasing by 1 atmosphere with every 10 metres.

made CPO Veer's ascent faster than the stipulated rate. Surfacing too quickly can cause decompression sickness due to a sudden drop in pressure, a condition called 'the bends'. The sickness is the consequence of a sudden switch from a high-pressure environment to one with low pressure. It causes the formation of potentially fatal nitrogen bubbles in the tissues and bloodstream of deep-sea divers. The bubbles can block arteries and trigger a stroke or heart attack in extreme cases.

Before the completion of every dive, divers are mandated to make safety stops at prescribed depths to control their ascent rate and expel the extra nitrogen built up in their bodies.

Standard procedure for a dive up to 60 metres prescribes three safety stops during the ascent—at 9, 6 and 3 metres from the surface. The ascent has to be paused for five minutes at 9 metres, another five minutes at 6 metres and fifteen minutes at 3 metres. The number of safety stops and their duration, spelt out in the Navy's dive table, vary with the depths at which the divers are operating.

CPO Veer had decided against making the mandatory safety stops during ascent that day as he was in a rush to take Lieutenant Kiran's body to the surface. INS *Matanga*, alerted by dive supervisor Dahiya, had launched another boat minutes earlier to bring the body back and arrange for it to be flown to a naval hospital in Goa by helicopter.

If a diver chooses to ascend without making safety stops for any reason, as CPO Veer did, he either has to return to the prescribed depths for the stops within nine minutes or complete the drill in a recompression chamber on board the diving ship to rid the body of extra nitrogen.

'I went straight up and delivered the body, and within five minutes I was back in the sea at the 9 metre depth for the safety stops. We didn't have a recompression chamber on the

Gemini. It was on board INS *Matanga* and I needed to get it done quickly,' says CPO Veer.

By 3.30 p.m., the dive teams were back on board INS *Matanga*, still processing the speed with which they had managed to complete the most critical part of their mission. The divers watched in silence from the deck of their vessel as an Indian Navy Sea King helicopter picked up the body of Lieutenant Kiran, rising and then peeling away towards Goa.

It was a quiet night on board INS *Matanga*. Responding to questions from the younger divers on the team, Commander Ashok and CPO Veer shared lessons from the day's dive.

'If I can do it, so can you,' Commander Ashok said. 'Trust your instincts and always remember this is what we train for. This is the life we have chosen. Unexpected twists will be there. But the best part is when the time comes, you will know exactly what to do.'

It had been a day of deep success and deep tragedy. After a briefing on follow-through protocols and missions for the next day, the squad retired to their bunks for the night.

In his bunk, CPO Veer couldn't sleep. He knew he would never forget those images from the shattered cabin of the Dornier. That hand. That wrist. That watch. He had learnt over dinner that night that Lieutenant Kiran traced her roots to Khetri town in Rajasthan's Jhunjhunu district.

'What are the odds of retrieving someone's body from the bottom of the sea and that someone turns out to be from your own town,' says CPO Veer.

As sleep finally overcame the exhausted squad, its final thought was most likely a single one. The Dornier's co-pilot Sub Lieutenant Nagori was still a missing piece in the tragic story, and the truth about what happened to the aircraft would only be known if the dive team was able to locate and retrieve the aircraft's black box.

The squad on his vessel was up before sunrise, Commander Srivatsa remembers, fully charged up and ready for a second day of dives, determined to complete the mission.

The operation to locate the missing Dornier and the two crew members was being monitored at the highest possible level, with then chief of the naval staff, Admiral Robin Dhowan, rushing to Goa from Delhi to monitor the mission firsthand. Aircraft were on standby at INS *Hansa* for Admiral Dhowan, to carry out reconnaissance of the crash site, one of the first things he did after landing in Goa. That the chief was personally on the scene to keep tabs wasn't just an act of solidarity, but a message of urgency that filtered down and energized all ranks involved.

The previous day's dive had been a successful one. But that was no guarantee that further descents would turn out the same way. Each mission down to those depths carried with them the same as well as additional risks. With each passing hour, the Dornier wreckage, sitting on loose diatomaceous earth on the seabed, could potentially drift down to further depths.

At the dawn briefing, Commander Ashok made it fully clear to the squad that optimism had to be balanced with caution for the mission's success.

'You remember what I said last night. When the time comes, you will know what to do. Just focus on what you are doing and have a great dive. The bottom time is non-negotiable,' Commander Ashok told the two men in the build-up to the dive.

By 9 a.m., the first pair of divers was given the thumbs up by MCPO Dahiya to flip backwards into the sea from their Gemini. The dive team was cleared to go down to the wreckage and find and recover Sub Lieutenant Nagori's body as well as the Dornier's black box.

Based on inputs provided by Commander Srivatsa, the divers were also equipped with information on the two possible ways to access the cockpit in which Sub Lieutenant Nagori's body was likely to be trapped. Fortunately for the team, underwater visibility was as good as it was the previous day.

If visibility hadn't been that good, the divers would have had to use what is known as a distance line, a coiled reel fastened to the sinker or shot-line, to navigate through the murky waters and return safely to the starting point. A distance line also serves as a critical dive-site navigation tool when the sea current is high.

'The latest dive team was sent down with a Nikon camera for underwater photography. The photographs and footage would be of enormous help to other divers to understand the conditions in which the operation was being conducted as not all of them would get a chance to explore the wreckage,' says CPO Veer.

But for all the preparation and benefit of first-hand advice, that first dive attempt on day two was unsuccessful.

The two divers could neither locate Sub Lieutenant Nagori's body nor the black box. They entered the wreckage from the Dornier's port side taking the same route as CPO Veer and Commander Ashok had after forcing the cargo door open. What had seemed like a straightforward task when the dive team set out from INS Matanga for the crash site that morning was turning out to be far more complicated than the divers might have imagined.

'Sir, I don't think Sub Lieutenant Nagori's body is there in the wreckage. We did a thorough search. It may have drifted away,' said one of the divers. The limiting line of fifteen minutes at 60 metres left the two divers with no time to scan the wreckage further.

While they had hoped that the divers would make some headway in at least locating Sub Lieutenant Nagori's body, if not retrieving it, CPO Veer and Commander Ashok weren't really surprised. They had themselves not detected any signs of the co-pilot's body in the mangled aircraft the previous day, though their focus on Lieutenant Kiran left them with little time for a thorough look at the cockpit area.

Back on the Gemini, the dive team downloaded the photographs and videos they had recorded during the dive on to a laptop for closer analysis. Commander Ashok and CPO Veer looked closely at every frame.

'There were no leads in the photographs or the video footage. We didn't have enough time to look for Sub Lieutenant Nagori's body the previous day, but I was convinced it was in the wreckage. I don't think the divers made it to the cockpit or whatever was left of it. The bottom time restriction may have played on their minds and diluted their focus. It can happen. But we still had a fighting chance,' says CPO Veer.

There was no question of calling off the mission. It was tantalizingly close to completion, but there was no telling how long this final stretch could wind on for.

Within fifteen minutes of the first two men resurfacing, a second pair of divers was launched into the sea. Before they disappeared beneath the surface of the water, CPO Veer had some advice.

'The body has to be in the cockpit. The fuselage is badly crushed, and the cockpit will not look like how you imagine it to be. Go for the cockpit door on the port side. This is your chance,' he said to them.

But the second dive also failed to locate the co-pilot. This was a disconcerting turn of events, with the mission appearing to hit a wall of questions: where could Sub Lieutenant Nagori's body possibly be? Was it trapped inside the wreckage? Had it drifted away? Did he make it out of the cockpit?

The team was fully focused on Nagori. The black box would have to wait.

A third pair of divers volunteered to go next but after deliberations on board, Commander Ashok decided that he and CPO Veer would make the third descent themselves.

'Let's stick to the limiting line this time,' MCPO Dahiya said, minutes before the two men dived. He made little effort to hide his scowl. It was his duty to make sure that the divers conformed to the safety protocol to the maximum extent possible, but he knew what he was dealing with.

The only silver lining to the diving operations till that point on the second day was that the divers, who had operated at depths where they weren't even supposed to be in the first place, were not involved in any incident that could have diverted the team's focus and delayed the search.

Familiar with the wreckage site, CPO Veer and Commander Ashok descended fast and hit the bottom in exactly three minutes. They wanted to squeeze every minute they could of bottom time to search for Sub Lieutenant Nagori.

After spending a full minute examining the battered fuselage from outside, the two divers noticed the Dornier was not sitting upright on the seabed, something that had escaped their attention earlier and that of the other dive teams. It hadn't been noted in discussions and debriefs since the wreckage had been located either. They were looking at the wreckage afresh now.

The front portion of the fuselage housing the cockpit had slammed right into the seabed and was buried a few feet in the mud. It was hardly surprising therefore that attempts to approach the cockpit from the cabin had proven futile. 'It was buried in the seabed. The co-pilot's body and the black box had to be in there,' thought CPO Veer.

The two men quickly made for the fractured cockpit door that was partly buried in the soft soil, once again using sheer strength to try and remove the big, mangled piece of metal. From the Gemini above, MCPO Dahiya reminded the team not to go silent for any period of time. The two divers had been given a respectful earful from Dahiya the previous day, and fully understood his consternation. They reported with updates every twenty seconds on this dive.

Time moves quickly when you're at 60 metres and busy as hell, using every ounce of your strength to break free a jagged, heavy piece of metal jammed into the seabed with shattering force. It took seven whole minutes for the two divers to break the door free.

'You have five minutes of bottom time left. Do you see him?' shouted Dahiya from above.

CPO Veer and Commander Ashok exchanged a quick glance of ironic relief. They both saw the body at the same time.

Sub Lieutenant Nagori was in the co-pilot's seat, still strapped in with his seatbelt.

'His seat was also partly buried in the seabed. We unfastened the safety belt and gently pulled him from the wreckage. As Commander Ashok held the officer's body, I returned to the cockpit to retrieve the black box,' says CPO Veer.

The black box was entangled in a jumble of wires that CPO Veer had to cut away with his knife. He inserted the device into his safety harness and quickly exited the cockpit. Nearly seventeen minutes had passed since the two men made the dive. The prescribed bottom time had elapsed again, just like it had the previous day. But this time Dahiya was calmer since the team had kept him posted at every step. No paralysing silences from the depths this time.

The two divers completed the recovery of Sub Lieutenant Nagori's body in exactly the same manner as Lieutenant Kiran's.

'The only difference was that the buoyancy of the co-pilot's body was taking me back to the surface even faster this time,' says CPO Veer. 'I clearly recall Commander Ashok holding my legs to slow my ascent. I could have released the body closer to the surface but decided against it as it could have drifted.'

When they broke the surface, a third Gemini boat was on site from INS *Matanga* to carry the body back to the ship from where it would similarly be flown to Goa in a helicopter.

Triumph and tragedy mixing like blood in water, the divers returned to INS *Matanga* early that evening. The sorrow of losing two personnel would always be the core of what had happened. But with two grieving families awaiting news after the shock of the accident, it was upon the shoulders of the divers to deliver the possibility of closure quickly. An endless search would have protracted their agony and bereavement. The divers weren't celebrating the recovery of two corpses from the depths of the ocean. But they knew they had the right to bask in the simple glow of a job well done.

So upbeat was the mood on board that night that the dive squad discussed the possibility of recovering the Dornier wreckage using salvage bags the following day.

'The team's morale was sky high,' says CPO Veer. 'We talked about how we would go about recovering the wreckage and the role each squad member would play. However, we were later informed that the responsibility of salvaging the wreckage had been given to the Oil and Natural Gas

Corporation (ONGC), which has specialized diving crews and sophisticated equipment.'

The Navy honoured CPO Veer and Commander Ashok with the Nao Sena Medal for gallantry for rising above and beyond the call of duty and leading the operations under the most trying circumstances. Their citations for the military honour brought out in detail the tough and many challenges the men encountered and how they overcame them to earn a place in the Navy's diving history.

'He dived repeatedly and even exceeded the stipulated limiting line, which exposed him to great danger. He personally recovered the bodies as well as the black box by innovatively gaining access through the damaged fuselage by sheer strength and brute force. His courage and determination percolated to other members of his team leading to the accomplishment of the task and brought closure to the families of the deceased aircrew,' reads CPO Veer's citation.

CPO Veer, since promoted up the ranks, has gone on to serve with a submarine rescue unit based in Visakhapatnam.

Commander Ashok's citation also acknowledged the courage, selflessness and perseverance he demonstrated while recovering the two bodies and the black box from the seabed. 'His valiant efforts at the age of fifty-plus led to recovery of the bodies of two officers and the flight data recorder (black box) in adverse circumstances,' his citation added.

Commander Ashok retired in 2018 and settled down in his hometown Pathankot, Punjab. The memories of the mission, which was an extreme test of physical and mental strength, are still fresh in his mind.

'It's my firm belief that when you lead from the front, your men will give their 100 per cent. They will not hesitate to even put their lives on the line for the mission. We were honest in the pursuit of our goal and constantly thinking of what the families of the two officers must be enduring. I believe that the sincerity of our approach even aligned the forces of nature in our favour. You get what I am saying?' he asks.

'The sea was as calm as a swimming pool when we were out there,' he concludes.

Acknowledgements

To our readers, our deepest thanks. They've taken what began as a collection of stories in 2017 and transformed it into a series that has a life of its own.

Thanks to the chiefs of the armed forces, General Manoj Pande, Air Chief Marshal Vivek Ram Chaudhari and Admiral R. Hari Kumar, and their predecessors, General Manoj Mukund Naravane, Air Chief Marshal R.K.S. Bhadauria and Admiral Karam Bir Singh, who permitted us unfettered access to units, documents and front-line personnel—the very core of what makes India's Most Fearless perhaps the only authentic series on Indian military operations.

Thanks to the several military personnel who helped in the journey, many of whom cannot be named for operational reasons. But among those who can, our deepest thanks to the Indian Army's additional director general (strategic communication), Major General Mohit Malhotra, and his team of officers, including Colonel Pankaj Gaur and Lieutenant Colonel Vivek Tripathi, as well as the spokespersons of the Indian Air Force and Indian Navy,

Wing Commander Ashish Moghe and Commander Vivek Madhwal, for seeing our vision.

Our friend and comrade Sandeep Unnithan, whose gritty, heartfelt illustrations of the heroes adorn this book. You are one of the most talented, knowledgeable and generous people we know.

To Sanjay Simha, one of India's greatest military and aviation photographers, our respect and gratitude. He gave us the stunning photograph you see on this book's cover.

To Milee Ashwarya, our friend and comrade at Penguin Random House India who, along with her amazing team, has ensured *India's Most Fearless 3* is every bit the book we hoped it would be when we committed it to her hands.

This book would not have been possible without the steady hand of our organizations. Thanks to the India Today Group leadership, Aroon Purie, Kalli Purie and Supriya Prasad; and the HT Media leadership, Shobhana Bhartia and Sukumar Ranganathan.

Our incredible families that have watched us disappear for months—now years—to finish these books, ever patient, ever supportive. Tavleen, Torul, Aryaman, Agastya and Mira: you know where you stand in the endless river of this writing.

Thanks to our parents—Prakash and Usha, Mahabir and Archana—who've been proud ambassadors of our work, like all Indian parents!

Above all, our humblest thanks go to the soldiers and officers we've written about. No words—certainly nothing in a few sentences—can express how deeply grateful we are for their deeds, their fortitude, their sacrifice and their time for us. As we've promised in the earlier books of this series, their stories will never be forgotten.